Quod scriptura, non iubet vetat

The Latin translates, "What is not commanded in scripture, is forbidden:'

On the Cover: Baptists rejoice to hold in common with other evangelicals the main principles of the orthodox Christian faith. However, there are points of difference and these differences are significant. In fact, because these differences arise out of God's revealed will, they are of vital importance. Hence, the barriers of separation between Baptists and others can hardly be considered a trifling matter. To suppose that Baptists are kept apart solely by their views on Baptism or the Lord's Supper is a regrettable misunderstanding. Baptists hold views which distinguish them from Catholics, Congregationalists, Episcopalians, Lutherans, Methodists, Pentecostals, and Presbyterians, and the differences are so great as not only to justify, but to demand, the separate denominational existence of Baptists. Some people think Baptists ought not teach and emphasize their differences but as E.J. Forrester stated in 1893, "Any denomination that has views which justify its separate existence, is bound to promulgate those views. If those views are of sufficient importance to justify a separate existence, they are important enough to create a duty for their promulgation ... the very same reasons which justify the separate existence of any denomination make it the duty of that denomination to teach the distinctive doctrines upon which its separate existence rests." If Baptists have a right to a separate denominational life, it is their duty to propagate their distinctive principles, without which their separate life cannot be justified or maintained.

Many among today's professing Baptists have an agenda to revise the Baptist distinctives and redefine what it means to be a Baptist. Others don't understand why it even matters. The books being reproduced in the *Baptist Distinctives Series* are republished in order that Baptists from the past may state, explain and defend the primary Baptist distinctives as they understood them. It is hoped that this Series will provide a more thorough historical perspective on what it means to be distinctively Baptist.

The Lord Jesus Christ asked, *"And why call ye me, Lord, Lord, and do not the things which I say?"* (Luke 6:46). The immediate context surrounding this question explains what it means to be a true disciple of Christ. Addressing the same issue, Christ's question is meant to show that a confession of discipleship to the Lord Jesus Christ is inconsistent and untrue if it is not accompanied with a corresponding submission to His authoritative commands. Christ's question teaches us that a true recognition of His authority as Lord inevitably includes a submission to the authority of His Word. Hence, with this question Christ has made it forever impossible to separate His authority as King from the authority of His Word. These two principles—the authority of Christ as King and the authority of His Word—are the two most fundamental Baptist distinctives. The first gives rise to the second and out of these two all the other Baptist distinctives emanate. As F.M. lams wrote in 1894, "Loyalty to Christ as King, manifesting itself in a constant and unswerving obedience to His will as revealed in His written Word, is the real source of all the Baptist distinctives:' In the search for the *primary* Baptist distinctive many have settled on the Lordship of Christ as the most basic distinctive. Strangely, in doing this, some have attempted to separate Christ's Lordship from the authority of Scripture, as if you could embrace Christ's authority without submitting to what He commanded. However, while Christ's Lordship and Kingly authority can be isolated and considered essentially for discussion's sake, we see from Christ's own words in Luke 6:46 that His Lordship is really inseparable from His Word and, with regard to real Christian discipleship, there can be no practical submission to the one without a practical submission to the other.

In the symbol above the Kingly Crown and the Open Bible represent the inseparable truths of Christ's Kingly and Biblical authority. The Crown and Bible graphics are supplemented by three Bible verses (Ecclesiastes 8:4, Matthew 28:18-20, and Luke 6:46) that reiterate and reinforce the inextricable connection between the authority of Christ as King and the authority of His Word. The truths symbolized by these components are further emphasized by the Latin quotation - *quod scriptura, non iubet vetat*— *i.e.,* "What is not commanded in scripture, is forbidden:' This Latin quote has been considered historically as a summary statement of the regulative principle of Scripture. Together these various symbolic components converge to exhibit the two most foundational Baptist Distinctives out of which all the other Baptist Distinctives arise. Consequently, we have chosen this composite symbol as a logo to represent the primary truths set forth in the *Baptist Distinctives Series*.

Intercommunion
Inconsistent, Unscriptural
and
Productive of Evil.

J. R. GRAVES
1820-1893

INTERCOMMUNION

INCONSISTENT, UNSCRIPTURAL,

AND

PRODUCTIVE OF EVIL.

BY

J. R. GRAVES, LL.D.,

EDITOR OF "THE BAPTIST," AUTHOR OF "THE GREAT IRON WHEEL," "OLD LANDMARKISM; WHAT IS IT?" "BIBLE DOCTRINE OF THE MIDDLE LIFE," "TRILEMMA," ETC., ETC.

With a Biographical Sketch of the Author by John Franklin Jones

SECOND EDITION.

"Because there is one loaf, we the many [members of the one Church at Corinth] are one body; for we all partake of the one loaf."—1 Cor. 10: 17.

"Now I praise you, brethren, that you keep the ordinances as I delivered them unto you."—1 Cor. 11: 2.

MEMPHIS, TENN.
BAPTIST BOOK HOUSE;
GRAVES, MAHAFFY & CO.
1882.

he Baptist Standard Bearer, Inc.
NUMBER ONE IRON OAKS DRIVE • PARIS, ARKANSAS 72855

Thou hast given a *standard* to them that fear thee;
that it may be displayed because of the truth.
-- Psalm 60:4

Reprinted 2006

by

THE BAPTIST STANDARD BEARER, INC.
No. 1 Iron Oaks Drive
Paris, Arkansas 72855
(479) 963-3831

THE WALDENSIAN EMBLEM
lux lucet in tenebris
"The Light Shineth in the Darkness"

ISBN# 1579784127

This Little Work is Dedicated,

AND

Its Dissemination throughout the Denomination committed

TO

THE BAPTIST MINISTRY AND BAPTIST CHURCHES,—

"THE TWO WITNESSES,"

To whom Christ committed the Gospel and its Ordinances to
be preserved and perpetuated, in their Pristine Purity
and Form, among
All Nations and in all Ages,
"Till He Comes,"

BY

THE AUTHOR.

Memphis, *April* 10, 1881.

OPINIONS OF DISTINGUISHED AUTHORS AND SCHOLARS ON THE MERITS OF "INTERCOMMUNION OF CHURCHES UNSCRIPTURAL," ETC.

Rev. E. J. Fish, D. D., Mich., Author of "Ecclesiology."
Rev. J. R. Graves, LL. D.

Dear Brother:—For years I have been accustomed to say that the question of communion roots itself in the greater question of the church, and will not be satisfactorily answered until that greater question is answered. It was with much gratification, therefore, I opened your treatise on "Intercommunion," to find that you had gone to the very root of the matter—a work for which your many years of ecclesiological study and discussion, your loyal heart and logical acumen had given you rare qualifications. I have now read, re-read and studied your interpretations and reasonings, and give my emphatic verdict in favor of your main conclusions, viz, that the church of Christ is exclusively a local body of prescribed doctrinal and structural form, and that the Lord's Supper is a memorial ordinance to be observed only within and by a local church. You thus make church ordinance observance, and church disciplinary protection exactly coextensive—as manifestly sensible, as it is a scriptural order. On fundamental ideas of the church, your two brief chapters (Part II., chapters ii, iii,) are worth more than a wagon-load of ordinary treatises. **On the Symbolism of the Supper you are without a peer**, so far as I know, and deserve, as in time you will receive the thanks of all true Christians. With great pleasure, therefore, I commend your work to all ministers and church members as **without an equal in its line**.

Rev. S. H. Ford, LL. D., Editor "Ford's Ch. Repository," St. Louis:
"One thing at least is done in this work, with a **clearness and thoroughness surpassing any work on the Lord's Supper that we are acquainted with**—the development of the symbolism of the ordinance. He has shown that the Supper is the covenanted members of a particular church symbolically preaching Christ—showing forth his death. We hold that the object of the Supper, the radical idea of the symbolism, **confines it to a particular church.**"

The "Central Baptist," leading paper of the West, St. Louis, Mo.:
"This book is so compact that to summarize its contents is almost impossible. The conclusion sought in the argument by the author is, that the Lord's Supper is a (local) church ordinance, and that, therefore, neither by right nor courtesy, can the members of different churches be asked to celebrate it together. The old points of conflict have been along the line between our denomination and others, and 'close communion' has been the reproach cast upon us. Dr. Graves transfers the contest to the narrower lines which surround each local church, maintaining in a masterly way that the ordinance was put there by Christ and his apostles, and by its significance must remain there, within the limits of church discipline. To his argument we have seen neither scriptural nor logical reply. His reasoning, by itself, must be well nigh convincing to a candid reader; and if there is another side to the question, which will modify the conclusion, it has not been brought out. **That the ordinance is within the local church we think the author most conclusively proves.** We have seen no specific law authorizing courtesy or establishing rights beyond church membership, and those who advocate intercommunion among Baptist churches must assume the proof of their position. The general law is against them; if that law is modified by precept or example, the burden of showing such modification is theirs."

CONTENTS.

CHAPTER I.

Reasons for offering a new book in defense of Scriptural Communion—Because 1. Grounds and arguments by which our present practice is supported manifestly untenable and unsatisfactory; 2. Concessions made by our standard authors fatal to the existence of Baptist Churches; 3. A new treatment of the whole subject can be offered 9–16

CHAPTER II.

Facts and axioms, with their logical inferences demonstrative of the one fact, that, of the thirty-four sects in America, only one can be an Evangelical Church 17–29

CHAPTER III.

The definition of the terms "Scriptural," "Evangelical," "Gospel," "Christian," "Orthodox," etc.—The admission of Baptist authors that the leading denominations are Evangelical, Christian, Gospel, etc. 30–42

CHAPTER IV.

The unwarranted and fatal admission made by Baptist authors on Communion—that in all things essential to salvation, in all the fundamental doctrines of grace,—Baptists agree with other denominations 43–53

CHAPTER V.

The statements of many of our authors concerning the evangelicalness of the leading denominations examined.—The criterion by which they are to be judged, not Charity, but the Word of God.—Do Baptists agree with Presbyterians? . . . 54–64

CHAPTER VI.

Do Baptists agree with Methodists as to the essential doctrines of salvation? 65–74

(v)

CHAPTER VII.

Baptist authors have generally misstated the real issue between Baptists and others touching Communion . . . 75-87

CHAPTER VIII.

The Author's positions sustained by the Editors of the "Christian Review," Dr. F. Wilson, Dr. G. B. Taylor, by the late Dr. A. M. Poindexter, of Va., and by Facts 88-98

PART II.

CHAPTER I.

A CHURCH OF CHRIST—WHAT IS IT?

Definitions of a Scriptural Ecclesia—by Catholics, Protestants, and Baptists—Baptists divided among themselves, etc. . . 101-114

CHAPTER II.

There can be no more excuse for this confusion of ideas respecting the meaning of ecclesia, than respecting **metanoeo, pistuo,** or **baptizo** 115-124

CHAPTER III.

The scriptural use of Ecclesia.—It is used to designate a specific organization—a Church of Christ only; by a figure of speech, the churches or kingdom of Christ 125-139

CHAPTER IV.

THE KINGDOM OF CHRIST.

The views of our standard writers variant and contradictory—Some advance none.—False theories of the kingdom of Christ give rise to unscriptural and pernicious practices, and maladministration of the ordinances.—Views of Authors . . . 140-163

CONTENTS.

CHAPTER V.

THE SUPPER A CHURCH ORDINANCE.

Definition of church ordinance.—The Supper demonstrated to be a church ordinance. 164-184

CHAPTER VI.

Christian Baptism—Is it the pouring or sprinkling of water upon, or the immersion of the subject "in or under water?"—Authorities, etc., etc. 185-202

PART III.

CHAPTER I.

The inspired accounts of the institution harmonized—Was Judas at the Lord's Supper—Was feet washing connected with the ordinance or enjoined as a Church or Christian duty? . . 205-220

CHAPTER II.

The Supper first given to the apostles as a family who were instructed to commit it with baptism to the churches; 1. Accounts of its observance; 2. Scriptural names; 3. Qualification of the subjects 221-240

CHAPTER III.

THE SYMBOLISM OF THE LORD'S SUPPER.

Of the bread; 1. Of the one loaf; 2. The unbroken loaf; 3. The wheaten loaf; 4. The unleavened loaf; 5. The broken loaf; 6. The eating of the one loaf 241-273

CHAPTER IV.

THE WINE.

1. The Fruit of the Vine; 2. The unleavened Fruit of the Vine; 3. The One Cup; 4. The drinking of the One Cup . . 274-285

CONTENTS.

CHAPTER V.

THE PRACTICE OF THE APOSTOLIC CHURCHES.

They observed the ordinances as they were delivered to them.—The Supper was delivered to be observed as a church ordinance.—They had no authority to change any rite in the least respect.—They were commanded to judge all whom they allowed to eat with them, and they can not judge the members of sister churches.—Intercommunion was unknown among the apostolic churches in the earliest ages of Christianity . 286-306

CHAPTER VI.

The inconsistencies, and the evils of Intercommunion among Baptists 307-323

CHAPTER VII.

FALSE PRETENSIONS EXPOSED.

Pedobaptists, the most rigid of Close Communionists, by their own Statutes, Standards, and Practice.—The Presbyterians are so.—The Methodist's, the Episcopalian's, the Campbellite's Open Communion a sham and fraud 324-339

CHAPTER VIII.

OBJECTIONS TO CHURCH COMMUNION REVIEWED.

1. " Paul and his eight companions, belonging to different churches, communed with the church at Troas." 2. A local church has the RIGHT to invite members of other churches to her table. 3. It tends to destroy fellowship between the churches, and creates an extreme independency 340-355

APPENDIX.

(A.) The recognition of unevangelical churches . . . 356-358
(B.) No church at Troas in the first century . . . 358-361
(C.) The beauties of open Communion 361-366

Intercommunion,

Unscriptural and Inconsistent.

CHAPTER I.

Reasons for offering a new book in defense of Scriptural Communion—Because 1. Grounds and arguments by which our present practice is supported manifestly untenable and unsatisfactory; 2. Concessions made by our standard authors fatal to the existence of Baptist churches; 3. A new treatment of the whole subject can be offered.

WHY a new book on "Communion," about which so many books have been written? Why a pair of new shoes when you have bought so many? What better answer can be given than "Because the old ones are no longer serviceable?" The fact is—and it is but the part of candor to admit it—that the old current arguments by which Baptists have attempted to vindicate our entire consistency in restricting our Communion to our own denomination have been shown to be **untenable,** and our principal argu ments **sophistical**. The result is, dissatisfaction with our present practice of restricted Communion is manifestly increasing yearly, both in the ranks of our ministry and the masses of our thinking membership.

This state of the case imperiously calls for a thorough re-examination of the whole question, to ascertain whether the cause lies in the fact that our present practice is wrong, or our arguments illogical, or both. Then it is the conviction of the writer that our standard authors, who have written in defense of our practice, in order to escape the charge of "bigotry," "illiberality," and "uncharitableness," have conceded so much to the denominations opposed to us, that Baptists have, in fact, no foot of ground left to stand upon, and no alternative seems left us but to search for other and more defensible ground and arguments, or surrender at discretion. I do not say this because my confidence in a scriptural warrant for strict Communion is shaken; since I firmly believe that all the teachings of Scripture and all arguments based upon reason, are in favor of **strict** Communion, as it has been conceded by a distinguished affusionist that all the arguments are in favor of immersion as the apostolic act of baptism,[*] but, in my humble opinion, the true line of defense—the **impregnable** scriptural argument—has never been clearly laid down; while, as I have suggested, an indefensible

[*] Olinthus Gregory.

line of argumentation has been hastily adopted, and, in attempting to defend it, concessions have been made fatal to our existence as a denomination.

In addition to this, our churches, while holding fast to the form of sound words, have been insensibly beguiled by the fraternal feeling and the plea of courtesy into the practical surrender of **Church** for **denominational** Communion, thus immeasurably weakening the whole line of defense, and, in fact, abandoning our chief bulwark to the enemy, and, by our practice, perverting the sacred symbolism of the Supper.

It seems to me evident, that if our arguments in support of the practice of our churches were scriptural and our practice consistent, they would have been like the shoes of God's ancient people, imperishable,—

"'Till all the ransomed Church of God
Is saved to sin no more."

So fully convinced am I of the truth of the above, that, for years past, I have chosen an altogether new line of battle, and developed defenses which the most powerful of our opposers have been compelled to pronounce impregnable. It is my personal conviction that of all questions pertaining to Baptist faith or practice, this one of "Close Communion" has been the most **superficially** and **inefficiently** treated, which must be the reason for the general and growing dissatisfaction in the very bosom of our churches. This can not be said of our views of the subjects, design and act of Christian baptism, and is it not because these have received a more **scriptural** and **logical** treatment?

Numerous, therefore, as are the books, tracts, and treatises upon "Close Communion," I trust I will be pardoned for offering for the consideration of my people and the public an altogether new treatment of the whole subject of Church Communion, developing what I consider its impregnable strength from four sources—(1.) The constitution of the Christian **Ecclesia**; (2.) The divine symbolism of the ordinance itself; (3.) From the positive teachings of the Scriptures forbidding denominational Communion; and (4.) The practice of the primitive churches and not from mere **"analogy,"** or, as it is denominated, "orderly example." I shall prove, if I know what constitutes proof, that it is not only unscriptural, inconsistent, and productive of evil for Baptist churches to invite members of other denominations to their Communion tables, but wrong so to invite members of our sister Baptist churches—*i. e.*, that **denominational** Communion,* as at present practiced by Baptists, is unscriptural, inconsistent, and fraught with manifest and manifold evils. I only asked to be impartially

---

*In this book I shall, for convenience, use the term Denominational when applied to Communion, to designate the common practice of our churches in inviting all members of the Baptist denomination present, and even district associations and State Conventions to partake of the Supper with them:

heard, if such a thing is possible. If I do nothing more than to awaken a general discussion of the whole question, or offer a **clew** that will conduct our churches out of existing confusion, my effort will not be altogether fruitless. Other and abler pens may take the direction indicated, and lead the denomination into "all truth" upon this subject.

I propose, in the first place, to show—

1. That the many concessions, so fatal to Baptists, made by all our standard writers who have volunteered to defend our restricted practice, are not sustained by the facts in the case—indeed, are disproved by the self-same authors themselves!

2. That the principal positions hitherto taken by our own writers in defense of Restricted Communion, not only force wide open the doors of our own tables, which they seek to close, but surrender every just claim we have to exist as Christian churches.* Like soldiers attempting to defend the outposts, surrender the citadel itself; so very many of our authors on Communion, while attempting to defend our present practice of Communion,

---

* It is a fact, as regretful as true, that an enemy could, with little trouble, by collecting and arranging all the admissions made by our prominent men in favor of the denominations opposed to us, and what they have asserted adverse to our historical succession as churches, establish the claims of these denominations to be scriptural churches, and that the rise of Baptist Churches was many centuries this side of the apostles! Touching our history this has already been done, and the book is before me!

have surrendered the denomination. There can be no question but these false positions should henceforth be abandoned.

3. That the scriptural argument used by our writers, is, to say the very least of it, the very weakest the word of God affords, and that these are rendered wholly uninfluential by the concessions of our standard authors on Communion.

The ground being properly cleared of these obstructive matters, I shall make "my best endeavors" to bring to the front and establish, "beyond successful contradiction," the clear, positive, and impregnable scriptural arguments in support of **local Church Communion,** as opposed to the modern practice of indiscriminate denominational Communion.

During the thirty-four years of my uninterrupted editorial connection with "*The Baptist,*" I have written little upon the subject of Communion, as all my brethren have noticed. The reason has been not that I was not a staunch believer in **restricted** Communion, but satisfied of the inconclusiveness of the current arguments, "hackneyed and worn," and suspicious of their logical accuracy, I hesitated with that most sagacious remark of the wise man before my eyes, "Whoso breaketh a hedge a serpent shall bite him," warned me, that before presuming to encounter such a peril in attempting to break the "hedge" of an old and popular usage, I should be thoroughly convinced it was my duty to break it. Now fully convinced as to my duty, I boldly cleave through the hedge with "the sword of the Spirit, which is the Word of God," and offer a new line of argumentation that is equally adapted to offensive as to defensive warfare. The great Wellington sagely remarked, that a position only adapted to defensive operations was a dangerous one, and such is the position Baptists now occupy upon the Communion question—only fitted for defense; and that it is both a weak and dangerous position, has been demonstrated by the immense losses we have sustained as a denomination by occupying it.

My aim will be to indicate the scriptural position of the Lord's Supper in the Churches of Christ, and to defend that position with unanswerable arguments, which will not only establish the fact that different denominations can not intercommune without perverting and profaning the ordinance, and eating and drinking condemnation to themselves, but as conclusively show that **intercommunion**, now so generally practiced among Baptists, is not only unscriptural and inconsistent, but is working many and serious evils, and immense loss to our denomination.

To all those who regard this plan and purpose as sufficient to warrant one more "little book" by an old editor on the subject of Scriptural Communion at the Lord's table, these pages are affectionately commended.

In justification of what I have said, I submit the following from the pen of Rev. George B. Taylor, D. D., our present missionary to Rome, when editor of the *Christian Review:*

"The most prominent of our denominational journals have, within the last half year, contained communications from Baptists, in different parts of the country, expressing, to say the least, the absence of satisfactory conviction that baptism is 'the true limit to Communion;' and, recently, in some of these journals have appeared communications which, in view of the prevalence of inquiry on the subject, **call for another treatise in defense of Restricted Communion.** We mention these circumstances, unimportant in themselves, as straws which show how the winds of opinion and feeling are blowing. The author himself is aware of not a few prominent Baptists—ministers and laymen in different States—men not suspected of heterodoxy—who, more or less cautiously avow, at least, **that the arguments commonly used in favor of Restricted Communion to the baptized, seem to them not entirely satisfactory.** How many there are, practicing this restriction, who do so because they have received it from their fathers, or find it practiced by those around them, it were difficult to say, and not pertinent to our present object to inquire; though the fact that there are **many** such, would **certainly be a reason for the re-discussion of the whole subject.**"

CHAPTER II.

Facts and axioms, with their logical inferences demonstrative of the one fact, that, of the thirty-four sects in America, only one can be an Evangelical Church.—"The Branch Church," "The Army Church," "The Breastplate Church," "The Rainbow Church," "The Currency Church," and "Universal Church," theories refuted.—The admission that opposing sects are Evangelical Churches fraught with disastrous consequences—(1) It yields the claims of Baptist Churches to be evangelical; (2) It must have a direct influence to infidelize the nation.—Infidel France.

THAT the reader may clearly apprehend the objections I am about to make to the statements of most Baptist authors who have preceded me in the discussion of the Communion question, it will be necessary for me to lay down a few fundamental facts, which every intelligent, unprejudiced Christian will, I think, admit.

FIRST FACT.

That Christ, while upon earth, did set up a visible kingdom, of which each local church is an integral or constituent part.

It is enough to refer the reader to the fact that

all the prophets which foretold the coming of Israel's Messiah and the world's Redeemer, declared it to be a part of his mission to "set up a kingdom" on this earth, unlike earthly kingdoms in the beneficence of its mission, the character of its subjects, and the unchangeableness of its duration. Daniel says: "In the days of these kings"—the Roman Emperors—"the God of heaven shall set up a kingdom"—but **one** kingdom and **visible**— "which shall not be given to other people, but it shall stand forever." Christ did appear on earth in the days of the Cæsars—the kings of the fourth Universal Empire—and his herald announced this fulfillment of the prophecy in these words: "**The kingdom of heaven has approached**," and, subsequently, the king himself, in the same language.

From this we learn that this visible kingdom of visible saints did not exist upon this earth prior to or in the days of Daniel (600 B. C.); and, since it is composed of visible churches as its constituents, we decide that Christ had no visible Christian Church or churches prior to his advent. We learn from his own lips that he did have a visible kingdom on earth. He could say in truth, that "the publicans and harlots go into the kingdom of God before you," which would have been impossible if that kingdom had then no **visible** existence. He could in truth declare that "from the days of John the Baptist until now the kingdom of heaven suffered violence—*i. e.*, was assaulted—and that the violent—his enemies—take it by force"—violent persons are endeavoring to ravage or destroy it. Christ explained what he meant in the next verse, but the translators have put other words in his mouth than those he used. "For," said Christ, as recorded by Matthew, "all the prophets and the law prophesied until John"—and Luke finishes the sentence (xvi: 16)—"since which time the kingdom of heaven is preached, and every one is violently opposing it,"*—not all men are pressing into it, which would make Christ contradict his statements throughout the whole chapter and the preceding one, but his general statements throughout the Gospels (read especially vs. 16–26). John the Baptist bore direct testimony to the statement of Christ, that all men (comparatively) opposed his kingdom. "He that cometh from heaven is above all; and what he hath seen and heard that he testifieth, and **no man receiveth his testimony.**"—Jno. iii: 32.

Christ, in definite terms, declared that his kingdom was present; and upon the soil of Judea, and

---

*The natural force of the terms **biazo** and **harpazo**, in Greek usage, is to indicate the violent action of an enemy, and not the loving movement of friends, *e. g.*, **biazesthai ton parthenon** and **biazesthai auton**, to do oneself violence—to kill oneself. **Eis** before the accusative, with **biazo**, indicating hostile intent, means to *force against*, *i. e.*, to assault, to violently assail. See Harrison on **Eis**, with verbs of hostile motion, p. **213**.

within the jurisdiction of Herod, "my kingdom is among you, not within you."—*See Alford*.

SECOND FACT.

Christ never set up on earth but ONE kingdom, which is a visible one, composed of his true churches as constituencies.

THIRD FACT.

Christ did not "set up" his kingdom of constituencies in deadly antagonism to each other, and in open rebellion to his authority also—a kingdom CONSTITUTIONALLY divided against itself—of materials so heterogeneous and discordant that they could never be "fitly framed together."

Christ, the Founder, hath said:

"Every kingdom divided against itself is brought to desolation."

But Christ's kingdom is never to be brought to desolation, but is to stand forever; and, therefore, it is not divided against itself—composed of discordant and antagonistic constituencies—churches.

Direct Inferences from these Facts.

First Inference.—That these constituencies of Christ's kingdom are each and all the equals of each other in every quality that constitutes logical **differentia**—*i. e.*, essential qualities.

In a Christian **ecclesia**—church—the essential features are—1. The character of its members; 2. Organization; 3. Ordinances, with their respective designs or symbolisms; 4. Fundamental doctrines, etc.

I shall take it for granted that my readers will admit that the essential features of a visible church of Christ are clearly revealed to us by Christ and his apostles, so that we need not err in the description; and—

That no organization, however old, numerous or respectable, or however pious and saintly its members, can rightly be called a Christian or **evangelical** church, unless it possesses the divine essentials of a true church of Christ.

This statement of the late Bishop Doggett is in place here:

"We do not suppose that any unprejudiced mind would call any body of men or women the true church—**so particularly described by the inspired writers as the true church has been**—unless it comes up fairly and fully, in every minute particular, to a description proceeding from that wisdom that could not err in the description in any remote or conceivable degree."

The churches of Christ, then, are not diverse the one from the other, but the equals of each other, having the same character of **membership**, the same **form of organization**, the same **ordinances** in form and design, and holding and teaching the same fundamental **doctrines**.

SECOND INFERENCE.—That the popular "church-branch theory" is a bald absurdity. This theory—which is so popular with all those ministers and members who pride themselves upon being "undenominational Christians"—is that all the leading popular "sects," at least, variant and antagonistic though they be, are branches of "The Church" of Christ—the constituents of his kingdom visible! Branch is a relative term, and necessarily implies a **trunk** or **body**; but these people are unable to tell us what or where the **trunk** of this tree is! The absurdity of this conception must be apparent to the dullest comprehension, when one thinks of a tree bearing **natural** branches of **sixty-three different kinds of wood, and without a body!**

THIRD INFERENCE.—That the "Church Army" theory is equally absurd with the former. This theory, so popular with the "broad-gauge" preachers and members, is that all the different denominations compose but one allied army, Christ being the "Captain," and the various sects the regiments, brigades, etc., and the different **creeds** the **flags** under which they fight, etc.

This theory sadly breaks down when we recall the fact that the various parts of an army are all under the **same laws** and **regulations**, drilled by the **same tactics,** and not in deadly conflict with each other,—regiment against regiment, and brigade against brigade, as the different denominations called "churches" have ever been from the day they were originated, are to-day, and must be to the end of time, so long as they hold and teach different and antagonistic doctrines. They are not fighting a common foe, but are endeavoring to betray and deliver each other over to a common enemy.

FOURTH INFERENCE.—We learn that the "Breastplate theory," and the "Rainbow theory," (Dr. Burrows), and the "Currency-Church theory" (gold, silver, nickel and copper, representing the different churches of different values—Lorrimer), are all equally fallacious and God dishonoring, though so popular with all our "go-easy" preachers and members. The simple fact being, that **paste, in a breastplate, or anywhere else, is not a gem,** however illusive, no more than an unscriptural Church is a ray of real light, or a counterfeit coin, currency, in any sense, but a cheat and a fraud.

FIFTH INFERENCE.—The above facts equally lay bare the absurdity of the "Universal Church theory"—a church theory so popular with all pedobaptist theologians, and those Baptists who are their disciples.

This theory is, that all the different and opposing sects—the respectable ones at least, taken together constitute "The Church and Kingdom of Christ visible." The fatal disease of this theory is, that it squarely antagonizes with the first **fact**—that the constituencies of Christ's kingdom must be concordant and equal the one to the other, else Christ would have a kingdom divided against itself. But the various denominations which "liberalists" call

Christian and **Evangelical** Churches, are discordant and irremediably divided against themselves, and engaged, like the men who sprang up from the dragon teeth, in destroying each other. If any one should succeed in obtaining the universality it is striving for, it would annihilate every other Church of Christ from the face of the earth! One part of the kingdom destroying and swallowing up all the rest! As I have said, it is too **preposterously absurd** to be put forth by men who have any respect for the wisdom of the Divine Founder of the Christian Institution called a Church of Christ. Infidels could wish for no better argument against Christ or Christianity. I honestly believe that more infidels are made by those who teach these absurd and unscriptural church theories than by all the speeches and writings of avowed infidels themselves. Convince a man that Christ did originate all these diverse sects, and that he really is the Author of all the absurd and contradictory doctrines and systems of faith, if not **a fool**, he must **be an infidel.** Christ has no more two Churches, one visible and the other invisible, than he has two kingdoms.

FOURTH FACT.

There are in America alone fifty-four distinct sects of professed Christians, all diverse, and most of them radically differing from each other in the **essential elements** of a Church of Christ, but each claiming to be alone conformed, or at least, more than any other conformed—to the scriptural model of a Christian Church. Now the unthinking multitude is taught, from the pulpit and the press, to believe and to call all these antagonistic sects, **Evangelical** Churches, which means Scriptural Churches of Christ, and equally entitled to our Christian consideration; and that it is proof of "intolerant bigotry" to deny that they are not all Churches of Christ, or that any one is more conformed to the scriptural pattern than any other, or that one alone is so conformed. This is a plain statement of an existing fact.

The honest Christian has but one alternative, either to stultify his reason and common sense, and admit what he knows to be false, or he must dare the burning fiery furnace of a perverted public opinion, which modern and idolatrous liberality has prepared, heated to a sevenfold intenser heat by sectarian hate than it is wont to be heated for any other offense.

There is no proposition easier demonstrated than that two—much less two score—different and unequal things can not be equally true or equal to a third thing.

I will state two Axioms that will apply to this subject as well as to mathematics.

FIRST AXIOM.

Things equal to the same thing are equal to each other.

And its converse—

SECOND AXIOM.

Things unequal to each other can not all be equal to the same thing—one, and only one, may be.

This is but the equivalent to the truth stated in another axiomatic form.

THIRD AXIOM.

Of contradictory propositions, if one be true all the others are false.

Now apply these axioms. There are fifty-four sects in America, each claiming to be equal to the same thing—an Evangelical Church—but are they equal to each other in all the elements essential to an evangelical church? Ask each one separately to testify concerning the others, and each will deny that the others are equal to itself or to the evangelical model. The question is thus answered by themselves: Try their claims by the second axiom. Are these fifty-four sects unequal to each other—any two of them essentially alike? Put the question to their respective representatives, and they will affirm that each is widely, if not vitally, unlike the others, and this unlikeness is their sectarian glory. It is the boast and glory of Methodists that they are radically unlike the Presbyterians in doctrines and organization, and in all the distinguishing features of Methodism. So it is of the Presbyterians, that they are unlike the Methodist, and so of each of the other denominations. They all can not be equal to the same thing—an evangelical church; if one is evangelical, whether that one be the Catholic, or the Methodist, or a Baptist Church, **only that one** is an evangelical or scriptural church.

Try these sects by the third. That the creeds or faiths of those sects are diverse and contradictory, needs no proof. Who could conceive of two creeds, touching the vital doctrine of grace, more contradictory than the Calvinism of Presbyterianism and the Arminianism of Methodism in common with Catholicism? or that of the Baptists and Campbellism? They are the very **antipodes** of each other. All these fifty-four **contradictory** sects, built upon as many contradictory propositions, can not be equally true—if one is evangelical, only one can be. Now, if this be a fact, ought not every honest Christian—and can a Christian practice habitual dishonesty, falsehood, and deception?—to say so, though the burning fiery furnace stands in appalling fierceness before his eyes? Has he not a God able to deliver, if not to place on his brow a martyr's glorious crown?

I have said all this to prepare the reader to see the force of this irresistible mathematical conclusion. If I should affirm that the Catholic is an **evangelical** church, would I not thereby affirm that Baptist churches, and all the other fifty-three sects, were not evangelical? And so of any other one, should I admit any one to be evangelical, it would be affirming that only that one is evangelical; while, if I should admit that all were evangelical, I would convict myself of—what? I will not say of hypocrisy, but of **self-stultification**.

The reader can now understand the force of my complaint, that so many—nearly all—Baptist authors, who have written on the Communion question, have admitted that Protestant denominations —if not Campbellites also—are "**Christian denominations**," "evangelical churches," "Christian churches."

I complain for two reasons—1. The admission is fatal to the claims of Baptist churches to be evangelical, or Christian, as we have seen above. In attempting to defend strict Communion, every one who has made this admission, has surrendered his denomination; 2. It is a concession to infidelity fatal to Christianity. (1.) It admits that Christ is the originator of fifty-four conflicting faiths, and that he, himself, originated, or authorized the origination, of fifty-four antagonistic organizations, that must, from their very constitution, be in perpetual conflict until one shall have exterminated all the rest,— a kingdom divided against itself, which the founders of earthly kingdoms would not think of doing; and (2.) It concedes to infidels, that the oceans of blood that have been shed in religious persecutions, all the martyr fires that have been kindled, and all the racks and instruments of infernal torture that have been invented, have been shed, and kindled, invented and used by the **evangelical** churches of Christ, upon evangelical churches, Christians playing the **role** of infernal **fiends** upon their fellow Christians! Make the world believe this, and will it be strange if it should rise up with demoniacal frenzy and spurn Christianity from the land as the red-armed butcher of innocency, **a fraud** upon human reason, and a damning **curse** to the race? It was the like of this that smote France with centuries of infidelity. It was the Catholic church, claiming to be the very embodiment of Christianity, while she proved herself the direst foe of humanity. **Scarlet,** but with the blood of saints and the purest and truest patriots of earth. **Mother,** indeed, but of those twin evils, and direst of all abominations, civil and religious tyrannies which she hung in double conjunction over the sky of Europe and France for half a century,— like the plague-struck sun of the apocalypse, tormenting the nations. It was with respect to **Catholicism,** as Christianity, and not toward **Christianity** itself that France was infidel; and unless we would impregnate the veins of our populations with the **virus** of a like maddening unbelief, let us not, in God's name, teach them that Christianity has been the torture-armed inquisitor of the centuries; that evangelical churches have gored their spotless robes in the blood of their own children, or even denied to mortal man the divine and indefeasible boon of absolute religious freedom.

CHAPTER III.

The definition of the terms " Scriptural," " Evangelical," " Gospel," " Christian," " Orthodox," etc. The admission of Baptist authors that the leading denominations are Evangelical, Christian, Gospel, etc.—Drs. Howell, Arnold, Samson, etc.

IT is urged, in defense, by those who apply the terms "Evangelical," "Christian," "Orthodox," to opposing sects, that they are not synonymous with **scriptural**, and they do not mean that they are conformed to the scriptural pattern of a scriptural church. If they do not mean this, the world and those sects understand them to mean it. "Liberalists" have no right to use words with opposite or different significations from their definitions in our standard Lexicons. Let us refer the question to Webster's Unabridged:

"**Scriptural**. — 1. Contained in the Scriptures; 2. According to the Scriptures or sacred oracles.

"**Orthodox**. — 1. Sound in the Christian faith; 2. According with the doctrines of Scripture—as an orthodox creed, or faith, or church.

"**Christian**.—1. Pertaining to Christ, taught by him, or received from him, as the Christian religion, Christian doctrines.

"**Gospel.**—1. Accordant with the Gospel.
"**Evangelical.**— 1. According to the Gospel; consonant to the doctrines and precepts of the Gospel published by Christ and his apostles."

With these definitions before the reader's eyes, he needs no word of ours to see clearly that they are as nearly synonymous as words can be. They mean substantially the same thing, and "Evangelical" is the strongest of them all, if, indeed, one implies a greater degree of accordance with the teachings of Christ and his apostles. No church can truthfully be called "Evangelical," unless, in all the essential elements of a church, it conforms to the teachings of Christ and his apostles. This covers all the ground. Friends of Christ and his truth should persistently refuse to allow liberalists to use this term to mean any thing more or less than Webster's definition, which they seem determined to do.

I will now call the reader's attention to a few noted examples of the real use of these terms.

Dr. Howell asserts and implies it throughout his elaborate work on Communion, though admitting it **once** would accomplish all the harm to our cause that a thousand repetitions of it could do:

"Between Baptists and the members of **all the surrounding evangelical denominations**, we cherish for them, as the people of God [?], the sincerest affection."

If it be true that all the surrounding denominations are evangelical, or the various Protestant bodies—for I will grant the author means no other—then his work on Communion, and all he ever wrote in a long life against Pedobaptists, was but a ruthless assault upon the kingdom of our Lord Jesus Christ, as will be shown in a subsequent chapter:

"And it is evident that all the respectable writers we have quoted, and others of all the **evangelical churches,** concur with them."—p. 117, Lon. Ed.

He refers to all Protestant Pedobaptist societies, at least, here, as in the former quotation, and the reader will mark that he in the one sentence pronounces them "**evangelical denominations**," and, in the latter, "**evangelical churches.**"

"They [the views alluded to] originated with the churches in Switzerland [Pedobaptists], but, with some modification, are now the prevailing sentiments of evangelical Pedobaptists."—p. 195, Lon. Ed.

Whether we understand the term "evangelical," as applied to **Pedobaptists** personally, or to their **societies**, he admits that they are "evangelical."

"The **evangelical** portion of them [Pedobaptists] will, I doubt not," etc.

It can not be denied that this author admits that the **members** of Pedobaptist denominations are "evangelical Christians," and their societies "evangelical churches."

Prof. Curtis, in his very able work on Communion, as frankly admits, throughout his book, that Pedobaptist societies are **"Christian"** and **"evangelical churches."**

It must be supposed that **he** used the term "church" according to his own definition, given on pp. 36 and 37:

"Whoever carefully studies the New Testament, will find the word Church, when applied to a Christian assembly, is used in two distinct senses: (1) For a particular congregation of **professed** believers [mark him, not a mixed body of professed believers and unconscious infants]; (2) For the Universal Church—the general assembly and Church of the first born."—p. 36.

"Each separate Church, then, is recognized in Scripture as a **divinely** organized society, having its own special prerogatives and relations independently of all other bodies, and for the employment of which it is answerable to the Head of the Church alone."— p. 37.

This being his own definition, he can not be justified in calling any organization a Church that is not a "divinely organized society of **professed believers existing independently of all other bodies**," etc.; for to apply it to any **humanly** organized society, religious or otherwise, **not of professed believers**, would only serve to confuse rather than instruct his readers, and confirm members of such societies in their errors.

Prof. Curtis, through five entire chapters, 112 pages, seems studiously to avoid applying the terms "evangelical," or "orthodox," or "Christian Church," to Pedobaptist societies; but occasionally applies the term **Church** to them, *e. g.*, "belonging to **churches** of other denominations."—Page 96.

"That we do not participate in the occasional celebration of the Lord's Supper with **churches** of other denominations, whose members we do not consider baptized."—P. 97.

He here, contrary to all standard writers, whether Baptist or Pedobaptist, concedes that there can be a Church, and a **Christian Church**, without baptism, where not a member of the body is baptized!

But when he comes to meet the objections of Pedobaptists, that we unchurch them by our terms of Communion, he seems to break down altogether, and disowns and throws overboard his own previous definitions, to make fair sailing under Pedobaptist skies. After admitting that almost all Pedobaptists—he could have said all, without an exception, known or heard of by us—regard baptism as essential to a Christian church, he says, "We shall, however, express in all candor our own opinion," just as though he had not done so in his first definition given above!

"The **original** word for church is used with different significations in the Scripture. [Not in its **primary** sense, which is the only one we have any thing to do with.] In one sense even the tumultuous assembly at Ephesus is so designated (**ecclesia**) Acts xix: **22**.* Any Christian congre-

* Not the multitude (**demos**), nor the disorderly crowd (**ochlos**) was designated here (**ecclesia**), but a specific body

UNSCRIPTURAL AND INCONSISTENT. 35

gation, especially if assembled for worship, would have been thus called in the time of the Savior and his Apostles (Matt. xviii: 17).* All organized religious bodies acknowledging the Headship of Christ, and assembling for the worship of the Father through him, we [Professor Curtis] regard as Christian churches. We only do not consider them as **regular** churches, according to the New Testament pattern: 'If a company of believers without any **baptism** at all—as, for instance a body of Quakers—claimed the title, we should have nothing to say against it.'"—Pages 117, 118.

In thus repudiating his first, and, so far as it goes, a correct definition of a Christian church, Professor Curtis concludes that any organization of professed believers, with or without any kind of baptism, claiming to be a church, is a church in his estimation! Is such a writer a safe instructor upon this subject? He furthermore states that a company of believers, **not organized according to**

of qualified citizens whose names were enrolled—a body corresponding to the House of Commons in England. This **ecclesia** convened at its accustomed place of meeting, the theater, and the disorderly multitude rushed in. It was not a tumultuous **ecclesia**, but **demos**—populace. When the officers of the **ecclesia** could not learn from the multitude any definite charge for the **ecclesia** to consider, he dismissed that body and dispersed the crowd.

* Here Professor Curtis errs again, for the **ecclesia** referred to here by Christ was an organized body empowered to exclude, from its fellowship and membership, an offending member who would not be governed by its judicial decision—and, therefore, it was a judicial body—a Christian Church.

the New Testament pattern, may be considered a Christian church! This means, in plain English, that a body organized in open manifest violation of the teachings of Christ, is a Christian church, which means, is **organized according to the teachings of Christ!** If this is not a palpable self-contradiction, we do not know what is one.

Dr. Arnold, professor in Madison University, in Hamilton, N. Y., in his work "Prerequisites to Communion," yields the question he attempts to defend by the fatal admission—

"But, strictly, **evangelical** Pedobaptists, with whom we have chiefly to deal in the present controversy," &c.—p. 16.

Dr. Hovey, the distinguished president of the Newton Theological Seminary, Massachusetts, in his little work on Communion, also admits it:

"From what has been said, it appears that the principles which require Baptist churches to limit their invitation to the Lord's Supper to Christians of their own faith and order, are identical with those which determine the action of **other evangelical churches** in this matter. Hence we can not perceive the fitness of calling their practice 'Close Communion.' In principle it is as open as that of most orthodox churches; as open as the New Testament allows them to make it."—p. 68.

Here, in three sentences, in one paragraph, and on one page, Dr. Hovey admits that Pedobaptist societies are "evangelical churches," and "orthodox churches."

Dr. Samson, late president of Columbia College, D. C., in his little book, "The Christian Law of Union in Communion," is in accord with the above, in admitting the **evangelical** character of the **members** of Pedobaptist societies as well as of the societies themselves—

"Discussions in all **evangelical** churches, since the alliance, have turned on the issue of union and Communion, this being the natural result of that conference."—p. 6.

"Mission of Baptists among **evangelical** Christians."—page 8.

"**All evangelical** Christians agree in the general statement," etc.—p. 9.

"Believing with all other **Christian denominations**," etc.—p. 20.

"Injustice to other **Christian denominations**," etc.—page 31.

"The experience of **churches**, other than Baptists," etc.—p. 36.

"The variety of views, arising in great degree from different constitution of human minds, has given origin to varied denominations of **evangelical Christians**, which are sometimes said to have different missions."—p. 45.

And Dr. Samson nowhere offers the least protest to this view, only claiming that "the Baptists certainly have a very important mission."

"By common consent, the assembled delegates of the **evangelical** alliance, representatives of **evangelical** churches of every name and nation."—p. 50.

From a perusal of Dr. Samson's book no one

would receive the impression that he even imagined that Pedobaptist societies were a whit less **churches** of Christ than Baptist churches, but everywhere speaks of them as "evangelical churches," and "evangelical denominations," and of their members as "evangelical Christians."

Rev. Henry Colby is another author who, through the American Baptist Publishing Society, essays a defense of restricted Communion of the Lord's Supper in a twenty-one page Tract.

He contributes his influence to impress Pedobaptists and the world, as well as Baptists, that Pedobaptist societies constituted, as Dr. Osgood says, upon principles subversive of the whole scheme of Christianity, are indeed the true churches of Christ, only somewhat "irregularly constituted," yet truly **evangelical**, and possessed of the ordinances—administering the Lord's Supper, but only "**prematurely!**"

I quote a few statements:

"The **real question** we understand to be this:

"**Ought we to acknowledge that evangelical Pedobaptists are qualified to partake of the Lord's Supper?** We say **evangelical** Pedobaptists, because those with whom we have to do chiefly in this discussion do not ask us to receive any others."—pp. 3 and 4.

He must mean all the Protestant Pedobaptists as opposed to Catholics.

"We simply declare, concerning Pedobaptist **churches,**

that, in our judgment, they are **irregularly constituted**; and, as for the table which is spread by them, the bread is there, the wine is there, the prayers are offered, and the elements duly distributed to many devout persons, who partake of them in faith, and find the occasion a precious **means of grace**" [?], * * "We have no disposition to deny that it is the Lord's Supper. But since baptism scripturally precedes the Supper, our view is that they partake of it **prematurely**."—p. 14.

"The declaration that our practice casts **contempt** upon their churches or their table is a misrepresentation of our [Mr. Colby's] attitude."—p. 15.

This author allows no one to mistake his qualified indorsement of Pedobaptist societies as **scriptural churches**, and the rite professed to be observed by them for the Lord's Supper as really and truly the Supper. I can not resist the question here: If organizations irregularly constituted—which means in violation of the law of Christ—are, indeed, Christian churches; and if it is the Lord's Supper, though "**prematurely**" observed—which means in violation of the **order** in which it was commanded—then why not say their sprinklings of water are **evangelical baptisms**, though a different **act** than Christ commanded?

I could fill pages more with like admissions, but these must satisfy all that I have not misstated the fact when I say that all our leading writers, in defense of Close Communion, have admitted that Pedobaptist societies are evangelical churches and in substantial agreement with us on the fundamental doctrines of grace and teachings essential to salvation.

In addition to these frank admissions, all these authors, and the hosts who follow their leadership, seal their teachings with the highest possible **practical** indorsement of the evangelicalness and real scriptural character of "all the leading denominations around us." They, one and all, advocate the validity of the immersions of all these sects; and, as often as they have opportunity, receive them into Baptist churches, where they believe that no organization on earth is authorized to administer Christian immersion, except a true Church of Christ.

They, one and all, practice and defend the policy of pulpit exchange and pulpit affiliation with the ministers of all these sects, thus accrediting them, before all men, as truly **ordained ministers of Christian churches**—since no organization, save a true Church of Christ, can ordain and commission a man to preach the gospel.

It is useless to say that such ministerial affiliations and fellowships do not accredit and indorse them as scriptural ministers, for it does indorse them as such. These ministers so understand it, and have a right to so understand it. Their people so understand it, and have a right to do so; and the world so understands the act, and have no right to understand it otherwise (see App. A.).

These admissions are far from being only expressions of "courtesy"—mere "trifles light as air." These logically necessitate the following grave—

CONCLUSIONS:

I. **That there** can be an "evangelical" or "Christian" Church **without scriptural baptism,** and practicing infant baptism.

All the above writers concede this cardinal principle with Baptists, by admitting that Pedobaptist societies are Christian churches; and Prof. Curtis makes the admision in so many words—"churches baptized or unbaptized."

II. **That all EVANGELICAL churches are SISTER churches.**

No one can, with reason, question this. No church can be more than evangelical any more than one circle can be rounder than round, or than one square can be more square than another. Baptist churches are denominated "sister churches" because they are, one and all, evangelical.

The third irresistible conclusion is—

III. **That "all the leading denominations around us," and Baptist churches, are sister churches, and, consequently, of the same faith and order..**

Then, what other conclusions invincibly follow?

If members of sister churches, of the same faith and order, can scripturally commune together, as all the above writers admit and advocate, then it follows—

IV. That Baptist churches may scripturally practice open communion with "all the leading denominations around us."

This is a clear surrender of the **citadel**. But another conclusion—

V. Baptist churches can properly and consistently dismiss members by letters to, and receive members by letters from, "all the leading denominations around us."

This certainly follows, for we say dismissed when joined to another church of the same faith and order; and if they are evangelical churches, they, most assuredly, are of "the same faith and order."

But the crowning consequence of the admissions of our brethren is—

VI. Baptist churches are not evangelical churches, and, therefore, have no moral or scriptural right to continue their existence.

And thus, in attempting to defend an outwork, our defenders surrender the citadel and the garrison at discretion!

CHAPTER IV.

The unwarranted and fatal admission made by Baptist authors on Communion—that in all things essential to salvation, in all the fundamental doctrines of grace, Baptists agree with Congregationalists, Presbyterians, and Methodists—Our agreement with Presbyterians examined.

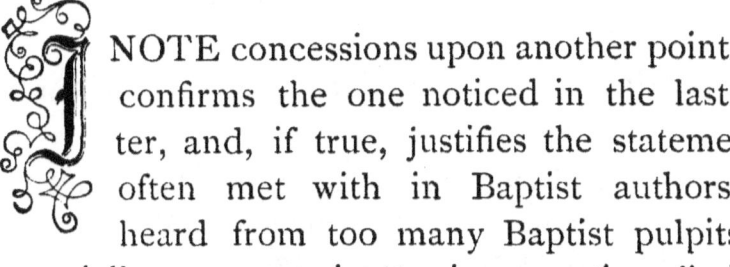NOTE concessions upon another point which confirms the one noticed in the last chapter, and, if true, justifies the statements so often met with in Baptist authors, and heard from too many Baptist pulpits, and especially common in "union meetings," that in all the essential doctrines of Christianity Baptists and all the leading denominations agree. Then it is upon the non-essentials of Christianity that Baptists exist, and about which they differ from other denominations. If this be so, the sooner Baptists are exterminated out of the land the better for Christianity and the world.

The form this idea assumes in some of our most popular books on communion is about this:

That in all the fundamental doctrines of grace and things essential to salvation, Baptists substantially agree with Protestant denominations.

It is far from being a pleasure to me to call public attention to their unfortunate concessions in favor of denominations so diametrically opposed to us; concessions that strengthen them with the public and weaken Baptists; it is with pain I do it, as it is with painful astonishment I read their admissions, but I do it to correct a false public opinion created largely by the unwarranted admissions of Baptists, and in hopes that these brethren may see fit to modify their statements in future editions of their works; and others who write hereafter may be more careful of their statements.

Dr. Gardner in his popular work on "Church Communion," says:

"With some of them, as the Congregationalists, Methodists, and Presbyterians, we agree **substantially in what is essential to salvation**," etc.—p. 22.

Again, on page 53 we find this—

"Hence we see that the Baptists and others agree as to the qualifications for Communion. All agree (1.) That the **new birth** is a scriptural qualification; (2.) That **valid baptism** is a scriptural qualification; and (3.) That regular church-membership is a scriptural qualification.

"Such, then, are the **points** of **agreement** between Baptists and others; (1.) As to the **nature**; (2.) As to the **design**; and (3.) As to the qualifications for the Lord's Supper."

Dr. Gardner must have written this in a moment of forgetfulness, for no statement could be wider of the **facts** in the case, as he himself abundantly proves in the latter part of his book, where few, who read his book to ascertain his position, would be likely to find it, and of little force also, whatever else he might urge after having conceded; 1. That in **all** things fundamental and essential to salvation Baptists agree with Protestants; and 2. Concerning **all** the scriptural qualifications for the Lord's Supper Baptists agree with Methodists and Presbyterians.

Why should the inquirer read further? or how otherwise conclude but that Baptists are, indeed, unscripturally close and bigoted sectarians if they refuse to commune with those with whom they agree both as to the doctrines of grace and the **qualifications** for, and the **design** or symbolism of, the Supper? Though I propose to devote the next chapter to the refutation of these concessions, I must say here to the reader—who may lay down the book at the close of this, satisfied with the evangelicalness of these denominations, and the correctness of their practice, indorsed so fully and by such high authority, and satisfied also that Baptists are indeed a bigoted sect—that neither Methodists nor Presbyterians, much less Baptists who think, will indorse these statements of Dr. Gardner, and, as we have said, he himself refutes them nearer the close of his book.

Do not both these sects hold and teach that both baptism and the Lord's Supper are **sacraments of salvation,**—God's appointed media through which the blessings of salvation, pardon, regeneration, and sanctification are offered, communicated and sealed to the soul of both the unconscious infant and the unregenerate adult? Do not Presbyterians hold and teach that the ordinances are **seals** of the covenant of grace? Do not both agree that "in the ordinary way" one or both are necessary to salvation; so that "out of **the** church there is no ordinary possibility of salvation."—*Presbyterian Confession*, p. 112. Do Baptists agree with these sects touching the way an infant or an adult is to be saved? I trow not.

But do we agree with Methodists as to the qualifications for the Lord's Supper? They hold and teach, and on this faith practice, that all men, baptized or unbaptized, should partake of the Supper as a means of pardon, regeneration, and salvation,—that no qualifications are required except to know and feel one's self fit for hell.

Wesley says:

"Every one who knows he is fit for hell, being just fit to come to Christ in this as well as all other ways of his appointment."

He says all such should come to have their "souls renewed in the image of God;" and he makes it the duty of his ministers to invite and urge all sinners to partake of the supper for this purpose, and they do it all over the land. Do Baptists agree with them in either the qualifications for or design of the Supper?

Presbyterians do not require regeneration as a qualification for the Lord's Supper, so they be church-members and not absolutely scandalous in life, and are not infidels or scoffers. This all intelligent Presbyterian ministers and elders know full well, and Baptists should know it. In the late Pan-Presbyterian Assembly that met in New York last September, Dr. Bannerman, of Scotland, a celebrated scholar and theologian, read a paper on "sealing ordinances," which was unanimously approved. I copy one sentence here:

"Applicants for the sacraments, therefore, do not profess to be Christians except in an outward way. They simply declare that they are not infidels or scoffers, and that they wish church privileges for themselves and their children." —p. 525 of Report, etc.

From this we learn two things; 1. That all except infidels or scoffers are qualified to receive Presbyterian baptism; 2. And on baptism and membership their unregenerate wives and all their ungodly children are baptized and taken into church relations, and entitled to the Lord's Supper. Do Baptists agree with Presbyterians either as to the qualifications for baptism and the Supper, or the design of those ordinances? Do we believe that by them pardon, and regeneration, and salvation are secured—that they are effectual unto salvation, with or without faith? Let no Baptist say, then, that the faith of Baptists and Protestants is the same, or that we indorse their teachings on the above points. See next chapter.

Prof. Curtis in his work on Communion makes the same statement slightly modified:

"But it is true that baptism is **the chief** thing that prevents us from affiliating with those Pedobaptist churches **which are of similar faith** and of congregational government."—p. 118.

Here is the **threefold** admission; 1. That Pedobaptist societies are **churches;** 2. That there are Pedobaptist churches of **like faith with** Baptists; and 3. That baptism is the chief thing that prevents our intercommunion with them! It really pains one to admit here that Dr. Howard Osgood, of Rochester University, New York, a brother whom I so highly respect as an authority, in his little work "Protestant Pedobaptism," etc., makes the misleading admission, that, touching the **doctrines of grace,** Baptists and Protestant Pedobaptists are generally agreed, and thanks God for it!

He says:

"The central point of controversy between Baptists and Protestant Pedobaptists **is not the doctrines of grace—for thanks be to God, we generally agree there**—but it is the constitution of a church."—p. 8.

"Baptists are thought to be great schismatics, because **agreeing with evangelical Protestants on the great doctrines of the gospel,** antecedent to the doctrines of a church," etc.—pp. 8, 9.

Now, this was not written to mislead, but it does mislead—nor to deceive, but it does deceive, and greatly contributes to the much already written calculated to confuse and bewilder the people, and to confirm Pedobaptists in their **doctrinal** errors.

What other impressions are these statements calculated to make? what other can they make upon the masses who read them, or hear them quoted, than this, that in all things essential to the salvation of men, Baptists and Pedobaptists substantially agree, and the things about which they differ are mere **non-essentials?** I do not intend to say, or imply, that these good brethren think this, but I do say, this is the impression their unfortunate admissions are calculated to make, and do and **must** make. How often is it spoken and written by Baptist ministers and writers, that the points of agreement between Baptists and Protestants far outnumber those about which we disagree, and the impression sought to be made by those who make this declaration is, that we should not permit these few and non-essential differences to separate us in Christian **work** or **Church** Communion. Now, if this was the truth, no one would glory in it more than the writer of these pages; but alas! it is not the truth, and it ought not to be spoken, or written, to deceive the world. The stern, sad fact is touching the fundamental doctrines of grace; and all that is essential to the plan of salvation, Baptists differ from Protestant Pedobaptists, *toto cælo*, just as far as salvation by the "sovereign grace of God alone," and salvation by the deeds of law—any law, moral, ceremonial, or ecclesiastical. As far as the East is from the West are these two grounds of salvation asunder,—the **whole revealed word of God**

lies between them. Protestant Pedobaptists have made the whole plan of salvation and grace of God of none effect by their **traditions.** Instead of teaching salvation by grace, they teach that union with Christ and salvation, is by and through the ordinances which they have in common with the Romish Church, converted into **sacraments,** thus teaching that **through the church,** can and must the sinner, "in the ordinary way," come to **Christ;** and **through the water** of baptism gain **access to the blood** that alone cleanseth from all sin; and through the ministration of an ordained minister can one alone be savingly introduced into the everlasting covenant, and sealed an heir of grace! This doctrine, as the thoughtful reader can see, converts the simple minister of the gospel, and **servant** of the church, into a **priest,** practically possessed of the keys of heaven and hell, at his own will opening so that no one can shut, and shutting so that no one can open! Not only is the sinner's regeneration thus made by them dependent on the will of men (John 1), but "their churches, so called, are all formed in direct contravention of God's way of salvation."

I have said, and I must continue to repeat it, that I would as soon have a **sacrament** from the hands of a Romish priest, as from a Protestant minister (whose creed makes him a priest), and sooner, as a mercy to the perishing, would I approve of **seven** sacraments than but two, as multiplying the "means of grace." I can not refrain from allowing Dr. Osgood, whom we heard just now thank God for the agreement of Baptists with Protestant Pedobaptists on the great doctrines of grace, and the gospel of our salvation, an opportunity here to refute his own hasty declaration:

"And this point of difference, *i. e.* [concerning church constitution], involves not merely that which is outward and subordinate, but draws in its train immediate consequences which **affect the doctrines of God's grace to sinners.**"—page 10.

That is the stern fact. Their views of church constitution subvert what Baptists regard as the fundamental doctrine of salvation, and therefore our disagreement from all Pedobaptists is nothing less than *toto cælo*.

Hear him again:

"Their churches are, to our view, formed in direct contravention of God's way of salvation; their constitution is **AT WAR WITH THE DOCTRINES OF GOD'S GRACE.**"—p. 11.

"But this we say, that while we may so highly regard them [not as churches, but personally], we are compelled to bear our testimony—unequivocal and earnest—against what we esteem to be **grievous errors against the doctrines of God.**"—p. 12.

Is not the good doctor manifestly inconsistent, here with himself, when, in one breath, he thanks God that Baptists generally agree with Pedobaptists on the doctrines of grace, and, in the next breath, bears his testimony, unequivocal and earnest, against "their grievous errors against the doctrines of God?" But Jupiter sometimes nods.

On page 13, Dr. Osgood charges upon all Pedobaptists that they put **the Church in the place of the Word**; and, on page 20, that they put **the Church in the place of faith**; and, on page 24, he draws this very just conclusion:

"When the Church is put in the place of faith in the order of salvation—when one is said to be united to Christ, a member of Christ, before he exercises faith—they reverse the whole gospel scheme of salvation. By that act, it is practically declared **that salvation is of works, not of faith.**"

Even these charges are not all, or the severest. On pages 30 and 31, he says:

"To put the Church before faith, to put it before the work of the Spirit, to put it before the Word, is to attempt to put it in the place of God's sovereignty and secret will; and there it breaks upon the bosses of Jehovah's buckler. The constitution of that Church can not be scriptural which thus wages incessant war, not only with distinct and separate truths of God's word, but [in Dr. Hodge's words] with the relation in which the several parts of the divine plan stand to each other."

On pape 32, he says:

"Put the ordinances of a church entirely out of view for the moment, and **beyond them how wide is the difference between us!** What **puny superficiality**, then, to assert, that the form of one ordinance is all that makes a Baptist Church to differ from others, or that Baptists exist merely to uphold that form! If there are any Baptists so blind as to acquiesce in a statement so far short of the truth, I pity them

What noble testimony this would be if Dr. Osgood did not nullify the whole force of it by the declaration and thanksgiving (which Pedobaptists alone will use), that "touching the doctrines of grace, and on all the great doctrines of the gospel antecedent to the doctrine of a Church, Baptists and Protestants, thank God, are agreed." How wide the difference between this statement and his statement last quoted! Who can reconcile them? Pedobaptists will not quote what the doctor says **against,** but **for,** them.

CHAPTER V.

The statements of many of our authors concerning the evangelicalness of the leading denominations examined.—The criterion by which they are to be judged, not Charity, but the Word of God.—The sources of our information as to what they hold as their acknowledged doctrinal standards.—Do Baptists agree with the sects of Presbyterians touching how adults are to be saved?—An appeal to their standards and their scholars.

PROPOSE, in these chapters, to develop, from the standards of the leading sects, their faith and teachings touching the one great vital doctrine of Christianity, viz.: How a sinner is to obtain the benefits of Christ's death—pardon, regeneration and salvation. If the system of a sect is diseased at this point, the malady is mortal, the body is as good as dead, and, like a contageous corpse, should be buried out of contact. It has become a bounden necessity to determine the question, whether all the leading denominations agree with Baptists touching the essential, vital doctrine of grace—the way a sinner may be saved—since so many of our authors—through ignorance (it is the most charitable judgment) of the doctrinal standards of the sects—are so free to

affirm a substantial agreement. The latest work, by a popular author, scarce dry from the press, not only indorses the evangelicalness of Presbyterians, Methodists and Congregationalists; but extends the circle of Christian charity (?), and embraces Reforming Campbellites (a sect unheard of by me, and unknown to the world), Reformed Lutherans, Low Church Episcopalians, and even **Old Catholicism**, whose divinely written name is "Mystery, Babylon the Great, Mother of Harlots and Abominations of the Earth;" and the teaching is, that all these agree with Baptists as to how a sinner is to come to Christ for pardon, regeneration and salvation. If this statement is not true, it is time for such a misleading and dangerous untruth to be no longer published from our press and our pulpits; but, if true, for Baptists to cease from the earth, and no longer trouble the Christian world with their ceaseless contentions about empty forms and ceremonies not essential to either the life of Christianity or the salvation of a soul.

To ascertain the doctrinal belief of any denomination, we are not to take the faith of this or that man, but its published symbols, and acknowledged standards, and the concurrent testimony of its founder, and the publicly recognized and indorsed exponents of its doctrines, as its theological professors, etc.

And it is befitting to say, here, that Christian charity has no office to perform in this task—it is not her province. I am aware, that, by a large class, it is denounced as the lack of Christian charity to question the essential orthodoxy of the creed of any sect! What term in mortal language is more wrested and abused than "charity"—"Christian **charity**"—or used for a fouler purpose, so unworthy of her heavenly origin, since they would force her to be an accomplice of the most deadly errors! What has charity to do with printed propositions—articles of faith, or formulated systems of religion? Her office is but two-fold—(1) To succor the needy; (2) To kindly construe motives. Creeds need no alms, and articles of faith have no motives for us to judge kindly. No; this talk about charity being applied to Christian doctrines or ordinances is all delusive, deceptive and fraudulent. The mandate of the divine Father to all his children is: "Prove all things, and hold fast to that which is good"—the true; and to abstain from and reject every form of evil, and to hate every false way, for Christian charity alone rejoices in the truth, and is never an accomplice of error.

Before we can decide whether these various sects all agree with Baptists as to the way a sinner is to come to Christ for salvation, it will be necessary for the reader to know what the Baptists do hold and teach upon this point. I can state our faith in a few sentences.

Baptists teach that a sinner must come to Christ

by personal faith before he comes to the Church; that the plan of salvation is, not through the Church and its ordinances that a sinner comes to Christ, but by faith through Christ to the Church and its ordinances—**Christ before the Church.**

Stated in another form:

The sinner must, in every case, come to the blood of Christ, that cleanses from all sin, before he can come to the water of baptism, which is the figure of his having been cleansed.

It is **through Christ**, by faith, **to the water;** and not **through the water to Christ.** It is **Christ** before **water.** He must go down into the water **with** Christ—formed within the hope of glory; and not go down into the water **for** Christ. We see, then, it is:

Blood before water.
Salvation before baptism.
Possession before profession.

Let us first notice—

The Presbyterian Denomination. The forty-nine* sects which constitute it, I understand, accept the Westminister Confession of Faith with more or less or no modification.

I do not expect that any statement made in these

---

* At the first Pan-Presbyterian Assembly, which met in Edinburgh, July, 1877, twenty-two sects of Presbyterians were represented, and twenty-seven others expressed a desire to be represented—forty-nine!

pages concerning the doctrinal teachings of the various sects will be received as true that I do not prove to be so, beyond all possible contradiction, by their doctrinal standards. I protest I have no desire to misrepresent their views in the slightest degree, and shall therefore confine myself strictly to the Confession of Faith and the most distinguished exponents of it.

The first question to be settled is, what is the distinction between the Presbyterian "church" and all other denominations, claiming to be churches? If we turn to its Confession of Faith, chapter xxv, section 2, we will find this definition:

> "The visible church, which is also Catholic or Universal, under the gospel (not confined to one nation as before under the law), consists of all those throughout the world, that profess the **true religion, together with their children,** and is the kingdom of the Lord Jesus Christ, the house and family of God, **out of which there is no ordinary possibility** of salvation."

To say the least of this definition, it denies that Baptist churches, and Campbellite societies to be visible churches of Christ. If the reader should ask a Presbyterian minister if he believed that Baptist churches were conformed to the apostolic churches, he would answer, No.

We draw two legitimate conclusions from this definition, helpful to the settlement of the question of inter-denominational Communion—

1. That Baptist and Campbellite communities

are not churches of Christ. Presbyterians can not, except by abandoning their own principles of confession, invite them to their tables; but they do, and hence their insincerity and inconsistency.

2. That Baptists and Campbellites, being out of the visible church, there is no ordinary possibility of their salvation.

3. The first step for a sinner to take toward salvation is to join the Presbyterian Church, to which alone is committed the ordinances and their administration.

The reason of this will be seen when we understand their views of the saving efficacy of the ordinances. We will first notice what they hold and teach concerning

BAPTISM.

"Baptism is ordained by Jesus Christ, not only for the solemn admission of the party baptized into the visible church, but also to be unto him a sign and seal of the covenant of grace, of his engrafting into Christ, of regeneration, of remission of sins, and of his giving up unto God to walk in newness of life."—Chapter 10.

Of this language, Dr. Howell says: "Much guarded caution characterizes the language of this passage; indeed it appears almost a jumble of nonsense; but the doctrine of baptismal regeneration is, nevertheless, fully embodied and maintained." We turn to the Shorter Catechism and find this additional light:

QUESTION.—What is a sacrament?

ANSWER.—A sacrament is a holy ordinance instituted by Christ; wherein, by sensible signs, Christ and the benefits of the new covenant are represented, sealed, and applied to believers.

Q.—Which are the sacraments of the New Testament?

A.—The sacraments of the New Testament are baptism and the Lord's Supper.

The explanation of the operation of the sacraments we will find in Larger Catechism, answer 161:

Q.—How do the sacraments become effectual means of salvation?

A.—The sacraments become effectual means of salvation, not by any power in themselves, or any virtue derived from the piety or intention of him by whom they are administered; but only by the working of the Holy Ghost, and the blessings of Christ by whom they are instituted."

William Norton, of England, commenting on this language, says:

"Except as to the **intention** of the administrator, this is precisely the doctrine of Rome.

Lest we possibly put a wrong construction upon these teachings, let us inquire how the most eminent Presbyterian divines and professors of their theology, understand and explain this.

Matthew Henry was ordained in 1687. In his "Treatise on Baptism," he says:

"The gospel contains not only a doctrine, but a covenant. Baptism wrests the keys of the heart out of the hand of the strong man armed, that the possession may be surrendered to him whose right it is. The water of baptism is designed for our cleansing from the spots and defilement of the flesh. In baptism our names are engraved upon the breastplate of the high priest. This, then, is the efficacy of baptism; it is putting the child's name into the gospel grant. We are baptized into Christ's death; that is, God doth, in that ordinance, seal, **confirm,** and make over to us all the benefits of the death of Christ.

We begin to see why there is ordinarily no salvation out of the Presbyterian "church," since regeneration, sanctification, salvation,—indeed all the benefits of Christ's death are made over to us in the act of baptism! And Christian baptism can only be administered in the Presbyterian "church," since the ordinances are in, and not out, of the visible church.

Dr. Dwight was elected president of Yale College in 1795. In his "System of Theology," first sermon on baptism, he says:

"When children die in infancy and are scripturally dedicated to God in baptism, there is much and very consoling reason furnished to believe that they are accepted beyond the grave."

The converse of this cautiously worded statement must be true, viz., that there is **little** or **no consoling reason** furnished by the Scriptures that unbaptized infants are accepted beyond the grave. This is said of the unbaptized infants of believers, what then are we left to suppose is the horrid fate of the unbaptized infants of all unbelievers?

Well wrote a Pedobaptist against this doctrine when put forth by Dr. Pusey:

"Strange doctrine! which leaves us in doubt of the eternal salvation of millions of millions of hapless infants, because they have not been subjected to a rite which depends **wholly on the will of another;** nay, which may be withheld by the parents precisely because they have conscientious scruples on the subject; in obedience, as they suppose to the will of God."

But hear her theologians, the exponents of her faith. Dr. Hodge, of Princeton, says:

"We are baptized in order that we may be united to Christ, and be made partakers of his benefits. This baptism unto repentance is a baptism that the remission of sins may be obtained."—Pritchard, *Infant Baptism*, p. 124.

Dr. Nevin, formerly professor at Princeton, and finally president of the Mercersburg Seminary of the German Reformed Presbyterian Church, says

"The church (Presbyterian) makes us Christians by the sacrament of holy baptism, which she always held to be of supernatural force for that very purpose."—Pritchard, *Infant Baptism*, p. 124.

John Calvin, the father and founder—the author and finisher of the Presbyterian faith, says:

"By baptism God promises remission of sins, and will certainly fulfill his promises, etc."

If we open the standard hymn-book we find that the same doctrine is sung as well as preached.

These are specimens:

UNSCRIPTURAL AND INCONSISTENT. 63

> "Abr'am believed the promised grace,
> And gave his son to God;
> But **water seals the blessing now**
> That once was **sealed with blood.**"
> —*121st Hymn, 1st Book.*
>
> "Baptismal **water** is designed,
> To seal his **cleansing grace.**"
> —*141st Hymn, 2d Book.*

Now, if baptism is the seal of the covenant of grace, as Presbyterians certainly do teach, then no one unbaptized, young or old, has been saved, or ever will be. Baptists hardly agree with these views, and they do most certainly involve all that is essential to salvation and the whole system of Christianity and the character of a scriptural church, and we think thoroughly subversive of both. Indeed, if Presbyterianism is the system of Christianity, Baptists have never held or taught it; and if the Presbyterian denomination is a church of Christ in any sense, no Baptist church can be so considered.*

I close this chapter with the strong and pungent language of Dr. Osgood, of Rochester University, New York:

> "Their views of Church constitution subvert what Baptists regard as **the fundamental doctrines of salvation,** and, therefore, our disagreement from all Pedobaptists is

---

* According to the definition of a church given in the confession, there is no church of Christ save one composed of those who profess the true Presbyterian religion, together with their children.

nothing less than *toto cælo* . . Their churches are, to our view, formed in **direct contravention of God's way of salvation; their constitution is at war with the doctrines of God's grace.**"—*Com.*, p. 11.

We ask the Baptist authors and editors of America, if this statement be true—and we have proved it in this chapter to be so—can we call the Presbyterians an "evangelical" or a "Christian church."

Is it telling the **truth** to do so? They have no Lord's Supper to invite us to; since the ordinance, as perverted by them, is no more of the Lord's Supper than the Mass of the Catholics is the Lord's Supper, and a Baptist would eat and drink unworthily should he partake of either the one or the other. I would as soon participate in a Romish **mass** as a Protestant **sacrament.**

Some Christian Presbyterian, who has experienced regeneration of heart by the exercise of a personal faith, may say, I do not believe or profess the above doctrine of sacramental salvation. But so long as you are identified with, you do profess it, uphold and teach it by all your influence; and if you were baptized in that body you did profess it personally or by proxy. If you do not believe it, and as you would not by your influence teach others to do so, and to depend upon sacraments for salvation, you should renounce the doctrine by leaving the Presbyterian church at once. So long as you are a member you can in no way effectually protest against those unscriptural doctrines.

CHAPTER VI.

Do Baptists agree with Methodists as to the essential doctrines of salvation?—What does Methodism teach sinners they must do to obtain the remission of sins and regeneration?—The teachings of Mr. Wesley, the founder and finisher of its faith.—Bishop Morris—The Discipline—The Hymn Book—The General Conference—The Church before Christ, and Water before Blood in every case!

WHERE are we to look for the doctrines of the Methodist "church"—those that every minister has professed to believe, and has obligated himself to teach, and every Methodist is pledged to uphold and defend? Bishop McTyeire tells us in his work, "Wesley's Sermons and Works," "The Discipline," "The Methodist Hymn Book," and the works issued by their Book Concerns. To these, then, let us go to ascertain the way of life and salvation as preached by Methodism. It is presumable that the father and founder of a system of faith understands that faith. Let us now hear what John Wesley taught and required his followers to believe and teach concerning the way of salvation.

THE EFFICACY OF BAPTISM.

In his "Treatise on Baptism" Works, vol. 6, pp. 15, 16, New York edition, 1832, issued by the "Book Concern" of that church, Mr. Wesley says:

"By baptism, we who are by nature the children of wrath, are made the **children of God.** And this **regeneration**, which **our church** in so many places ascribes to **baptism**, is more than barely being admitted into the church, though commonly connected therewith. Being grafted into the body of Christ's Church we are made the children of God by adoption and grace—John iii: 5. By water, then, as a means,—the water of baptism, we are **regenerated and born again**, whence it is called by the apostle 'the washing of regeneration.' In all ages the **outward** baptism is a **means** of the **inward**. Herein we receive a title to, and an earnest of, a kingdom which can not be moved. In the ordinary way, there is no other way of entering into the Church or into heaven. If infants are guilty of original sin, then they are proper subjects of baptism, seeing, in the ordinary way, they can not be saved unless this be washed away in baptism."

The very last book Wesley ever wrote was his "Notes on the New Testament." In reference to the baptism of Paul on the words, "Arise, and be baptized, and wash away thy sins, calling on the name of the Lord," he observes: "Baptism is both the **means** and the **seal** of pardon, and God did not ordinarily, in the primitive church, bestow this **grace upon any save through this means.**"

In his note on Col. ii: 12, speaking of "the faith of the operation of God," Mr. Wesley says:

"**Which** he wrought in you when you were, as it were, buried with him in baptism."

On John iii: 5:—

"Except a man be born of water, **and of the Spirit**; except he experience that great inward change by the Spirit, and be baptized (wherever baptism can be had) as **the** outward sign and **means of it;**" *i. e.*, **the** means of the baptism of the Spirit, or regeneration.

There can be no doubt as to the doctrinal sentiments of Wesley, and these are adopted and indorsed by the General Conference to-day without modification, and they are bound never to reject them.

I will quote a paragraph here from the sermons of Bishop Morris:

"Baptism is one **of the means of grace;** and, therefore, suitable for penitents, who need all the help they can get. So Peter understood it, as it appears from the advice he gave those who were smitten under his preaching: 'Now when they heard this they were pricked in their heart, and said unto Peter and the rest of the apostles, Men and brethren, what shall we do? Then Peter said unto them, Repent, and be baptized every one of you in the name of Jesus Christ, for the remission of sins, and ye shall receive the gift of the Holy Ghost.' Here, Acts ii: 37, 38, we can but mark the difference between the system of some Calvinistic teachers and that of the gospel. Their system is; 1. Conversion; 2. Repentance; 3. Pardon: and lastly, Baptism. But Peter's arrangement is: 1. Repentance. 2. Baptism; 3. **Pardon;** and, 4. The witness of the Spirit."—*Morris's Sermons*, p. 243.

Methodism teaches practically to-day that baptism precedes pardon and regeneration, and is the divinely appointed means of securing them. Let us open the Discipline and examine the office for the baptism of adults, and see if we do not meet throughout with the self-same expressions as in the office for infants, and which Wesley says teaches there is no salvation without baptism. We must admit they mean the same thing in both offices. I, therefore, insert adult for infant, and reassert Wesley's language.

It is certain that the whole office for the baptism of an **adult** proceeds upon the fact that every adult baptized by the Methodist Episcopal "church" is an unregenerated sinner, and comes to baptism to seek release from his sins, and to receive regeneration of heart in the act of baptism.

Let us notice the wording of each part of the Ritual—1. The exhortation the minister is required to make to the applicants: "I beseech you to call on God the Father, through our Lord Jesus Christ, that of his bounteous goodness he will grant, unto **these persons**, that which by nature they can not have!" [this **thing** is regeneration of heart, unquestionably], "that they may be **baptized with water and the Holy Ghost.**" By this latter baptism every Methodist understands the spiritual baptism, or regeneration of heart. The language teaches that the applicants have never received what they here seek in baptism, and what the congregation is exhorted to pray they may have.

The first prayer—

"We call upon Thee for **these persons** now to be baptized. Receive them, O Lord, as thou hast promised, by thy well-beloved Son, saying, Ask and ye shall receive; seek, and ye shall find; knock, and it shall be opened unto you. **So** give **now** unto us that ask; let us that seek find; open the gate unto us that knock; that these persons may enjoy the everlasting benediction of thy **heavenly washing.**"

This washing prayed for is the washing of regeneration, and therefore implies that those who apply for baptism have never received it, but come to baptism for it. If there is the least doubt of it, the instructions of the minister following will remove it:

"Then the minister shall speak to the persons to be baptized on this wise: Well-beloved, who are come hither, desiring to receive holy baptism, ye have heard how the congregation hath prayed that our Lord Jesus Christ would vouchsafe to receive you, and bless you, TO RELEASE YOU OF YOUR SINS, to give YOU THE KINGDOM OF HEAVEN, and everlasting life. And our Lord Jesus Christ hath promised in his holy word to grant all those things that we prayed for, which promise he, for his part, will most surely keep and perform."

Then the last prayer—

"O merciful God, grant that the old Adam **in these**

persons may be so buried that the new man may be raised up."

This supposes that the old man has never been put to death in them, nor the new man raised up in them—and they depend upon their baptism to accomplish this in and for them:

"Grant that all carnal affections **may** die in them, and that all things belonging to the Spirit may live and grow in them."

This is a statement on the part of the minister, and an admission on the part of the applicants for baptism, that they have never died to sin, or risen in the new life in Christ, and that they come to baptism seeking this change from nature to grace, from death in sin to spiritual life:

"Regard, we beseech thee, the supplications of this congregation; and grant that the persons now to be baptized **may receive the fullness of thy grace.**"

This grace had never been received, or it would not be sought in baptism.

Every intelligent reader knows that this ritual was copied, almost *verbatim*, from the ritual of the Church of England, concerning which Bishop Melville, one of the most eloquent ministers of the Church of England, of this generation, speaks:

"We really think that no fair dealing can get rid of the conclusion that the Church holds what is called **baptismal regeneration**. You may dislike the doctrine; you may wish it expunged from the prayer-book, but so long as I officiate according to the forms of the prayer-book, I do not see how I can be commonly honest and yet deny that every baptized person is, on that account, **regenerated.**"

The office does not recognize or admit the idea that they are already Christians saved, pardoned, or regenerated, **or that they can be without baptism.** There is no ceremony, or prayer for the baptism of a believer, of a recognized regenerate person, in the Discipline! Therefore, the baptism of a **professed Christian,** is unknown in the Methodist Episcopal church. Every one baptized by Methodist ministers must be baptized as a **confessedly unregenerate sinner,** and baptized to receive the grace of remission, regeneration.

I now open the Hymn-books of two divisions of Methodism, and examine the hymns on baptism. In the Northern book, besides the invocation, there are nine hymns—eight are for infants, and one that may be used for infants or adults; but each teach the self-same doctrine—baptismal efficacy, spiritual regeneration effected by baptism, as a sacrament!—that it is the seal that imparts and ratifies the benefits of the covenant of grace. I will give one, found in both, No. 280:

> "Father, in these reveal thy Son;
> In these, for whom we seek thy face,
> The hidden mystery make known,
> The inward, pure baptizing grace.

"Jesus, with us thou always art;
 Effectual make the sacred sign;
 The gift unspeakable impart,
 And bless the ordinance divine.

"Eternal Spirit, from on high,
 Baptizer of our spirits, thou
 The sacramental seal apply,
 And witness with **the water now.**"

These hymns teach that in no one who comes to baptism has Christ been revealed; to no one has the hidden mystery of baptism been revealed, or the inward grace of the Spirit; and the prayer is that the sign may be made effectual in the act, and the unspeakable gift of pardon and salvation be imparted, and the seal of the Covenant of Grace, which is sacramental, be applied to the subject who comes, not professing to have been pardoned or regenerated, but as a seeker of them only, in and by the rite.

Finally and conclusively—

THE ACTION OF ITS GENERAL CONFERENCE

Establishes the fact that Methodism, like the Roman Catholic Church and the Campbellites, teach that baptism is essential to regeneration, because the appointed means of it. I refer to this because the leaders of the unreading people aver that, "however they might have viewed some things in Wesley's day, the Methodists of this day do not believe or practice baptism as a means of regeneration." I reply, Do they not still use the self-same **Discipline**? repeat the same **Ritual**? pray the **same prayers**? and for the same thing? Are not Methodist ministers bound by the same vows to hold, teach and practice the same doctrine?

The last Methodist General Conference, that met in Memphis, indorsed an official report declaring that the present growing practice among Methodists—to baptize persons on the profession of regeneration before baptism—was an evil that should be discontinued! I copy a part of that report:

"Baptism, too, has been unnecessarily deferred, not only in case of children, but sometimes postponed to an indefinite period in case of adults. The practice of requiring a public **profession of regeneration before baptism** has resulted in **evil**; and that the design of the sacrament is perverted, and the people encouraged to expect the divine blessing without the use of means [baptism]! We call attention to these **evils** that we may seek diligently to remove them."—Copied from the *Methodist Advocate*, official Conference paper.

This is conclusive that this denomination, as such, holds and teaches that there can be no remission or regeneration without baptism!

What Baptist will presume to say that it is an " Evangelical Church," a " Christian denomination," and in full agreement with Baptists touching the essential doctrines of salvation? Or can we say that any one, though immersed by Methodists, with the above design, and for the above purpose—as every one baptized by them is—has received scriptural baptism? Can we accredit such baptisms as scriptural and valid? Can we claim to be in our right minds if we say that such an organization—originated less than one hundred years ago, holding doctrines that are subversive of the whole plan of salvation, as they are of the ordinances of the Church of Christ—is, indeed, any church at all?

CHAPTER VII.

Baptist authors have generally misstated the real issue between Baptists and others touching Communion— That it is the lack of immersion that prevents Baptists inviting others, which is not the case.

THE very first position our authors generally lay down, in defending our practice, is as manifestly untenable as it is false and fatal to Baptists—

"**That the mere act of baptism is the real issue between Baptists and other denominations—i. e., because they have not been immersed in adult age, Baptists can not invite them to the Lord's Table.**"

The reader will find that in nearly every book and tract published, and sermon preached, and discussion held, in defense of our practice, the main position taken is, that it is not "close communion" but "close baptism" that separates us at the table. We meet this statement every-where; we hear it every-where; it is our sheet-anchor argument. The impression made by our authors and speakers is, if other denominations would only immerse adults, instead of sprinkling or pouring water upon them, all obstacles to intercommunion with them would be removed. Of the mass of books, tracts and treatises issued in the last fifty years, I can examine but a few of the best known.

Dr. Howell, in his work on Communion, published by the American Baptist Publication Society, and republished in England, makes the following statements:

"We can not commune with Pedobaptists because, not having been immersed, they are not **baptized**."

"These, briefly, are our reasons, and we believe they are good and sufficient reasons, for refusing to recognize the rite when administered in infancy. Pedobaptists have received no other baptism but this, which is a nullity. They are not **baptized**, and, **therefore**, we dare not, until they are, admit them to the Lord's Table."—*Howell*, pp. 146–7, Eng. Ed.

It is clearly implied here, that if Pedobaptists would only adopt immersion every obstacle to intercommunion would be removed. Again:

"Nothing would be more pleasing to us than to go with them to the Lord's Table, but we are repelled by the fact that a preliminary duty [baptism] is essential, and with this they have not complied."—p. 23.

No one can mistake this language. Baptism is indicated as **the** only essential barrier that separates Baptists from the communion tables of Pedobaptists. Again:

"We have shown that we can not commune with Pedobaptists, because Jesus Christ expressly, as nearly all of them confess, requires baptism as a preliminary to Church

Communion; and they have not, in our view, been baptized," etc.—p. 452.

The impression is clearly made upon the minds of Pedobaptists that their societies are all right, as correct in all things as Baptist Churches, with the solitary exception—the lack of immersion!

We do not think this, by any means, a true statement of the case; and this author proves that it is not—in another part of his book, in which he shows that Pedobaptists administer both baptism and the Lord's Supper—for illegal purposes—*i. e.*, as sacraments of salvation; and that by communing with them, or in any way to recognize them as Churches of Christ, is to recognize the unregenerate as church members. He fails to show what the symbolism of the ordinance teaches or requires; indeed, the reader would not learn from this author that it had any symbolic signification whatever, which constitutes one of the radical defects of his work.

Rev. W. W. Gardner, D. D., late Professor of Theology in Bethel College, Ky., in his work on "Communion," in many respects an excellent work, falls into the same error of emphasizing the want of immersion as **the principal bar** to intercommunion with other denominations. He says:

"We learn, etc., (3) That it is not 'close communion,' in fact, but 'close **baptism**' that separates the Baptist and others at the Lord's Table."—p. 255.

The great question, then, that here divides us is,

"What is **Scriptural baptism?**" Here is **the real issue** between us, and here the battle must and should be fought.—p. 251.

"In the language of Dr. Hibbard, 'The **only question,** then, that divides us [*i. e.,* from Methodists] is, What is essential to valid baptism?'"—*Communion*, pp. 163 and 251.

He adds, on page 252, another obstacle:

"Until they [how many denominations he saith not] commune with us in believers' **immersion** and church **government,** we can not consistently and scripturally commune with them at the Lord's Table; and, as has been shown, it is both unkind and uncharitable in them to ask it. Hence, we see the charge of 'close communion' is no more applicable to the Baptists than to others. It is not 'close communion,' in fact, but 'close baptism' that separates us and others at the Lord's Table. This is admitted by the ablest advocates of mixed communion."

Whatever objections Dr. Gardner may suggest, here and there, in his defense, we see that he emphasizes his perfect agreement with Dr. Hibbard, that **the "only question that divides us from the Methodists and others is valid baptism."** Dr. Hibbard must have been aware that, could he lead Baptists into this snare, he would thereby secure their indorsement of the **doctrines** of Methodism!

But Dr. Gardner, elsewhere in his book, shows that to commune with other denominations, would be **to pervert the design** of the Lord's Supper, since they hold and teach that it, like baptism, is "**a sacrament**"—an efficacious means of salvation. Also "**a test of brotherly love;**" and "a proof of our Christian liberality," and should **we** partake with **them,** we would indorse this unscriptural design. The impropriety of our inviting them to our table consists in our indorsement of their unscriptural form of baptism!

In our opinion Dr. Gardner, like all his predecessors, has signally failed to occupy the strong impregnable ground of defense of Close Communion, namely: "**The symbolic teachings of the ordinance.**"

"Restrictions of the Lord's Supper" is the title of a little treatise by Rev. H. Colby, and issued by the American Baptist Publication Society, Philadelphia, and therefore the exponent of the views of that society.

He, like the authors quoted, falls into their error, and poises the whole question upon **the lack of immersion** on the part of Pedobaptists.

"Our unwillingness, therefore, to invite to the Lord's table Christians who have **not been immersed,** is so far from expressing a reluctance on our part to promote Christian union 'that it emphasizes our anxiety for the establishment of union upon the only real foundation.'"—p. 9.

This foundation, he leaves no one to doubt, is the immersion of professed believers.

Dr. T. G. Jones, in "*The Baptists,*" says:

"**The real issue** between Baptists and their Pedobaptist opponents **respects baptism** rather than the Lord's

Supper." . . . "In common with others, they believe that only the **baptized** are entitled to a place at the Lord's table. And they believe that only such as have been **immersed upon a personal profession of faith** are baptized. Hence they can not, without gross inconsistency, as well as moral guilt, invite to the table of the Lord any, however pious and exemplary who have not, upon such profession been immersed."

Dr. Hovey, president of Newton Theological Seminary, Massachusetts, so cautious and reliable in his statements, in his tract, "Close Communion," page 68, says:

"In reality, the great question between other denominations, and the one for which we have endeavored to speak, relates to the subjects and the rites of baptism."

Professor Curtis's work on Communion, published by the American Baptist Publication Society, we consider, on the whole, the ablest Treatise that has yet appeared upon the "Lord's Supper."

Though he by no means discusses the symbolic teachings of the ordinance to any extent, or develops their real strength in support of strict Church Communion, yet he makes his strongest point in its favor, by **asserting**—not **proving**—from the one loaf itself, that "the Supper is a symbol of church relations, subsisting between those who unite together in the participation of it."

Professor Curtis does not concede as much as the above-quoted authors, yet he makes the same unfortunate and fatal admission "that it is true that baptism is **the chief thing** that prevents us from affiliating with those Pedobaptist churches which are of similar faith and of congregational government." —1. This concedes that their lack of baptism is **the chief thing** that bars us from their Communion; 2. His language implies that there are Pedobaptist churches—a church means that organization, or one equal to it, which Christ set up; and 3. That there are "Pedobaptist churches which are of similar faith" with Baptists! If our **faith and government** are identical, then it is true that baptism is the only thing that hinders intercommunion with them, **if intercommunion among Baptists is admissible.**

The very latest defense of our Communion, is a sermon on Communion, by R. M. Dudley, D. D., president of Georgetown College, Kentucky, published in "Baptist Doctrines," which proposes to be an exponent of Baptist faith. He follows in the beaten track:

"This brings to the surface the fact that **the real difference** between Baptists and Pedobaptists is **not one of Communion at all,** but of baptism. And for our Pedobaptist brethren to cry out Close Communion, is not only wide of the mark, but ignoring the real issue. As has been said the thousandth time, perhaps, 'It is close baptism;' they will not give the Supper to the unbaptized. We say no more than that, so the question between them and us is, 'What is baptism?'"

Now exactly where Dr. Dudley stands, practically, on the Communion question we can not divine, for he advocates the validity of immersions by Campbellites and Pedobaptists, if not of Mormons and Universalists. Consistency compels him to advocate Communion with all who have been immersed on profession of their faith.

While many pages more could be filled with like statements, these must suffice to indicate how generally the position is taken by those able brethren who have been accepted to defend the practice of the denomination; and every author* whose book bears the *imprimatur* of the American Baptist Publication Society, Philadelphia, that has come under my notice, takes this position, so that in the eyes of the world American Baptists are fully committed to this position.

Now Pedobaptists, our own members and the thinking world, have seen and felt that it is not true that immersion is the **only** or the main thing that hinders Baptists from inviting all other denominations to our table, else our **professions** are insincere, and our practice wrong and inconsistent.

The New York *Independent*, a standard Pedobaptist journal, has recently made a show of this openly, and greatly to our damage. The editor says:

"When remonstrated with for their 'Close Commun-

---

*All the above works, save Gardner's, are published by the American Baptist Publication Society, Philadelphia.

UNSCRIPTURAL AND INCONSISTENT. 83

ion,' our Baptist friends offer the following defense : ' We are no more **close** than others,' say they. ' All churches practice Close Communion so far as to invite to the table none but the baptized. We differ from others only in not regarding sprinkling as baptism. They will Commune with us, because they regard us as baptized; we do not Commune with them, because we do not regard them as baptized. We are **close** in our definition of baptism ; but in regard to the Communion we are no more close than others. If you Commune only with these whom you consider to have been baptized, why do you blame us for communing only with those whom we regard as having been baptized ? '

"But this defense (whatever its value in part) does not cover the whole case. Here are the Free-will Baptists and the Adventists, all of whom have been immersed. Here are many in Methodist and not a few in other congregations who were immersed on being converted and joining the church. Here are persons, once members of Baptist churches, and immersed, of course, who, having removed to places where there was no Baptist meeting, or for other reasons in no way impeaching their Christian character, have become members of other churchers. Do Baptist churches invite these to the Communion table—these whom Baptists, as well as others, acknowledge to have been baptized ? By no means. The general form of invitation to Communion in Baptist churches is to ' members of sister churches **of our own faith and order.**' In other words, though one be a Christian, and an **immersed** Christian, they will not welcome him to the Lord's table unless he be a member of a regular Baptist church ! Call you this being ' no more close than others ?' Other churches invite to the Commuion all Christians whom they regard as baptized. The Baptists are the only ones who narrow down **the invi**tation to members of their own denomination."

In addition to the above, this editor urges the fact that all **our orderly churches** exclude those of their own members who persist in going to the Communion tables of Pedobaptists, Campbellites, and do not permit those to return to our table after they have joined other organizations. We can not say that these have not been scripturally baptized, for they received immersion at our hands.

Now, it is evident in these cases, as in the case of Free-will Baptists, Adventists, Campbellites, and Mormons, and the tens of thousands of immersed Pedobaptists who do not practice or believe in infant baptism—if the lack of immersion is, in fact, the only or the essential bar, then, to be consistent, we should invite all these to commune with us, which would be an open communion upon a pretty large scale. So strongly have some of our leading ministers felt the pressure of their own argument; *i. e.*, that immersion was the real barrier, that they have been seriously impressed that it was their duty to invite all **immersed Christians** of all denominations to their tables. As for the matter of church government being a bar, as suggested by Prof. Gardner, he could not shut out Congregationalists, Adventists, Universalists, or Campbellites, since all these sects have Democratic governments like our own!

The matter of the **act** of baptism is, in my opinion, the very least thing that separates us from other denominations. If effusion was discontinued to-day, and the immersion of professed believers adopted in its place, the same measureless distance would stretch between us—the teachings of the whole word of God upon this subject. Nor would the adoption of the Baptist form of church government lessen in any conceivable degree this distance. I trust that, after this showing, this old argument which would effectually drive us into a limited open communion, will never be put forward again by any intelligent Baptist; and I trust that it has been said for the last time that our Communion is no closer than that of others, because it is, and it should be; for Methodists invite all the professedly unregenerate, openly ungodly, to come to the Lord's table as well as to baptism, as a means of grace, and teach that, in observing it, they may hope to obtain the pardon of sin and regeneration and salvation.*

A Baptist pastor in the State of New York, discarding the old reason for not inviting immersed Christians of other denominations, proposes four new and different ones, while the one **real** and **scriptural** reason he has left untouched. I give them here in support of my position, that the lack of Christian baptism is by no means the **only**, or

---

* How much more scriptural, reasonable, and satisfactory for Baptists to say this Supper is a church ordinance, like voting; and, therefore, only members of this church have a scriptural right to celebrate it with this church. **We invite no other Baptist church.**

the **essential,** or the great reason why Baptists can not invite Pedobaptists, Campbellites, Hardshell and Soft-shell (Free-will) Baptists to their Communion table:

"1. He might [should he invite all immersed Christians to the table] reasonably expect to see devout Universalists, and members of other denominations, whose views of doctrine no evangelical church fellowships, availing themselves of it, and appearing at the Lord's table on his invitation.

"2. The excluded members of his own church and of other Baptist churches, believing themselves to be regenerated, and knowing themselves to be baptized, would be free to come to the Lord's Supper under such an invitation; and thus the force of church discipline would be greatly weakened.

"3. Such an invitation is a weakening of what seems to be the least guarded point of the Baptist defenses. It is the first question asked by an inquirer, it is the first objection raised by an opponent. It is the first step to mixed communion, which inevitably leads to mixed membership, and that ultimately to the neglect of the ordinance of baptism, and to the unscriptural observance of the Lord's Supper. The sooner Baptist pastors learn to yield no point of our defenses the better for them, for their influence and for the cause. If the camel once gets his head into any man's tent, he will be very sure to thrust in his body also.

"4. Such an invitation includes a baptized member of a Pedobaptist church. And the Baptist pastor is not authorized by the word of God to invite to the Lord's table such an one, because he belongs to and supports an organized system of disobedience to Christ, so far as his ordinances are concerned. He is a baptized member of an unbaptized 'church' [if such a thing could be.] Although he has in one instance obeyed the command of Christ by being himself baptized, yet the whole drift and influence of his life is given to uphold an unscriptural error, and it is a correct maxim which says that 'he who encourages wrong-doing is equally guilty with the wrong-doer.' Such a member of a Pedobaptist church, by his practice and example, does all in his power to give to the human devices of infant sprinkling and adult sprinkling equal validity with an ordinance of Christ; and by such disorderly walk he disqualifies himself for scriptural communion."

The great scriptural reason has not yet been suggested.

CHAPTER VIII.

The Author's positions sustained by the Editors of the "Christian Review," Dr. F. Wilson, Dr. G. B. Taylor, by the late Dr. A. M. Poindexter, of Va., and by Facts.

WISHING my readers to see that I am not captious, or altogether singular, when I say that most of the authors who have volunteered to defend our present practice of communion have unwittingly not only conceded that Protestant Pedobaptists and Campbellites are evangelical churches, and therefore scripturally baptized, and entitled to observe the Lord's Supper; but they have forced wide open the doors leading to our communion table, and, in fact, **surrendered our right to exist as a denomination.** I will quote here, at some length, from the *Christian Review*, when edited by those sterling Baptists, F. Wilson, D. D., of Md., and G. F. Taylor, of Va., 1858. The article is from the pen of Dr. Taylor himself:

"But may not Pedobaptists commune, and ought they not to do so? This is a question asked by the advocates of open Communion—asked with an air of triumph, as if the necessary affirmative answer must also involve free Communion; **and we admit that the answers given by** most writers for close Communion seem to tend to this. For instance, Prof. Curtis, in his work on Communion, admits that Pedobaptist societies are churches [and, we may add, nearly every Baptist writer on Communion—see Chapter III], and contends that the Supper belongs to churches. If this is true, these churches have a legal right to commune; and it would therefore be no more illegal for a Baptist to commune with one of them than with a Baptist Church to which he did not belong. This mode of argument ignores—not to say denies—the special connection between baptism and the Supper, which makes the former essential to the legality of the latter; it would, moreover, have no force, save with those who admit that a person may commune only with the particular (local) church to which he belongs. Even Prof. Curtis shrinks from this conclusion, to which, however, all his argument tends, and makes the Supper a symbol, not only of church relations actually existing, but of such also as might exist. Well, we think that, if Pedobaptist societies are churches, and legally entitled to all the privileges and prerogatives of churches, there are circumstances in which, both legally and properly, a Baptist might unite with one of these churches, reserving those rights which would be cheerfully accorded to him, in many such churches, touching his peculiar views; and, if this is so, he may, while not actually a member, commune with such a church, and symbolize his possible relation of membership to it. Other writers for close Communion leave open a yet wider door to the objector. They admit both—that the Supper belongs to churches, and that Pedobaptist societies are such; whence it follows that the observance of the Supper by these bodies is legal, while they do not contend for the peculiar restriction plead for by Prof. Curtis. If pressed, indeed, to tell why we may not commune with Pedobaptist churches, they say, 'Because that would sanction error.' **But how is their Communion an error, if they are churches, and if Communion belongs to churches?** The error must be in something else, and not in Communion. How is their error such that they may legally practice, and yet we may not sanction it? We deem the difficulty due to the admission that Pedobaptist societies are churches—**an admission, we believe, fatal to close Communion, and leading also to false conclusions in another direction;** since, if baptism admits to church membership, and Pedobaptists are already church members, Mr. Whitney's absurd conclusion, that Pedobaptists are not scriptural subjects for baptism, seems to follow.* But, as this reasoning is logical, and as the first premise is undoubted, we must deny the second premise, which admits Pedobaptist societies to be churches."

---

* How can Mr. Whitney be far from the exact truth, when the overwhelming majority—nine-tenths or nineteen-twentieths—of Pedobaptists were brought into their societies in unconscious infancy, and were professedly made the children of God by baptism; or, as adults, received baptism for the remission of sins and regeneration of heart; uniting with the Church in the belief that they were thereby united with Christ? It is confirming these already deceived millions to address them as Christians and brethren in Christ, simply because they are members of those human societies. It is a solemn and sad fact, that, as a general thing, the members of Pedobaptist societies are not scriptural subjects for Christian baptism, because they have not been "born from above"— have never been the subjects of the quickening and renewing influences of the Holy Spirit. Question them, as **we** have done, and the reader will soon be satisfied that **they** are strangers to regenerating grace.

Can any one resist reasoning so clear and conclusive? These editors are conservative men, and they are forced by logical exigencies to their conclusion. They could have stated the case more emphatically, viz.: If Pedobaptist societies are, indeed, evangelical churches, then Baptist churches can not be more so; then their ordinances, and sprinklings, and pourings, and communion, are as scriptural and valid as the immersions and Lord's Supper of Baptist churches, to all intents and purposes; then it is just as right, and just as much the duty of every Christian, under any and all circumstances, to join **them**, as to join Baptist churches; and then Baptist churches could be, and should be, dispensed with altogether. This is the end to which the **fatal** admissions, I have pointed out, with all the inexorable force of logic, drive every reasoning mind.

To the above I will add the testimony of a witness—than whom the South never produced a more intellectual, and, withal, a more logical mind—the late Dr. A. M. Poindexter, of Richmond, Va. When editor of the "*Commission*," he had occasion to review the work of Samuel Davidson (Baptist) on Baptism and Communion. He copies these two expressions of Dr. Davidson's:

"'Although we are in debate with the congregational body represented by Mr. Wood, etc. * * * There is much in that section of the Church that we admire and love,' and other language of similar import, by one who holds (p. 240, and elsewhere) 'baptism can be performed by immersion only, and was made by the inspired apostles a uniform and indissoluble prerequisite to church-fellowship; and hence to receive the unbaptized to communion would be an alteration of the basis upon which the Christian Church has been organized.'"

And says:

" We should like to be informed, without equivocation, how a body, composed of persons who have failed to comply with a uniform and indispensable prerequisite to church-fellowship, and which has altered in its very structure, 'the basis upon which the Christian church has been organized,' can be 'a section of the Church of Christ!' It is time to have done with such jargon. **If Pedobaptist societies are Christian churches, then Baptism is not a prerequisite to membership in a Church of Christ; and, if baptism is not a prerequisite to membership in a Church of Christ, then it can not be proved to be a prerequisite to Communion.** Why should we permit a **false** charity to cause us to obscure the truth on this subject? This is done whenever we use language so loosely—at one time calling any society of professedly converted persons a Christian church, and at another speaking of baptism as indispensable to membership in a Church of Christ."

The words of such a mind and such a man, should arrest the attention of the leaders of denominational opinion, and surely every friend of the truth should do his utmost in placing these considerations before the people. The reader can see that Dr. Poindexter fully indorses my position; that by admitting, by **word** or **act**, Pedobaptist and Campbellite societies to be evangelical churches, is admitting that there can be Christian churches without scriptural baptism, which Pedobaptists agree with all Baptists in denying; and then open communion and mixed membership inevitably follow, as they have in England.

We need no longer wonder at the increasing dissatisfaction among our own people—among our **ministers** as well as members—with the arguments adduced by those who have volunteered to defend this important ordinance of God's house. Can it be a matter of surprise that so many Baptists can see nothing improper or inconsistent in their going to the tables of Pedobaptists and Campbellites, when they are taught by such eminent teachers that the ordinance administered by them is indeed the Lord's Supper, and those bodies evangelical churches, and that the members of one sister or evangelical church can scripturally participate in the Supper with the members of any other sister church?

Does not this account for the rapidity with which books, tracts, and treatises on communion have been multiplied of late, they being efforts to satisfy the increasing inquiries of the people, but all in vain?

And does not this account for the thousands of Christians who join Pedobaptist and Campbellite societies yearly under the firm conviction received from their own writers and their preachers, that they are joining truly "evangelical" and "orthodox" churches? and for those other thousands of Baptists bearing letters of good-fellowship from Baptist churches, who, on removing "West," or into other neighborhoods where a Baptist church may not be altogether convenient, naturally "wanting to be in **some** church," unite with the nearest Pedobaptist or Campbellite society, and for the balance of life give their means and all their Christian influence to building them up; and dying, leave their children bound fast in the deception? These deluded Baptists have been taught that "all the leading denominations around them are evangelical churches," and that "in all the fundamental and essential doctrines of salvation they agree with Baptists," and they can see no impropriety in uniting with those bodies; and who that admits them to be evangelical can? And then they see and are made to **feel** that, by so doing the offense of the cross ceases, and they will thereby very materially enhance the social positions of their families in the community.

We learned when in California, in 1878, that there were multitudes of those who came to that State Baptists, who put their letters into Pedobaptist societies—Baptists being weak and poor as a general thing—and that in the one city of San Francisco there are lost Baptists enough to form a church financially stronger than any Baptist church in the city or State. We heard the name of an ex-

Baptist deacon who is the largest paying member in a fashionable Pedobaptist society. He was spoken of as an exemplary Christian man. He to-day, conscientiously no doubt, believes what his Baptist instructors have taught him, that he is a member of an evangelical church of Christ, and that there is no **essential** difference between Baptists and Pedobaptists; but he enjoys a far higher social position than he could among Baptists.

While penning the above, my eye has fallen upon this statement from the New York *Observer*, a standard Presbyterian paper, that has observed with great satisfaction what is transpiring among us on this question. He says:

"We have recently heard the names of some of the most eminent Baptist clergymen and professors mentioned as persons holding views favorable to the abandonment of the restricted Communion practice. They are not anxious to promote agitation, much less to disturb the peace of the church by the discussion of the subject unless it is necessary; but they are gradually disseminating those views and principles which will eventually work a change in the practice of the churches."

A full half score of these men, D. D.'s, have already left us for other denominations, and we doubt not scores of others are ripening to take their places of open dissent and protest, and are even **now** doing it. Does it not become us diligently to inquire what these "views and principles" are, that are so well calculated to betray the

Baptists into the hands of Pedobaptists? If they **have been doing this,** or if they **are doing this** in their books or papers, we must have met with them, whether we have recognized their tendency or not. Now the following views do characterize nearly all the writings of Northern authors, editors and newspaper writers, and we confess it with shame, some of our Southern writers and popular preachers—

1. That Pedobaptist societies are evangelical or Christian churches.

2. That they have a right to observe—and do observe—the Lord's Supper.

3. That their ministers are authorized to preach and to baptize.

4. That the immersions of such men are valid, and may properly be received by Baptist churches.

5. That it is right and expedient for Baptist ministers to affiliate with Pedobaptist ministers, and exchange pulpits, thus showing to the world that they are equals, **officially** and **ecclesiastically.**

6. That it is right and expedient to hold union meetings with such denominations and even to invite their ministers to participate in the ordinations of Baptist ministers.

In view of the considerations urged above, are we not justifiable in affirming that such views and principles do inevitably and more successfully than an out and out advocacy of the practice itself, lead our people into open Communion?

Subtle and far-seeing men have affirmed that a writer is far more likely to carry his point by laying down and establishing his **premises**, and leaving his intelligent reader to draw the **conclusion**, since, by announcing it himself, he might make an alarm and provoke opposition.

CONCLUSION OF PART I.

In closing this part of my book, I ask my brethren—ministers, editors, and authors especially—is it not high time to make a full end of all this "jargon," as Brother Poindexter calls it—these concessions so unfounded in fact, so prejudicial to strict Communion in any sense, and so utterly destructive of our existence as a distinct people?

If they are continued to be made under Baptist colors, are we not justified in marking these as the men among us who are insidiously working, "by complimentary words," the subversion of Baptist doctrine and polity? It is evident that the professed Baptist, who conscientiously believes that Pedobaptist societies are evangelical churches, can both conscientiously **commune and unite with them.**

May I not ask you, brethren, in the coolness of sound reasoning, if we have failed to hold our own for the past fifty years, by occupying this old line, in defending our communion—which was originally selected for **defense** only, can we hope to accomplish, by any means, as much in the fifty years to come, since this line has been successfully blown up, and irreparably breached in so many places that the confidence of its most valiant defenders has been materially impaired?

Are you not willing just to examine, without prejudice, the new line I propose, and which, in repeated charges, the enemy have found to be not only impregnable as a line of defense, but an incomparable position for offensive warfare? This is all I can ask of you; this I have a right to expect from you; *i. e.*, that you will prayerfully and honestly, as those who have to give an account unto God, examine my positions by the word of God.

In reaching scriptural convictions upon this subject, it will be necessary for us to get a clear conception of an evangelical church, and determine whether it is **one specific body**—organism—or many and diverse ones. This subject will be discussed in Part II.

PART II.

ECCLESIA,

CHURCH OF CHRIST:

WHAT IS IT?

"WHAT is the Church? is the great problem of this century."
—G. D. BOARDMAN, D. D.

"Unhesitatingly, therefore, do we set aside both of the theories of the church [the Invisible and Universal] which have mainly ruled the Christian world, together with the unfledged brood of correlated ideas, to fall back upon that which rules throughout the New Testament, and for a few centuries past **has been slowly rising like a morning sun above the horizon of confused thought,** changing, by degrees, Truth's twilight reign into the brighter light of growing day. The **real Church of Christ is a local body, of a definite doctrinal constitution,** such as is indispensable to the 'unity of the Spirit,' of which it is the embodiment, and of a specific form of organition."
—E. J. FISH, D.D.

CHAPTER I.

―∞∘⸰⦂⦁⦂⸱∘∞―

A CHURCH OF CHRIST—WHAT IS IT?

Definitions of a Scriptural Ecclesia—by Catholics, Protestants, and Baptists—Baptists divided among themselves, etc.

BEFORE entering upon the discussion of the Lord's Supper as a church ordinance, it is necessary for me to define what I understand by the term **church** when used in the New Testament as the English representative of the Greek word **ecclesia**—assembly.

1. Because there is such a diversity of views held by different denominations concerning it; and

2. Baptist writers do not agree among themselves as to its scriptural significancy. This last fact can not be too much regretted.

THE CATHOLICS—GREEK AND LATIN.

These hold that the term "church" in the New Testament in its general sense, means "all who are or ever will be saved, including the angels and the blessed now in heaven; the faithful on the earth; the souls of those suffering in purgatory, together with those yet unborn who are to be saved.

The church is defined by Canisius:

"The congregation of **all people** professing the faith and doctrine of Christ, which is governed under one next to Christ, the chief head and pastor upon earth" [the Pope].—*Dens. Theol.*, p. 164.

Cardinal Bellermine (A. D. 1600) thus defines it:

"Our opinion is, that the church is one whole, not two, and that the one and true church is an assembly joined together by profession of the same Christian faith, and participation of the same sacraments, under the rule of lawful pastors, and especially of Christ's only vicar in the world, the Roman Pontiff."—*Hag. His. Docts.*, ii, 291.

Practically, there can be, according to the Catholic theory, but **one** church on earth. No one of the various congregations worshiping in the one place, nor yet the aggregate of all these in one **country** or **nation,** is a church, but the infinitesimal parts of "The One Church," the seat of which is at Rome, and the supreme earthly head, the Pope.

The Lord's Supper being a church ordinance belongs, of **right,** to every member of the Roman Catholic hierarchy in any country of earth where a priest officiates.

THE PROTESTANT THEORY.

This is well represented by the Westminster Confession of 1646, and adopted by Presbyterians generally and the Congregationalists of America. They hold that the one term **ecclesia** is used to designate two **bodies** or **two conceptions**—a **Universal invisible**, and a **Visible universal church.**

The Confession speaks thus:

> "The Catholic or universal church, which is **invisible**, consists of the whole number of the elect that have been, are, or shall be gathered into one, under Christ the head thereof, and is the spouse, the body, the fullness of Him that filleth all in all."

The larger portion of this ideal church is yet unborn! The definition is borrowed from the Roman Catholics, and placing the General Assembly as head instead of the Pontiff, is quite the same.

> "The visible church, which is also Catholic or universal under the gospel (not confined to one nation as before under the law), consists of all those throughout the world who thus profess the true religion; [*i. e.*, the Presbyterian faith] together with their children, and is the kingdom of the Lord Jesus Christ, the house and family of God, out of which there is **no ordinary possibility of salvation."**

It will be seen that this " **visible** church" is, from the definition itself, as **invisible** as the former "invisible church." It never was assembled in one place; it never can be; it never was seen, is **unseen** and **unseeable.** It will also be noticed that the definition excludes all religious denominations from being churches in any sense that do not indorse the Presbyterian Confession of Faith, and embrace the children, young and old, of the parents belonging to it; and that the Church of Christ visible, is none other than the "Presbyterian church," out of which there is no ordinary possibility of salvation.

This theory, as practically exemplified, is this: No one of the thousands of worshiping congregations in America, which the people are taught to call and believe are churches, as the First, and Second, and Third Presbyterian "churches" in Memphis is, in fact, a church visible in any sense, but only integral parts of the one great Presbyterian church in America, of which the General Assembly is the visible head, having the sole authority to enact, repeal, and modify the laws, and determine the doctrines to be held by the membership. There can be no Presbyterian **churches** in America but only one Presbyterian **church**, national or provincial, of a specific sort, as Old School. And the same of the people called Cumberland Presbyterians, because originated (A. D. 1816) upon the Cumberland River. There is only one Cumberland Presbyterian "church" in America—the local societies are not churches.

Two facts are evident from the Presbyterian definition of church—

1. That the members of the various local worshiping societies can commune wherever the table is spread in **the** great church, since it is **one body**;

and, therefore, intercommunion is a constitutional right; and—

2. That Presbyterians can not constitutionally commune outside of the Presbyterian church, since the Supper can not be celebrated outside of **the church, and there is** no true church save the Presbyterian.

If Baptist churches were constituted upon this theory, the free intercommunion of the members of the various churches would be possible, since the symbolism of church relationship between the members partaking would be preserved.

The Episcopal and Methodist Episcopal definitions of church are very similar. There is but one Protestant Episcopal Church in America; the several worshiping congregations are not **churches,** but the parts which compose the church, of which the General Convention is the visible head. So of the Methodist Episcopal. It was decided by the Supreme Court of the United States, that the local societies, worshiping in any given place, are not **churches** in any conceivable sense, possessing none of the rights and privileges of churches, and having no voice whatever in the management or control of church affairs, but that the General Conference alone is the Methodist Church of America. Before the division it would not have been proper to say the Methodist churches of America, but the Methodist Church of America. Now there are only **two** Methodist

Episcopal churches in America. If the Episcopal were the true theory of church building there would be no violation of the symbolism of the Supper for the members of the local societies to Intercommune, for those of each are alike members of but one body.

There is still another accepted definition of Church of Christ not found in any confession, but is established in the Protestant literature of this age,—namely, that the Christian church is composed of all existing denominations professing to be churches, *i. e.*, that no one is the church, but only a church of "The Church," a **branch** of the one great universal one, though they are unable to tell us where the **trunk** or whole is. This is also called the universal visible church, though it is quite invisible, and never did or can assemble.

The reader can see that Catholics and Protestants, could they agree as to the earthly headship of "the church," are quite agreed as to its **definition**, and that both parties wholly ignore the idea of a local congregation being a church, or that the term can be literally used in the plural, although, as we shall see, it is so used no less than thirty-six times!

BAPTIST THEORIES.

Among Baptists of this age there is no general accord as to the scriptural definition of the term Ecclesia-Church, and among our theological writers there is a diversity that amounts to a confusion.

Often the same writer will hold to two definitions that are evidently contradictious, *i. e* , that it is used by the Holy Spirit to designate two radically different and opposite notions—as if it was claimed that baptizo means to sprinkle water upon a person or to immerse a person into water—opposite acts. The oldest confession put forth by English Baptists (A. D. 1643), thus defines a New Testament church :

"Jesus Christ hath here on earth a spiritual kingdom which is his church [*i. e.*, composed of his churches], whom he hath purchased and redeemed to himself as a peculiar inheritance; which church is a **company of visible saints**, called and separated from the world by the word and Spirit of God, to the visible profession of the faith of the gospel, being baptized into that faith and joined to the Lord and each other by mutual agreement; in the practical enjoyment of the ordinances commanded by Christ, their Head and King."—*Crosby.*

This, with but slight verbal alterations, purely **explanatory,** is just as I would define it to-day. They evidently use church in its true **collective** sense, implying all his churches compose his kingdom, and that each one is a company of visible saints, etc. The Baptists of that day knew no other **church.** Half a century later "many congregations" adopted, with but slight modification, the Presbyterian definition, which they in turn had modified from the Catholic definition. It runs thus—

"The Catholic or universal church, which (with respect to the internal work of the Spirit and the truth of grace) may be called invisible, consists of the whole number of the elect that have been, are, or shall be gathered into one under Christ, the head thereof, and may be called the spouse—the body—the fullness of Him that filleth all in all."

This confession, with this Romish definition of church, was adopted by the Philadelphia Association when it was organized in 1707 without alteration, and, doubtless, without **examination,** and very many of our earlier Associations adopted it, and thus this definition has been handed down from "sire to son." This will account for the tenacity with which it is held and defended by the fathers among us.

The New Hampshire Confession appeared fifty years ago, and has been adopted by the larger body of American Baptists,—gives no other definition of a New Testament church than a **local assembly,** and it had been well had no other idea ever been instilled into the minds of Baptists.

BAPTIST AUTHORS.

When we consult the writings of our own theologians, we will meet with the most confused and **contradictory** views. Dr. Dagg, in his "Church Order," stoutly maintains that the term **ecclesia**—assembly—is used by the inditing Spirit to denote two opposite notions—an assembly local and **visible,** and an assembly universal and invisible!

He defines the first—

"A Christian church is an assembly of believers in Christ, organized into one body according to the Holy Scriptures for the worship of God."

This is an **organized visible** body that can and must assemble in one place, and has officers, ordinances, and laws, etc. The latter thus—

"**Church universal** is the whole company of those who are saved by Christ."

This is an unorganized, invisible body that never did assemble, having no laws, officers or ordinances. Dr. F. Wayland gives this limitless definition:

"A church is the body of sincere disciples; the **form of** government is the manner in which **they** have chosen to administer the **laws** of Christ in their intercourse with each other."—*Wayland, Sermons,* p. 229.

Professor Curtis follows him in this—

"So any organized body of professing Christians, assembling from time to time for worship, may be justly considered a **Christian Church,** though if it be without valid baptism, an irregular church."—*P. and Progress,* p. 144.

And yet **this author** elsewhere insists that without scriptural baptism there can be no church, and all Pedobaptist authors admit this.

Dr. J. M. Pendleton, a clear and venerable name, says:

"In its applications to the followers of Christ, it is

usually, if not always, employed to designate a particular congregation of saints, or the redeemed in the aggregate."—*Christian Doctrines*, p. 329.

"It refers, either to a particular congregation of saints, or to the redeemed in the aggregate."—*Chris. Man.*, p. 5.

Here are two radically different notions given as the definition of one and the same term.

Dr. Wm. Everts agrees with Dr. Dagg that—

"In its most comprehensive and important (?) sense, the whole number of the redeemed called out from the world, and separated to Christ, compose the calling or Church of Christ—the Church for which he died, for which he intercedes," etc.

It is evident that all the members of this church could intercommune, if the Supper is a church ordinance in his acceptation of its meaning.

Dr. J. M. C. Breaker, another of our ablest denominational writers, thus defines ecclesia:

"In every place where the word occurs, it means either (1) a particular local congregation of professed Christians, or (2) the whole body of the professed disciples of Christ — that is, the aggregate, not of churches, but of the membership of all the local churches. Men are added to "the Church Universal" by becoming members of the local churches. No man can be a member of the Church Universal, who is not a member of a regular local gospel Church."—*Chr. Rev.* Vol. 21, p. 607.

It strikes me, if Dr. Breaker should affirm that the Lord's Supper is a church ordinance, the members of any local church could claim a right to it wherever it may be spread, on the ground that he is a member of both churches—the local and the universal.

We have, very recently, for the first time, heard brethren claim that members of one church had **equal rights** in all Baptist churches as in his own, which is utterly subversive of the fundamental principles of Baptist Church independency, since it could neither administer its own government, or control its own ordinances. This position is the natural outgrowth of Dr. Breaker's theory, which shows how important a correct theory is.

If Dr. Breaker will substitute "kingdom of Christ" for his "church universal," and hold that it is composed of all the **local** churches, I think it will materially relieve his definition from serious objections, and conform it to the teachings of the New Testament.

Rev. Mr. Adkins, in his "Polity and Fellowship of the Church," says:

"The word ecclesia, as applied to the disciples of Christ, is used in the New Testament in **two distinct senses—1.** In its broadest sense, it comprehends the whole collective body of true believers on earth and in heaven, all God's elect of every nation and every age, from the beginning to the end of time, as they will be finally gathered in heaven," etc.

This is purely the Romish idea. Then Christ has always had a Church, or he has none now, and never will have, until the end of time, when the last soul is saved!

"2. In its restricted sense, the word **ecclesia**—Church—is applied to the disciples of Christ as permanently associated and organized, in order of the gospel, for his worship and service, and to execute his commission, and fulfill his will on earth. This has been called the 'Visible Church,' with the same propriety that the other is called the 'Invisible.'"

He further says:

"The Lord's Table, on the other hand, is set within the pale of church relations. * * * It is the sacred banquet of the Church, to be served only within the **assembly** of the **Church**."—*The Church, its Polity and Fellowship*, p. 83.

Within the **assembly** of the Church! **Assembly** is **the** meaning of the term "Church." Would he say within the Church of the Church, understanding the **local** to be a **churchlet**, and the Universal the large one? Is not this confusing enough? This is Wesley's idea of **ecclesiola in ecclesia**—little churches in large ones.

The author of "The Great Iron Wheel," in 1855, defined ecclesia—Church—in its New Testament signification as a local assembly, and that its figurative use is grounded upon this idea, and that a universal invisible church is a **mere concept**—not existing in fact, but in the conception of the writer.

Dr. A. C. Dayton, in his "Theodosia Earnest," wholly discards the invisible church idea, and teaches that "the particular churches are in the kingdom of Christ, as courts and juries are within the State."

Had he said as the States of this republic are in it, and constitute it, his illustration could not have been improved upon.

Dr. E. J. Fish, in his work, "Ecclesiology," issued in 1875, has borne a manful part in aiding to put the much-abused term—"Church"—in its true light before the public. He denies the correctness of such a classification as local and universal, or invisible, unless it can be distinctly shown that the New Testament uses terms thus illogically. He says:

"The one is no proper collective of the other, since it collects materials wholly and extensively foreign to it. * * * Our proposition, then, is, that the **local, generic** and **collective** uses of the term Church **are its only uses** in the New Testament where it means the Lord's Ecclesia."—pp. 77 and 78.

We see among Baptists the definitions vibrate from the Presbyterian definition, borrowed and modified from the Catholics, as one extreme, to the unbaptized bodies of professed Christians, of Wayland and Curtis, as the other. It is the **true mean** between these that I shall attempt to find. It will be observed that the **trend of Baptist opinion is strongly setting toward the local idea,** the definition first put forth by Baptists, before they had been led captives by the Westminster Confession of Faith, through which the church universal idea has been engrafted upon, and ingrained into, the faith of our people.

The thoughtful reader can see, that so long as Baptists are confused and divided between these contradictious theories of a New Testament Church, there can be no general agreement touching all those questions of polity and practice that grow directly out of them—as church independency, the relations of baptism and the Supper to the churches, and of the churches to the kingdom of Christ; and especially the question discussed in this work: The Intercommunion of the Members of Different local Churches.

To this subject, then, I address myself.

CHAPTER II.

There can be no more excuse for this confusion of ideas respecting the meaning of ecclesia, than respecting **metanoeo, pistuo,** *or* **baptizo**—*No word can have two diverse or opposite meanings—The laws governing the definition of words, etc.—The classical use of the term* **ecclesia.**

CAN not for a moment grant that there is the least excuse for this confusion of ideas concerning the meaning of the term the Omniscient Christ selected to designate the institution he originated and established on earth, and with which he made it the duty of every one of his disciples to unite. If we can not unmistakably ascertain what he meant by this term, how can we claim that it is possible to know what he meant by any other term he used in commanding our obedience, as **metanoeo, pistuo, baptizo.** We can assert it with reference to **every word** Christ used with the same propriety we can with any **one word.** If a hopeless ambiguity attaches to any one or all the terms expressive of our duties and obligations, then it is certain that we are forever released from all efforts at obedience. It

is a reflection upon, if not a profanation of the character of Christ and the Holy Spirit, to suppose that either would select words of double or ambiguous meanings by which to teach us our duties. Words were invented to **express,** not to **conceal** ideas. Christ certainly designed to convey some definite idea by every word he employed. For a word to fill this office it must have been originated to designate some one specific notion, which we call the **meaning,** or **definition,** of the word. This meaning is always placed first in our lexicons, and is called the primary, natural, real, or physical meaning, and is, and can be **but one.** Christ must have designated some one specific act, designated some specific duty, or inculcated some specific idea when he enjoined obedience, or instructed us with respect to duty by every word he used; and just as certainly as it is possible for us to ascertain the exact meaning of the terms in which our **moral** duties are enjoined, so certainly is it possible for us to ascertain the meaning of the terms in which our **positive** duties are enjoined—**baptizo** as well as **metanoeo,** and **pistuo.**

The question arises, how can we ascertain, without doubt, the real meaning of any word? We usually refer to a lexicon, which, if standard, is good authority, but there is an ultimate authority to which all lexicographers go for their definitions, and that is—the use of the term by the best writers of the language in the age in which the word is used.

Now in ascertaining the meaning of the term under discussion, let us turn from the creeds of churches and the opinions of men, which we have found in hopeless confusion, to the original sources of information, and we will learn that the cause of the confusion is not attributable to any conceivable ambiguity in the term **ecclesia,** but to those teachers, who wrest the term, as they do the Scriptures, to uphold their false theories.

Now the sources of information are two—1. The general use of the term, by the Greeks themselves, which we call its classical usage; 2. Its general use by Christ, and the Holy Spirit, who selected the words used by the inspired writers.

Before doing this we should familiarize ourselves with a few, at least, of the leading rules of interpreting language, which I collate from Morus, Ernesti, and Blackstone:

"1. Every word must have some **specific idea or notion** which we call **meaning.** Were not this so, words would be meaningless and useless. In the Scriptures there is unquestionably assigned to every word some **idea** or **notion.**

"Sec. 14. "**Every word must have some meaning** [*i. e.*, definite, specific]. To every word there ought to be assigned, and in the Scriptures there is unquestionably assigned, some **one idea** or notion. This we call the **meaning** or **sense** of the word. . .

"2. The **literal** sense of words is the sense which is so connected with them, that it is first in order, and is spontaneously presented to the mind, as soon as the sound of the word is heard.

"3. The sense of a word can not be **diverse** or **multifarious** at the same time and in the same passage or expression, and, we may add, in the same letter or narrative. There can be no certainty at all in respect to the interpretation of any passage, unless a kind of necessity compels us to affix **a particular sense** to a word, which sense **must be one,** and unless there are special reasons for a tropical meaning, **it must be the literal sense.**"

"The first important diversion or distinction of words in respect to their meaning, is into **proper** and **tropical,** *i. e.,* **literal** and **figurative** or (better still) **primary** and **secondary.**"—*Morus, indorsed by Stuart.*

I may add here the reason Morus assigns for using a word tropically or figuratively, as—(1.) For the sake of variety in expression, and to this species of tropical language belong **metonymy, synechdoche,** and other similar tropes; (2.) "Tropical words, especially metaphors, are used for ornament." It will thus be seen that a figurative use of a word **does not create a new definition—a different sense**—but is the word **troped,** *i. e.,* **used in an artificial manner.**

Morus tells us that the most common figures used in our Scriptures are **metonymy,** and **synechdoche.** As I prepare this little book for the masses—the common people—I am confident they will hear me gladly if I explain these figures so they can know them wherever they meet them in the Bible—while the explanation has a direct bearing upon the two principal terms that enter into the discussion of the Lord's Supper.

1. **Metonymy is the use of one word for another—literally, a change of name.**

EXAMPLES.—These abound throughout the Bible.

1. "Jerusalem and Judea, and all the region round about Jordan, went out and were all baptized of him in the Jordan," etc. Here the **places** that contained the people are put for the **people,** as we say of a drinking man, he drank three glasses or bottles, or cups, the thing that contains is put for the thing—liquor—that is contained. A notable example, "On this rock will I build my **church**" —church instead of kingdom; or, if we understand that **one** of the constituents—a church—of the kingdom is put for the whole, it will be by—

2. **Synechdoche**—literally, a change of place. By this figure the **whole** is put for a **part,** or the **part** for the **whole**; one person or thing for the whole class, as the genus for the species; **man,** for all men, mankind—the **ox,** the horse, and for the whole species; or the species for the genus, as the bee, the fly, for swarms and multitudes of those insects. (See Isaiah vii: 18, 19.)

In these expressions—"The Indians hunt the buffalo, the bear, and the wolf." Man tames the horse, the ox, the mule, and cultivates the potato, the apple, and the melon; the **genus** is put for individuals in great numbers. So in the Scriptures we read that "Christ loved the **church**," that he is "the Head of the Church." One church is used for multitudes of the same kind, the **genus** for all contained under it. I would not call this the **generic or collective** use, but figurative, as will be more fully noticed. With these principles of interpretation, let us inquire for **the classical meaning of ecclesia, universally translated "church"** in our version, when referring to the Christian institution. **Ecclesia**, from **ek**, out of, and **kaleo**, to call.

Liddell & Scott:

"An **assembly** of citizens summoned by the criers—the **legislative Assembly**."

The citizens here called out from the people, **demos**, were the qualified voters only; and the qualified voters constituted a specific body—**organization**—for their names were enrolled, and it had its officers. The **ecclesia**, in Greece, then meant but **one specific** thing, and that an **organization.**

Donegan:

"**Ecclesia**—an Assembly of the people convoked by the heralds [never a mob]; also the **place** of Assembly."

But, as above, the people, convoked by their officers, were only those authorized to exercise the elective franchise, and these constituted a **specific body**—the legislative Assembly. By metonymy, only could it be used for the house in which the assembly met, as when we call the **house** in which a church worships, the church.

Dean Trench says:

"**Ecclesia**, as all know, was the lawful assembly in a free Greek city, of all those possessed of the rights of cit-

UNSCRIPTURAL AND INCONSISTENT. 121

izenship, for the transaction of public affairs. That they were **summoned**, is expressed in the latter part of the word. That they were summoned out of the whole population, a select portion of it, including neither the populace, nor yet strangers, nor those who had forfeited their civic rights, this is expressed by the first. Both the **calling** and the **calling out** are moments to be remembered, when the word is assumed into a higher Christian sense, for in them the chief part of its peculiar adaptation to its august sense lies."

The term "Ecclesia" had as **definite** and well understood meaning to the Greeks as the "House of Representatives" does to us, or "the Assembly" would to a Virginian's ear. The free cities of Greece were governed by **three** judicial **bodies:**

1. The **ecclesia**—assembly—which was composed of all the qualified voters of a free city, whose names were duly enrolled, and an officer selected by the body. At Athens, the ordinary fixed assemblies were called **ecclesiai,** of which there were four in each presidency; and an extraordinary assembly summoned for an especial purpose.

2. The **Boula** (Council) of five hundred, who were a committee of the **ecclesia** to prepare measures for that **assembly,** corresponding to our Senate.

3. The **Dikastries,** or Jury Courts.

The assembly being a legal legislative body, duly registered as such, was a permanent body, and at all times an **ecclesia**, whether in session or adjourned, as is the House of Commons of England, or House of Representatives of the United States. Of the powers of the ecclesia:

"Besides the legislative powers of the assembly—ecclesia—it could make inquisition into the conduct of the magistrates, and in turbulent and excited times exercised a power resembling that of impeachment, as in the case of Demosthenes and Phocion."—*North American Cyc.opedia*, p. 736.

It will be seen that all matters that affected the public interest and the welfare of the people, civil or religious, came under its cognizance.

The meetings of the **ecclesia** were usually held in the theaters of the free cities, as that of Dionysius at Athens and at Ephesus, as the regular sessions of our Legislatures are held in the capitol buildings of our State.

From these facts we learn:

1. That the terms **ecclesia**, the assembly, and the Council, Boule, in Greek, were used to designate **specific legislative** bodies, and were never applied to a lawless "mob" or promiscuous gatherings of the multitude for any purpose. The Greek has other terms to designate these, as **demos,** the populace; "**oklos**," the crowd; **sustrophe**, concourse; and **panegyrea**, general assembly—like those which convened at the public games.

2. We learn that writers and commentators are not justified in saying that it is sometimes applied to a riotous crowd or lawless mob, or a gathering of any sort for any purpose; **for it is never so**

used. In its classical signification it is used three times in the nineteenth chapter of Acts.

Paul preached in the free city of Ephesus: "And the word of the Lord powerfully increased and prevailed;" where Demetrius, a silversmith, thinking his craft in danger, made a great outcry, together with his fellow-workmen, and filled the city with confusion; and having seized Gaius and Aristarchus, rushed into the theater. This was the appointed place for the meetings of the **ecclesia**, and the reason why he took them there, and it may, at this time, have been in session. If not, it convened as was its wont and duty upon the outcry. "And some cried one thing and some another," and the **ecclesia** was confused by these varied cries, while no definite charge was brought to its notice for it to take cognizance of. Now, mark, it was not the **ecclesia** that was riotous, tumultuous; but the **oklos** (crowd) that had rushed into the theater where the Assembly was in session, or had gathered at this time to hold a session; for it was the **oklos** (crowd) and not the **ecclesia**, that the officer of the ecclesia—the secretary—quieted. See v. 35.

He informed them if they had any definite charge against any man, the Courts were held for that purpose, it was not the province of the Ecclesia; but if they sought any thing further—*i. e.*, concerning the weal of the city, etc., it would be settled in the lawful **ecclesia**. The Ecclesia was responsible for public tumults, insurrections, etc., and the officer appeals to the crowd to be quiet, and disperse; for, said he, speaking for the Ecclesia, we are even in danger of being accused about the tumult of to-day, there being no cause by which we can excuse this concourse—συστροφης, not Εκκλησια. And having said this, he dismissed (adjourned) the Assembly—**ecclesia**—not the **sustropes**.

Stephen in his speech before the Sanhedrim used the term in its classical sense when he said:

"This was he who was with the **assembly**—ecclesia—in the wilderness."—*Acts vii:* 38.

That was a specific organized body of men—the Jewish nation. All the instances in the Septuagint version of the Old Testament are of the **classical** use of this term, and refer to specific organized bodies, never to indefinite unorganized bodies. From the above examination of the classical use of the term, I feel justified in concluding that "ecclesia" is used to designate one specific body—*i. e.,* the Assembly of a free city of Greece, and never a promiscuous gathering, much less a riotous crowd or mob. It is like **Boule**, which is never used except to denote the senate or Council of five hundred, as we are wont to say "The Senate," "The House," when alluding to our State Legislature.

If ecclesia literally means any thing else in the New Testament than an **organized local assembly of adults,** its modified use must be learned from its New Testament usage alone.

CHAPTER III.

The scriptural use of Ecclesia.—It is used to designate a specific organization—a Church of Christ only; by a figure of speech, the churches or kingdom of Christ.

THAT the translators of our version of the Scriptures evidently understood the Greek term **ecclesia** to be a term of specific meaning, **in its religious use**, is evidenced by the fact that they employ but one English word to translate it, and that word is **church**, which universal usage has consecrated to designate that one divine institution of which Christ is the Founder; and only by a figure of speech—the **house** in which such a body is wont to worship. In the New Testament it is never used to denote a house. We start out, then, with this fact admitted by the translators, that, whatever the term "Church" signifies in the New Testament, it means one specific thing, and not many diverse things. This is in strict accordance with the rules given in the last chapter, viz.:

"Every word must have some **one** idea or notion, and this we call the **meaning**. The sense of a word can not be diverse or multifarious in the same passage or narrative, and when used with reference to the same thing; and the literal sense is the **real**, all others are **figurative**."

That this must be so, else, as Morus says:

"There can be no certainty at all in respect to the interpretation of any passage, unless a kind of necessity compels us to affix a particular sense to a word, which sense **must be one**; and, unless there are special reasons for a tropical meaning, **it must be the literal sense.**"

This must be conclusive with all Baptists who accept the reasoning as conclusive with respect to **baptizo.** Scholars find this term used seventy-nine times in the New Testament, and twenty of these instances, all admit, denote the physical act of **immersion in water**—the **literal** act of Christian baptism. In all the other instances, it has a **troped** meaning, derived from this literal meaning, which scholars agree to call the **figurative**, or **secondary** meaning. It is altogether absurd to call these fifty-nine secondary or figurative meanings distinct meanings, or uses of the term **baptizo.** They are **figurative** only, and the kind of figure is easily ascertainable.

Now apply this method to Ecclesia. We find it used one hundred and ten times in the New Testament, when applied to the Christian institution under discussion. All agree, that in ninety-one* of these instances, it refers to a local organ-

---

* Since the publication of "Old Landmarkism," my attention has been called to the fact that Acts ix: 31 is

ized assembly, since thirty-six of them are in the plural, which necessitates the local idea; and fifty-six in the singular, having explicit reference to a local organization, as a church in one city, in one house, or one place. Thus we see, at the outstart, that the local idea vastly rules the New Testament use of the term; and we are authorized to say that the literal, common, real meaning of ecclesia is a local organized assembly, and that an unorganized assembly is not the sense of the term. We are justified in saying that, in these nineteen remaining instances, the term is used **figuratively,** and that the idea that rules their true sense is that of an **organized assembly.**

It is concerning these nineteen secondary uses of the term that Baptist writers disagree, claiming, as they do, that they are different **senses** of the term—**real meanings.**

It is the faint hope that I may contribute something toward harmonizing the differences among my own brethren that I write this chapter.

One thing I claim, as already shown above, that, if ecclesia is used ninety-one, out of one hundred and ten times, to denote a local assembly, its natural, **literal** sense must be "a local assembly;" and that the remaining nineteen in-

found in the singular in the Vatican MS., and is claimed for the Universal Church theory. There are nineteen instances in which it is claimed as not referring to the local idea.

stances are certainly secondary or **figurative** uses of the word. This must and will be granted by all candid scholars. But, in this discussion touching the Lord's Supper, we have to do with its **literal, real meaning**, and not with its ideal or figurative.

But I do not admit that there are nineteen instances in the New Testament where ecclesia is used even figuratively. A careful examination convinces me that seven or eight of them undoubtedly refer to a **local** church, while the others are used **figuratively**, by metonymy or synechdoche, the ruling idea of each being an organized assembly, and no one giving the slightset support to the Universal Church Visible idea.

The following are all the instances where any one claims that ecclesia refers to a universal visible or invisible church:

Acts ix: 31; 1 Cor. xii: 28 and xv: 9; Gal. i: 13; Phil. iii: 6; Heb. xii: 23; 1 Tim. iii: 15; Eph. i: 22, iii: 10 and 21, v: 23, 24, 25, 27, 29, 32; Col. i: 18 and 24; Matt. vi: 18.

I can here give these but a brief notice, but sufficient to show that at least seven of them refer solely to a **local assembly**, and note the figure of the remaining ones.

1. Acts ix: 31 is lately brought forward with great confidence, upon the authority of the Vatican Codex, in support of the Universal Church theory, since, in that MS., ecclesia is in the singu-

lar—Church, instead of churches—as in our version. But there are many and formidable difficulties in the way that must be removed before this is granted.

(1) No less than four other words in the same verse would have to be changed from plural to singular to agree with Church, and authority for these changes is needed.

(2) But if that change could be established, it would not establish the fact that the churches of Judea, Galilee and Samaria were already so organized as to constitute but **one** Church, since Paul informs the churches of Galatia (i: 23) that, **at that time**, there were **churches** in Judea; and the Vatican Codex offers no different text for this passage. This, therefore, returns Acts ix: 31 to the local class of instances.

1 Cor. xii: 28 is claimed for the Church Universal theory, but it most evidently refers to the local churches that existed in the apostle's day, and the Church at Corinth especially; for these officers are not all in existence anywhere to-day, nor were they ever officers of the Church Universal or Church invisible, for those airy conceptions never had an officer of any kind; but all these were, at the time Paul wrote this, members of the Church at Corinth. So this passage refers to a local church, and can refer to nothing else.

2 I claim three others of the above as referring to the local idea, viz.: 1 Cor. xv: 9; Gal. i: 13;

Phil. iii: 6. In these, Paul speaks of himself as "persecuting the church;" but, until some one can prove that Paul ever left the city of Jerusalem to persecute Christians, until he left for Damascus, which he only reached to bless, I must claim what no one can dispute—that **it was only the Church at Jerusalem** that he persecuted.

3. 1 Tim. iii: 15 is claimed to refer to the Church Universal; but a literal translation—and omitting the definite article before Church, because not in the original—will show that Paul had the one Church only, of which Timothy was pastor, in his mind when he wrote this.

"That thou mayest know how thou oughtest to behave thyself in a house of God, which is a Church of the living God, a pillar and ground of the truth."

The term is manifestly used here in its **literal sense** of a local visible assembly, because, interpreted in any other sense, it would not express the truth. Timothy certainly needed no instruction how to behave himself in the Kingdom, for he had no office in it to perform; nor in the Invisible Church Universal, for there are no offices in that to fill; but he did need to be informed how to conduct the affairs of the Church of which he was an elder and pastor, and that Church Paul tells him was "**a** house of God, **a church** of the living God, a pillar and ground of the truth." This settles the meaning of the term here.

Heb. xii: 23 is another passage confidently

claimed, by Baptist authors in common with Pedobaptists, as a certain and sure proof-text in support of their alleged second **real meaning** of **ecclesia**, viz.: Church Universal, or invisible, consisting of all finally saved, including the angels even!*

Mr. Adkins, in "Church Polity," p. 15, says:

"In its broadest sense, it, ecclesia, comprehends the whole collective body of true believers on earth and in heaven—all God's elect of every nation and every age, from the beginning to the end of time, as they will be finally gathered in heaven, in the consummation of all things. A remarkable instance of this application of the term is Heb. xii: 23, etc. This has been called, properly enough, the "Invisible Church."

So with **all writers who advocate** the Church Universal theory.

Dr. Gardner quotes it as denoting the **spiritual** body of Christ—the Universal Invisible Church—the second **sense** of ecclesia.

That the two are here spoken of **antithetically,** a literal translation will make manifest:

"But ye have approached to Zion—a mountain and

---

* CURTIS, p. 27.—"But there is not a more scriptural or delightful doctrine than that of the spiritual communion of the whole Church—the living and the dead of all ages and of all climes."

To prove this "communion with saints in glory," he quotes but this **one** passage—". We are come," etc.

city of the living God—the heavenly Jerusalem; and to myriads—a general assembly of angels; and [ye have approached] to a Church of **first-born ones**, who have been enrolled in heaven; to a Judge who is God of all, and to spirits of just, or justified persons, made perfect; to Jesus—the Mediator of a new Covenant; and to the blood of sprinkling, speaking better things than that of Abel," etc.

Now, if this referred to a Church invisible, and ultimately to be gathered in heaven, or one already in heaven, the apostle could not have said **"ye have come to it,"** but ye are going to it. It must have been a Church which those whom Paul addressed were **then members** of.

Adam Clark offers a satisfactory exposition:

"In order to enter fully into the apostle's meaning, we must observe—1. That the Church which is called here the 'City of the living God,' the 'heavenly Jerusalem,' and 'Mt. Zion,' is represented under the notion of a **city**."

He says:

"**To the general assembly of innumerable angels** is probably the true connection.

"That the gospel first born, whose names are written in heaven, are here opposed to the enrolled first born among the Israelites. Exod. xxiv: 5; xix: 22. That the Mediator of the new Covenant, the Lord Jesus, is here opposed to Moses, the mediator of the old. And that the blood of sprinkling of Christ, our High Priest, refers to the act of Moses. Exod. xxiv: 8. * * * I see nothing, therefore, in these verses which determines their sense to the heavenly state; all is suited to the state of the Church of Christ militant here on earth; **and** some of these particulars can not be applied to the Church triumphant on any rule of construction whatever."

So Alford:

"So that * * there is no way left but to see, in the Church of first born ones, who are enrolled in heaven, the Church below. And this view is justified by every consideration — for, 1. Thus **ecclesia** is explained, **which, every-where, when used of men, and not of angels, designates the assembly of saints on earth.**"—*Notes in loco.*

Ecclesia, then, in this passage, is used in the local sense. Paul addressed these Hebrew Christians as belonging to local churches, and, therefore citizens of Christ's kingdom. This is made conclusive by his exhortation:

28th v. — "Wherefore we receiving [*i. e.*, having received] a kingdom that can not be moved, let us have grace whereby we may serve God with reverence and godly fear."

The typical kingdom of God—the Jewish—had been shaken, but these Christians were in possession of the anti-typical one, which Christ, the God of heaven, had set up, and which was never to be shaken, broken in pieces, or given to other people than the saints, and was to stand unshaken forever.—Dan. ii: 44; Matt. xvi: 18.

I have thus released seven of the nineteen instances in which church is claimed as referring to the Church Universal—leaving only twelve out of one hundred and ten instances where ecclesia can be reasonably claimed to convey any thing but the local idea. Surely, if any one will admit that baptizo has but **one** literal meaning, how much more and stronger evidence has he to say that ecclesia has but one meaning, and that of an **organized assembly?**

I have space but to quote the remaining twelve passages, and to indicate the figure employed.

Matt. xvi: 18.—"On this rock will I build my Church, and the gates of hell shall not prevail against it."

This certainly does not refer to the Church universal invisible, since against that the power of Death or Satan could not prevail; for the more slain by Death, or destroyed by the machinations of Satan, the larger would the Church in heaven become. But the Church invisible, or universal, as defined by its advocates, was never "built"—organized—and has no form, laws, or ordinances; and, more, it has existed from the days of Abel.

The figure here is **metonymy**, which means "a change of terms," and Church is used for kingdom, and is the fulfillment of the prophecy of Daniel (ii: 44):

"In the days of these kings shall the God of heaven set up a kingdom that shall never be broken in pieces," etc.

Eph. i: 22 and v: 23, 24, 25, 27, 29, 32 the figure is **synechdoche**. In all these seven passages, one Church being used for all the churches, and it is justified from the fact that, what can be logically predicated of a whole, may be of **each of its parts.**

One of these has been specially instanced as precluding the possibility of its referring to a local church—that it must refer to the redeemed in the aggregate, viz.:

Eph. v: 25-27.—"Christ also loved the Church, and gave himself for it * * that he might present it to himself a glorious Church, not having spot or wrinkle, or any such thing."

I answer, this use, by **synechdoche**, of one for all, is perfectly legitimate and logical, and need mislead no one. As I have before said, what is logically true of a whole, is true of each of its parts. It would not be absurd even to predicate this of each individual member of a local church. I can say that Christ also loved me, and gave himself for me, that he might present me to himself a glorious saint, not having a spot or wrinkle, etc., and it would be equally true of every other saved person in the world. In fact, Paul uses this expression in his letter to the Galatians (ii: 20)—"The Son of God who loved me, and gave himself for me," etc., but no more for Paul than for every other Christian on earth.

Eph. iii: 10.—"In order that now may be known to the governments and authorities in the heavens, through the **Church**, the much diversified wisdom of God," etc.

This wisdom could only be displayed through an organized **working force**—a visible, and not through an invisible and disorganized force. The singular is used for the plural—**one** for all. The figure in the remaining instances is **synechdoche**—one for all.

There are several passages, in which ecclesia is so used in connection with "one body," and "body of Christ," that it is claimed that it, as well as "body," refers to the "Church Universal," etc. To rescue these from misuse, I will collate them:

Rom. xii: 5.—"So we, the many, are one body in Christ, and, individually, members of each other" [*i. e.*, fellow-members].

Paul compared a true Christian Church, in any place, to a human body—a visible **organic unit**—**E pluribus unum**—one from many. He uses the same figure, with more specific applications, in his letter to the Church at Corinth:

1 Cor. x: 17—"Because there is one loaf, we, the many, are one body; for we all partake of one loaf."

1 Cor. xii: 12—"For just as the [human] body is one, and has many members, but all the members of the body, being many, are one body, so also is Christ. For indeed by one Spirit we were all immersed into one body," etc., a local church.

Paul does not leave them in doubt as to what **he** meant by "body of Christ," for in the same chapter he tells them that **their church** at Corinth was "a body of Christ." "Now ye are a [not "the," as in our version] body of Christ and members in particular " (chap. xii: 27), and nowhere in his epistle does he tell them of a great Universal Invisible Church or body, and we have no right to presume they had any idea of such a body; it was a conception of after ages, and gave rise to the Greek and Roman Hierarchies, and Baptists can not stand too clear of it.

Col. i: 18—" He is the head of his body, the church."

Col. i: 24—" . . On behalf of his body, which is the church."

Col. iii: 15—"And let the peace of Christ preside in your hearts for which you were called into a [not] one body, and be thankful," *i. e.*, called into an assembly—a Church of Christ.

It is clear to my mind that the terms "a body" and one body, and "the church" in these, and in all like passages refer to the same **organic unity,** and that is the local congregation in Rome, Corinth, Ephesus and Colosse, and that they could not make sense and refer to an unorganized and a mere ideal body. An invisible universal church is not an **organic** unity, and therefore not referred to by these terms. Here then are **ten** of the nineteen instances claimed as doubtful which a proper exegesis gives back to the real meaning, that of a local church, leaving but nine to be used in a strictly **figurative** sense, and the reader will find, by examining these instances, that the reasoning is from **one organic body** to another, and not from a real to a mere ideal body, and that real body is a local church, of which the brethren were members, to whom the epistles were addressed.

I claim to have proved, beyond successful contradiction, that the real and only true meaning of **ecclesia** throughout the New Testament, is an organized local assembly, and that the very few instances of its figurative meaning does not establish another definition or sense, any more than the figurative uses of baptizo establishes a secondary sense different from the primary.

I have shown that the idea of a great Universal Invisible Church, or a Visible Universal Church, composed of all the visible churches, or, as some claim, of all the baptized, independent of the local churches, can not, by any fair exegesis, be found. It is time for Baptists to be emancipated from the thralldom of such an idea.

Dr. H. Harvey, of Hamilton Theological Seminary, in his late work, says:

"The following uses of the word church, though now common, are not found in the New Testament **ecclesia**. 1. **As the designation of a universal visible church.** No officers of such a church are designated, for the apostles' office was plainly temporary and expired with them. No provision is made for assembling such a church, either actual or representative. No laws, ordinances, or discipline are given for such a church. All the elements, therefore, of such a body are wanting, **nor is there any intimation of its existence.** 2. **As the designation of a national or denominational church.** . . Every-where in Scripture a visible church is a local body."—*The Church*, pp. 28, 29.

The Lord's Supper, then, could not have been delivered as a denominational ordinance, but as a local church ordinance only.

I close this chapter by defining

AN EVANGELICAL CHURCH,

A body of professed believers in Christ, scripturally baptized and organized, united in covenant to hold "the faith," and preserve the order of the gospel, and to be governed in all things by the laws of Christ.

CHAPTER IV.

THE KINGDOM OF CHRIST.

The views of our standard writers variant and contradictory—Some advance none.—False theories of the kingdom of Christ give rise to unscriptural and pernicious practices, and maladministration of the ordinances.— Views of Dr. Williams, Dr. Gardner, Dr. Dagg, Dr. Fish.--The author's theory stated and illustrated.—A composite of the admissions of these authors.

THERE are, among Baptists, quite as many and as contradictory views of what constitutes "the kingdom of Christ" as there are concerning what is a Church of Christ. Scarce two authors take the same view, and hence the confusion of ideas that everywhere prevail among our people. Very few ministers, and scarce a member, if called upon, could give a clear definition of his own conception of what it is, having but an indefinable impression that it is **something,** or, possibly, several very different things— as Christ's spiritual reign over the heavens and the earth, or his spiritual reign in the hearts of his subjects, or the Christian dispensation, or the family of the regenerate, or the regenerate who have been baptized, etc.

The majority of our authors who have given us "Church Manuals," and able treatises on the church, and its polity and Communion, do not even mention the Kingdom of Christ, and only some few barely mention it without defining, or define it so indefinitely, that their readers can not apprehend what they really mean. Certainly no work on church polity is complete without a correct definition of the Kingdom, and of its relation to the churches.

It is but a natural consequence that unscriptural theories concerning the Kingdom of Christ inevitably give rise to unscriptural and pernicious practices, especially in administering the ordinances.

I submit the views of a few of our leading authors on Communion, and the practices, based on proof of my statements.

Dr. A. P. Williams, in his work on "Communion," says:

1. "Jesus Christ has a kingdom on earth, and he has churches. No one of his churches is his kingdom, but each one is an integral portion of his kingdom."

This, so far, is very clear. If a local church is an **integer** of the kingdom of Christ, then churches alone compose it, since its integral parts **must** be all of the **same denomination.** If churches are the **integers, or units** of its composition, **individuals can not be.** This I accept.

But the rest, Dr. Williams says, only makes manifest the confusion of his own ideas of the kingdom:

2. "It is by faith and baptism that we enter his kingdom. The eunuch, from the moment of his baptism, belongs to the kingdom of Christ.

3. "Any one belonging to the kingdom of Christ is eligible to membership in any one of his churches. [Not by **right**, however, for he says.] But in order to become a member, the consent of both of himself and of **the church** is necessary."—p. 92.

If the kingdom of Christ is composed of the local churches—a fact with which Dr. Williams starts—how can one become a subject of the kingdom without first having become a member of one of the **integral** portions of that kingdom? Impossible.

Dr. Gardner says:

"Baptism, therefore, is the **initiatory** ordinance into his **visible kingdom**, and the **vestibule to his churches in that kingdom**; and none have a divine right to cross the threshold and enter these sacred inclosures until they have received the print of the sacred name in the appointed way by a properly authorized administrator."—p. 13.

He further says that "all ordained ministers are the accredited officers of Christ's kingdom."—Page 203.

According to Dr. Gardner all the local churches are in the kingdom, and we know they can be in it only as its **constituencies**; or, as Dr. Williams says, "**integral** portions of it," and if so, visible churches alone, as such, are members of Christ's kingdom, and individuals, as such, can not be—therefore individuals can only be in the kingdom as units of the constituents or "**integral** portions of the kingdom," as I can only be a member of this Republic by being a citizen of some one of the States. But these excellent brethren both hold and teach that the kingdom has one ordinance, at least, (baptism), and that all true ministers are the accredited officers of the kingdom to whom this ordinance is intrusted, and that by baptism they introduce individuals into the kingdom before they become members of a church; and, therefore, they may live and die good members of Christ's kingdom and never become members of his church!

Here, then, we have two distinct and independent organizations, each having its laws, ordinances, and officers, and subjects, and, of course, separate jurisdiction, but the brethren fail to inform us how the officers of the one can officiate in the other!

Now the fatal defects of this theory, aside from its lack of Scripture warrant, are—

(1.) The kingdom of Christ has **no officer** save its one, King and Lawgiver, who never baptizes, and hence can not administer an ordinance to any one.

(2.) The kingdom of Christ has no ordinance, and therefore no one ever yet received baptism as an ordinance of the kingdom.

(3.) The kingdom of Christ is not composed of **persons,** as integral parts, but of **churches,** as kingdoms are of provinces, and therefore no person ever was, or can be, a member of it "only" as a member of one of Christ's churches.

(4.) But, if one ordinance belongs to the kingdom, then both do, for what God hath joined together let not man attempt to sever. The advocates of this theory will not admit that the Supper belongs to the kingdom, but to the churches, and therefore baptism belongs to the churches, since both were delivered to the same organization—the local church.

(5.) But, if the theory be correct, then, when the church excludes a member, she can only put him back into the Kingdom, where she found him. Think of it—all her excluded members are in the Kingdom of Christ, and there is no authority on earth to put them out!

(6.) A member of the Kingdom by baptism, applies to a local church for membership, and is refused, he still remains where he was, a citizen of the Kingdom of Christ, and there is no power to exclude him from it, however unworthy!

(7.) And more, the churches have no disciplinary jurisdiction over ministers, since they belong to the Kingdom, if they can administer its ordinance. If these are distinct organizations, as these teach, one can not interfere with the subjects of the other!

UNSCRIPTURAL AND INCONSISTENT. 145

(8.) These brethren can not find a command or exhortation to the members of the Kingdom to become members of Christ's church, or a reproof given to any one who failed to do so; and from what source can the members of the Kingdom learn that a further duty is required of them?

Thus we see that unscriptural theories inevitably beget unscriptural and harmful practices.

Those who accept and advocate the above theory, as a rule, teach consistently with it that the ordinances—baptism at least—was not delivered to the churches to guard and administer to those whose Christian experiences they can fellowship, but to the ministry to be controlled and administered by them when and where they please, and to whom **they** may judge qualified. They claim that it is their right to baptize applicants in a city filled with churches, as well as in remote rural districts where there are no churches, and to baptize in the very baptistry of those churches, if they can get the consent of the sexton, and even the members of one of those very churches, should they deem them unbaptized though the church does not, and would not give its consent if asked! If this is not presumptuously assuming the prerogatives of the local churches, I can not conceive what would be an usurpation, taking from them as it does the control of their own ordinance.

This theory compels its advocates to teach that persons, after their baptism, before they can be members, must make a formal application to some church, produce proof of their baptism, and be received by the unanimous vote of the church; that the vote of the church, **after baptism**, alone introduces into a local church. Now if this be so, then it follows that there is not a person on this continent, who is a member of a Baptist church, for there is no one, living or dead, who was ever so received, and the advocates of this theory are not themselves members of a Baptist church or entitled to come to the Lord's table, for they were not received into a church. And the last conclusion of this destructive theory is, that it annihilates every Baptist church from this continent, for "we have no such custom, neither have the churches of God."

But Dr. Dagg declares that both these authors are wrong, since their views are not authorized by the Scriptures:

"As theological writers have maintained that there is a 'visible Church Catholic,' distinct from the Spiritual Universal Church of the Scriptures, so some of them have maintained that there is a **visible kingdom** of Christ—a society of external organization, into which men enter by baptism. But the kingdom of Christ is not a society of men bound together by external organization, like a family, a nation, or a local church. This view of it is not authorized by the Holy Scriptures."—*Ch. Order*, p. 140.

He defines the kingdom of Christ thus:

"The kingdom of Christ is properly the **kingly au-**

thority with which he is invested; and the phrase is used, by **metonymy**, to denote the subjects of his reign, and especially the obedient subjects, on whom the blessings of his reign are conferred. But the tie which binds these obedient subjects to their King, and his reign, is internal. * * The family, the nation, and the local church [*i. e.*, all the churches], are all institutions in his kingdom, or under his reign; and the external organization of these institutions should be regulated according to the will of the Sovereign King; but the kingdom itself **exists independent of all external organization.**"

I understand him to teach that Christ has no **visible kingdom** on earth, and, therefore, no visible constituents, no laws, ordinances or officers; but that Christ's reign in the hearts of men is his kingdom, and that all regenerated men on earth, and all holy angels in heaven, are the subjects of it.

Dr. Geo. B. Taylor says:

"The kingdom of God is that community of professed believers in Christ peculiar to the new dispensation. * * Baptism is the appointed act for professing allegiance to the kingdom of God, and thereby becoming a citizen of that kingdom. * * A profession of subjection to the kingdom of God, made by baptism, constitutes regular qualification for participation in the Lord's Supper."

Since he holds that the Supper is a church ordinance, he must be understood as holding that baptism introduces into a local church, and that churches are the constituents of that **community** of believers peculiar to the New Testament.

Prof. Curtis defines it thus:

"The Christian Dispensation—all those living under the dominion of heavenly or spiritual principles; and all acknowledging one supreme head—Christ."

If this definition does not fritter away every thing visible and tangible from the idea of kingdom of Christ, I will submit one that certainly does.

Dr. E. J. Fish, in his "Ecclesiology," thus defines it:

"The kingdom is of such a nature that it may be spoken of as either **entering men,** or being entered by men. (Luke xvii: 21; Jno. iii: 5.) The kingdom is of such a nature that one **may enter it when already in it** (!)—that is, enter it still more deeply. (1 Thess. ii: 12.)

"A man is born into the kingdom by the second birth. The kingdom, considered as a collection of spiritual intelligences, proposes nothing. It does not even elect its executive, the Church. It simply is, believes, loves, expands, basks in glory. Stretching over the world's continents, islands and oceans, like an invisible empire of thought and experience, paying no regard to dynasties or powers earthly, it receives what Christ and his Church may impart!!"

I could fill pages with such like definitions, but these are sufficient to show that there is no generally accepted definition of the term which we may call standard among Baptist writers and theologians. I propose a definition which will commend itself for three reasons—

1. It will embrace all the ground **truths** of the

above contradictory theories, and harmonize them by omitting what is not truth; and—

2. It will have this advantage over them—agreement with the Scriptures and common sense; and—

3. Susceptible of being comprehended, at least, by the reader.

1. The term "kingdom," in all languages, implies **organization**, and, consequently, **visibility**. No definition of kingdom is correct that wholly ignores the above notions—as Dr. Dagg's theory most certainly does, making the language meaningless.

2. Throughout the Scriptures, the kingdom of **Christ**, whether spoken of as "the kingdom of God," or "of heaven," is spoken of as something that **was to be**—brought, or was brought, into existence at Christ's advent; and that its locality is on this earth, and nowhere else (See Psalms 2). John, the herald of the kingdom, proclaimed to the expectant nation of Israel—"**The** kingdom of heaven has approached." Christ's first proclamation was in the same words, which clearly imply, that, prior to that time, it had not existed.

Dr. Dagg's theory utterly ignores the prophecy of Daniel (ii; 44), because "the whole number of the saved" was never organized or "set up," and because the kingdom, as he defines it, existed from the days of Abel; and those were empty words uttered by Christ—"On this rock will I build my Church, and the gates of hell [even if it means death] shall not prevail against it"—for what could prevail, in any conceivable way, against the saved in heaven, or those God had ordained to save? This theory I can but esteem as violative of the laws of language, and the teachings of God's word.

THE KINGDOM OF CHRIST—WHAT IS IT?

I propose to construct it out of the ground truths admitted by our standard writers.

Dr. A. P. Williams, the profoundest thinker Missouri has produced, says:

"The **churches** are each **integral parts** of the kingdom of Christ."

If so—and I accept it—the churches, as such, are the **integers** of the kingdom of Christ. The local churches, then, compose the kingdom. Other able writers admit that a local church is not the kingdom, but a **constituent** of the kingdom, and I accept this also. Then, it follows that the **local churches** are the **constituents** of the kingdom of Christ. Then must the local churches constitute the kingdom of Christ—not **individuals** on earth or in heaven, but churches, are the units of which the kingdom is composed. And this is the fact to be kept in mind—

That the kingdom of Christ is not composed of **INDIVIDUALS**, as such, baptized or unbaptized; but of **CHURCHES**, as such, and only of individuals as composing local churches.

UNSCRIPTURAL AND INCONSISTENT. 151

This conclusion incontrovertibly follows:

That the visible kingdom of Christ, which is also called "kingdom of God," "of heaven," "of God's dear Son," can not exist without one or more of its constituents— local churches; and, therefore, it did not exist on earth before, or independent of, a local church.

But "the kingdom of heaven" did exist, not only during, but "from the days of John the Baptist"—the commencement of his ministry.

This can not well be doubted, since he proclaimed that it had approached.

The first public proclamation by Christ was that it had approached.

Subsequently, he declared that, "from the days of John, it had been assaulted, and violent men sought to destroy it; and that the law and the prophets were until John, since which time the kingdom of heaven was proclaimed, and all men were **opposing** it"—not pressing into it, as our version has it (see Chap. II). We know it could not be assaulted and outraged unless visibly existing. Christ further says, That while scribe and priest were endeavoring to shut up the kingdom against men, publicans and harlots were going into the kingdom before their eyes; and, when asked "**where his** kingdom was," he answered, that it was "among them"—upon the soil of Judea, although the Jews did not apprehend it.

But since the kingdom can not exist without one or more of its integral parts, or constituencies, then there must have been **one** Church, at least, in existence "from the days of John the Baptist," and that one was the only manifestation of the kingdom until other churches were multiplied; and during this period the church visible, and the "kingdom of Christ," were one and the same institution, and practically synonymous terms.

The Christian Church, in connection with the kingdom of Christ, may be considered as a progressive institution, and developed in three periods:

1. In its **inchoate,** or formative period, embracing the period from the ministry of John the Baptist until the close of the first Pentecost after the ascension of Christ.

During this period, the little stone was cut out of the mountain without hands—creative agency—and commenced rolling onward toward the image which symbolized all earthly opposing kingdoms (Dan. ii). During this period the little mustard seed germinated, and blade and stalk, with its tender branches and leaves, appeared in the garden of Judea; but the time of its blossoming, and full expansion into tree-form and fruitage, was not yet, but it was none the less " a mustard tree," or plant.

When Æneas, with his handful of heroes, having escaped from burning Troy, and the disasters of the sea, reached the Lavinian shore, and established his kingly jurisdiction, that little band was as much a Roman kingdom as it was when the legions of Cæsar had conquered all the known world.

Baptists have been tauntingly asked to show the semblance of a Church or kingdom of Christ before the days of pentecost; and some of our writers have strangely conceded that there was neither before pentecost. I think a kingdom can be found; and, if a kingdom, then a church, since the former can not exist without the latter. Let us carefully examine the inspired records.

John was sent to make ready a people prepared for the Lord, and he had a people in readiness for his Master, and the Lord accepted them and associated them as his disciples. In this body of disciples, under the authority of Christ, and obedient to his authority, we find all the elements of a Christian Church, viz.: Called out from the world by conversion and baptism, associated in a visible body according to the direction of Christ their only Head and King, and submitting in all things to his authority. This was Christ's Church in its inceptive state; and John applied to it the very name given it in the Apocalypse of Christ—the Bride (Rev. xxi: 9); that is, one day to be "the Lamb's wife." The name Christ ere long gave to this body of disciples was significant—an assembly; a body that could, and **must often**, be assembled in one place for worship, and the transaction of business. He several times assembled these disciples before he gave them the title of his "assembly"—Church.

The first full church-meeting—a gathering together of his disciples into one place for general instruction—is recorded by Matthew (v: 1):

"And seeing the multitude, he went up into a mountain, and having sat down his **disciples** came unto him, and he opened his mouth and taught **them**, saying."

These "disciples" were not the twelve apostles, nor yet the seventy merely, for **they** had not yet been chosen from the whole body, but the multitude of his disciples. So Alford:

"The disciples, in the **wider sense,** including those of the apostles already **called,** and **all** who had, either for a longer or shorter time, attached themselves to him as hearers. * * **The discourse was spoken directly to the disciples,**" etc.

Here, then, is a **real church** meeting; a visible assembly of men, possessing certain qualifications, called out from the **oklos** (multitude) for a specific purpose, and this is the essential signification of ecclesia in Greek. We may add an organized assembly, since they recognized the supreme authority of Christ over them. At this first general meeting of his disciples, which soon after he named his **ecclesia**—his assembly, church—he instructed them touching their individual Christian duties, and clearly indicated their mission as his assembly.

"Ye are the **light of the world**—a city set on a hill. Let your light so shine that men, seeing your good works, may glorify your Father who is in heaven."

This I consider Christ's first great commission to

his Church, and by which he made it the great missionary agency for the gospel enlightenment of the whole world; for it was of the whole world he constituted his church to be the light.

Here was a **Church,** of which Christ was the living present Head, and the source of all law and government: but as yet there were no commissioned officers, since the apostles, nor the seventy were chosen for some time after this. (See Matt. ix: 9.)

The second general gathering together of his disciples into one place was by a special summons. Luke thus records it (vi: 12)—

"And it came to pass in those days, that he went out into a mountain to pray, and continued all night in prayer to God. And when it was day, he called [summoned] his disciples [the whole body of them] to him. And having chosen from them twelve, whom he called also apostles. . . And having come down with them, he stood on a plain, and a **company of his disciples** [not all in this instance] and a great multitude of people from all Judea, etc., etc. And he lifted up his eyes on his disciples and said, Blessed are ye, poor ones: for yours is the kingdom of God."

Those disciples at this time alone composed the kingdom of God, and it was indeed literally theirs, being entirely of them.

"After this (Luke x) Christ appointed seventy other [officers], and sent them, two by two, before his face into every place whether he himself was about to come."

It is not much to infer that after these two general meetings of the whole or main body of the disciples, and the appointment of officers, that his disciples would understand Christ should he call them his **assembly,** and as constituting the **kingdom** which, as Messiah, he was to set up on this earth. This was soon formally announced:

> "And I also say unto thee, That thou art Peter, and upon this rock will I build my assembly—church—and the gates of hell shall not prevail against it. And I will give unto thee the keys of the **kingdom** of heaven; and whatsoever thou shalt bind on earth, shall be bound in heaven," etc.

There was a kingdom and a church in existence at this time, but not as separate organizations; for the kingdom included the church and the church composed the kingdom.

Soon after this the Lawgiver delivers to his church the fundamental law for dealing with all **personal** offenses among the members, which has never been modified or abrogated; and the giving of this law and the express mention of the body of his disciples as a **church,** puts it beyond all question that there was an organization at this time, since laws imply and necessitate organization.

The third general meeting of the brethren of his ecclesia was after his resurrection, where, at a place he appointed before his death, he met more than five hundred brethren at one time. (1 Cor. xv: 6.)

The number with Christ as witness of his ascension is not told, but it seems that one hundred and twenty upon their return, held a church meeting in an upper room in Jerusalem, where they, by popular vote, elected Matthias to fill the place left vacant by the death of Judas.

The body of brethren which Christ had three times gathered into an assembly, and had designated as his church, and spoken of as his kingdom, the Holy Spirit expressly calls a church after the ascension of Christ. We have not the slightest intimation that there was the least modification made in its organization, much less that a new and unheard of body was originated by the apostles. To the body which Christ left, the three thousand were added by baptism on the day of Pentecost; and it was to the church **then existing** that the saved were added daily for some time afterward. The closing days of this period were marked by great activity, since it entered with the zeal of a new convert upon the work assigned it by its risen Head; the gospel was preached, converts baptized in large numbers, and the Lord's Supper observed, the doctrine of the apostles steadfastly adhered to, and brotherly love abounded. Let this be borne in mind, that before the days of Pentecost and the great revival that marked those days, a church was in existence, and **that no church was organized during the days of Pentecost or afterwards in the city of Jerusalem,** and that this body of disciples constituted the kingdom of Christ during this period.

The Second Period of church development and extension of the kingdom of Christ, embraces the whole intervening space between the close of the first Pentecost, after the ascension, and the second advent and coronation of Christ upon the throne of his father David as "King of kings and Lord of lords." It is during this second period that the mustard plant of the last "becomes a great tree, so that the fowls of the air lodge in its branches"—that the prophetic stone reaches the feet of the image (Dan ii), crushes them and breaks the image in pieces.

Space does not allow me to trace at any length the development of the church Christ left on earth. We soon see it again exercising its democratic principles in electing seven deacons (Acts vi), to take the ministry of its **temporal** affairs that its ministers may the more fully give themselves to their **spiritual** vocations; and a little further on we see the church at Antioch clothed with, and exercising the full prerogatives of a complete and independent church, empowered to ordain and commission two of its members to go forth as foreign missionaries to carry the glad news of salvation into Asia and Greece.

The relation of the kingdom to the churches of Christ is thus indicated by Dr. Harvey in his late work, "*The Church:*"

"The church—[*i, e.,* churches] is the visible, earthly form of the kingdom of Christ, and is the divine organization appointed for its advancement and triumph. Organized and governed by the laws of the invisible king, and composed of the subjects of the heavenly kingdom, who, by the symbol of fealty, have publicly professed allegiance to him, the church [es] fitly represents that kingdom. Hence the apostles in receiving authority to establish, under divine inspiration, the form and order of the church, received 'the keys of the kingdom of heaven.' Whenever they gathered disciples they organized a church; and at their death they left this as a distinctive and only visible form of the kingdom of Christ on earth."—pp. 24-25.

The Third Period of the church's history, in connection with the extension of Christ's kingdom, will commence with the coronation and enthronement of Christ as the "One whose right it is to rule," the subjugation of all the nations of earth to his absolute dominion, and the association of all his saints, now fully redeemed and glorified, with himself as heirs and joint heirs with himself in the government of the nation as kings and priests.

The following scriptures refer to the kingdom in its third universal and glorious extension—Luke ix: 27; xxii: 16, 18; Acts xiv: 22; 1 Cor. vi: 9; xiii: 50; Rev. xii: 10; xi: 15; Matt. xiii: 41; xvi: 28; 2 Tim. iv: 1.

The Stone of Prophecy (Dan. ii) now becomes the great mountain [government] and fills the whole earth. The subjects of the kingdom in the former periods now inherit it, and become associated with their king in the administration of its government. All the nations and kingdoms of earth, as such, will become and constitute the kingdom of our Lord, and the subjects over whom the saints, with Christ, rule and reign. (Dan. vii: 27; Rev. v: 10; xx: 6.) Now will be fulfilled that prophecy "when the mountain [government] of the Lord's House shall be established on the tops of the mountains [over all governments], and all nations shall flow unto it." (Isa. ii: 2.)

It now remains to gather up the ground truths of the above standard authors, and construct a definition of kingdom of Christ that will be in accord with the teachings of scripture.

Dr. Williams says that "each local church is an **integral** portion of the kingdom."

Dr. Taylor: "That the baptized alone are in the kingdom."

Dr. Gardner: That all the true churches of Christ are **in** the kingdom of Christ.

Dr. Fish: The churches are the **executives** of the laws of the kingdom, and of course are in it. We must suppose he meant all the visible churches.

Dr. Harvey: That the church is the earthly form of the kingdom of Christ. * * The church fitly represents that kingdom.

This, then, must be the definition to embrace all these propositions.

The kingdom of Christ, of God, of heaven, is constituted of the sum total of all his true visible churches as constituents, which churches are the sole judges and executives of the laws and ordinances of the kingdom.

From this we learn:

1. That all the officers, save the king, belong to the **churches,** and receive their authority to officiate from the churches.

2. That the churches being intrusted with the administration of the laws and ordinances, they must be administered under their supervision and upon their fellowship, since they can not delegate their trusts to others.

3. That, by baptism, we become citizens of the kingdom of Christ, only because it introduces us into one of its constituents—a local church—just as we become a citizen of this Republic only by becoming a citizen of some one of its constituents —a State.

4. We learn that all our church rights, privileges, and franchises are limited to the particular church of which we are members, as those of a citizen are limited to the State of which he is a citizen. Nor can one church constitutionally extend her franchises or privileges to persons without and beyond her jurisdiction, any more than one State can extend her franchises to citizens of other States.

5. That since the Supper is one of the ordinances, and committed to the guardianship and administration of each local church, no member of another church has the least right or title to partake of it only in the church of which he is a member; **since Christ has not given him the right,** and since Christ has not authorized his

churches to legislate so as to change, in the least particular, his appointments, they can not grant, under the plea of "courtesy" or fellowship, a right or privilege which he has, for wise purposes, withheld.

OBJECTION.—That the kingdom of Christ had not come during the ministry of Christ, is evident from the prayer He taught his disciples to pray, which we call "The Lord's Prayer."

ANSWER.—Christ did not teach his disciples to pray that his Messianic kingdom might come—the prayer has no allusion to his kingdom—but that the Father's kingdom might come and embrace this ruined earth as it now does the heavens.

Often we mislead ourselves by our misreading. The Prayer begins thus:

Our Father, who art in heaven, hallowed be thy name. **Thy kingdom** come. Thy will be done in earth as it is done in heaven.

When this prayer is answered, **God's** will will be done on this earth as it is in heaven, and then earth will be heaven. This will take place at the close of Christ's mediatorial reign with his saints on this earth, when he shall have consummated the work he undertook to do in the covenant of redemption—have redeemed and regenerated the whole physical earth (Rom. viii:) making new heavens and a new earth (2 Pet. iii:) and have redeemed and saved enough of Adam's race to people it. "Then (Paul tells us) cometh the end when he shall have delivered up the kingdom to God, even the Father; when he shall have put down all rule, and all authority and power. For he [Christ] must reign till he hath put all enemies under his feet." (1 Cor. xv: 24.)

It is for this ultimate triumph, and the ample re-establishment of the prestine kingdom of the Father over this earth, that Christ taught his disciples to desire and to pray in that prayer; and it is what every child of God does desire, and for which he should pray.

CHAPTER V.

THE SUPPER A CHURCH ORDINANCE.

Definition of church ordinance.—The Supper demonstrated to be a church ordinance—1. Each church absolutely independent under Christ; 2. Each church is made the guardian of the ordinances, and enjoined to prevent the disqualified from partaking of them; 3. The symbolism of the Supper determine it beyond question to be a church ordinance, since it symbolizes church relations with the body celebrating the rite.—Christ appointed it as a church ordinance—could not have allowed his churches the right to contravene it. -The churches of the first ages observed it as a church ordinance.

WE have seen that the Supper can only be enjoyed by one—1. Who has been scripturally baptized; and thus, 2. Has become a member of a scriptural church; and 3. Is in hearty fellowship with its doctrines; and 4. Is walking in gospel order. I come now to notice further: **That the Lord's Supper is a church ordinance, and, as such, can only be** observed by a church, as such, and by a person in the church of which he is a member.

This statement indicates an observance of the Supper generally disregarded by our churches, as are other important matters connected with the sacred feast, as the character of bread and the kind of wine used, and it will, therefore, demand an investigation in spirit so unfettered by the prejudices of long usage and uninfluenced by the opinions of their powerful advocates, that comparatively few will be able to command; but, these few belong to the class of witnesses who have, through all ages, been the conservators of "the truth as it is in Jesus," and to whom the world is indebted for a pure gospel and scriptural ordinances. The truth of the proposition, as a whole, depends upon the truth of its first clause, *i. e.*, that the Supper is a **church** ordinance. It becomes me to define a church, from a denominational and social ordinance. There is no denominational ordinance of divine appointment—because such a thing as a denomination, in the sense of an organized body, embracing all the churches of a province or nation, was unknown in the first ages. I have denominated the Lord's Supper a denominational ordinance whenever it is opened to the members of any and all Baptist churches present. We do not allow a brother not a member, in however good standing, the right to vote in our Conventions,

Associations, Presbyteries, Councils, or church conference, but we do confer upon him the rights of a member, without the knowledge of his character, when we observe the Lord's Supper, the most sacred of all ordinances!

A social ordinance or act is one that may be enjoyed anywhere by any number of Christians, as individuals, baptized or unbaptized—as singing, prayer, exhortation and religious conversation.

But, the essential qualities of a church ordinance are,—

1. That it is a rite, the duty of perpetuating which is committed to the visible churches, as such.

2. The qualifications of its recipients must be decided by the members of the churches as such.

3. Any rite which symbolizes church relations can only be participated in by the members of the church celebrating, and is pre-eminently a church ordinance.

A church act or privilege is one that can be transacted or enjoyed by the constituent members of one particular church. Voting upon all questions relating to the choice of officers, the fellowship and government of the church, is a church privilege, or act, which, from the very nature and constitution of a gospel church, belongs to the members of that particular church alone, and can not be extended beyond its limits without peril to its very existence.

Baptism and the Lord's Supper are universally

admitted to be church ordinances, and yet few seem to apprehend why they are, or why they can not be administered by an officer of a local church without the action or presence of the church.

Of the Lord's Supper, especially, few seem to understand why it ceases to be a church ordinance when administered to those without and beyond its jurisdiction, or when those without and beyond the jurisdiction of a local church are associated in its celebration. It is my conviction that misapprehension of the true nature and limitations of a church ordinance has given rise to all the discussions, misunderstandings, all the misrepresentations, and bitter prejudices excited against us by other denominations, as well as to all the present disagreement among Baptists. If all parties could understand clearly why the Lord's Supper is a church ordinance, and why it must, from its very nature and in every instance, be observed by the constituent membership of each local church alone, it must be that all this unpleasant and harmful misunderstanding, and antagonism would be settled and pacified: and certainly this would be a consummation devoutly to be wished by every true child of God in every denomination.

In the not vain hope, I trust, of contributing something toward this so desirable a result, I submit this and the following chapters.

My first argument to show why the Lord's Supper is a church ordinance, and can not be scripturally observed only by the members of one particular church, is,—

1. That each church under Christ is absolutely independent.

The first church organized by Christ was a complete and perfect church, and yet it existed for years before other churches were formed. There were no new ecclesiastical relations originated, nor the slightest modification of the character of this church made, by the multiplication of churches. During the apostolic age, nor for ages after, was there the shadow of any confederation or con-association or constitutional *inter-dependence* recognized, any more than between the families of children of a common parentage. Love for the brotherhood and active charity for all in distress, and the doing of good, especially to the household of faith, was only enjoined   The idea of a constitutional inter-dependence, which is now imperceptibly taking root in the minds of the cultured leaders of our people, in the fourth century begot confederations and con-associations of churches, and these soon brought forth the centralized ecclesiastical hierarchism under the auspices of Constantine—which is known as the "Great Apostasy."

[A. D. 100-193]. "All congregations were independent of each other," etc.   (Gieseler, chap. iii : p. 53.)

"All the churches in those primitive times were independent bodies, and none of them subject to the jurisdiction of any other. It is as clear as noonday that all Christian churches had equal rights, and were in all respects on a footing of equality." (Mosheim, A. D. 100).

[A. D. 200.] "During a great part of this century all the churches continued to be, as at first, independent of each other, or were connected by no con-associations or confederations; each church was a kind of little independent republic, governed by its own laws."

[A. D. 300–400.] "Although the ancient mode of church government seemed, in general, to remain unaltered, yet there was a gradual deflection from its rules, and an approximation toward the form of monarchy. This change in the form of government was followed by a corrupt state of the clergy."

This was the vile offspring begotten by the idea of the inter-dependency of churches, which is finding strong advocates in our day. They sink the idea of churches into that of a Denomination.

The learned Dr. Owen, of England, asserts:

"That, in no approved writer, for two hundred years after Christ, is mention made of any organized visible professing church, except a **local organization**."—*Crowell's Church Manual*, p. 36.

Each church being absolutely independent, it must, from the very nature of the case, absolutely control its own acts; and can be responsible to no authority save Christ. It can not constitutionally allow the members of other communities to share its prerogatives, since such license would endanger its own independency and responsibility.

Should a church so far forget its trust as to fall

into the general practice of inviting, as an act of courtesy (which implies a discourtesy in refusing to do it), the members of all sister churches present to **vote** in the reception and exclusion of members, discipline, and even choice of pastors, as one prominent Baptist author advises, how soon the independency of the churches would be subverted! Usage would soon crystallize into precedent, and custom into law.

The independency of the churches is of Christ's special appointment, and it is our sacred duty to do nothing tending to imperil or contravene it. No one will presume to claim that Christ invested his churches with the power to contravene, at their pleasure, any one of his appointments. Their powers are all delegated, and delegated powers can not be relegated. A local church can not confer upon members of other communities any privilege or franchise that belongs exclusively to her own members.

But it is further demonstrable that the Supper, as well as baptism, is a local church ordinance, because—

2. **To each local church is committed the sole administration and guardianship of the ordinances.**

This will not be questioned, save by the few who hold that baptism, at least, was committed to the ministry as such; that they alone are responsible for its proper administration; and they can, therefore, administer it without the presence and voice of the church whenever and wherever they please. This must be settled, not by the will or opinions of men, but by the Scriptures.

Let us see what one apostle thought concerning this issue between a part of our ministry and the churches :

TO THE CHURCH AT CORINTH.

"I have received of the Lord Jesus that which I also delivered unto **you**."—(1 Cor. xi: 23.)

All the instructions and directions, both as respects the doctrine and the ordinances, Paul delivered, not to the ministry, but to the churches.

"Now I praise **you**, brethren [not you, **ministers** of the churches], that **ye** remember me in all things, and keep the ordinances as I delivered them unto **you**."—(1 Cor. xi: 2.)

Now note his command to this **church**, not to its ministers :

"Be **ye** followers of me, even as I am also of Christ."— (1 Cor. ii: 1.)

"I beseech **you**, be ye followers of me. For this cause I have sent unto you Timothy, my beloved son, and faithful in the Lord, who shall bring you into remembrance of my ways, which be in Christ, as I teach every-where in **every church**."—(1 Cor. iv: 16, 17.)

TO THE CHURCH AT PHILIPPI.

"Brethren, be **ye** followers of me, and mark them who walk so, as **ye** have us for an example."

He enjoins it upon the church to follow the directions he had given it, as well as to "mark" those who did not.

TO THE CHURCH AT COLOSSE.

"Though I be absent in the flesh, yet am I with you in the spirit, joying and obeying your order, and the steadfastness of your faith in Christ. As ye have received Christ Jesus the Lord, so walk ye in him. Beware lest any man spoil you through philosophy and vain deceit, after the traditions of men, after the rudiments of the world, and not after Christ."—(ii: 5–8.)

TO THE CHURCH AT THESSALONICA.

"Therefore, my brethren, stand fast and hold the tradition [which embraces all the instructions and ordinances] which ye have been taught, whether by word or our epistle.—(2 Thess. ii: 15.)

"And we have confidence in the Lord touching you [the Church], that ye both do and will do the things we command you."—(iii: 4.)

It would be useless to reason with those who could deny, with these Scriptures before their eyes, that the ordinances were not delivered in sacred trust to the churches, as such, and not to their officers; and that they are held responsible for their right observance.

It is further established, with respect to the Supper, by the duties especially enjoined upon each local church, as such. It is commanded to allow only members possessing certain qualifications to come to the Supper.

"Now we command you, brethren, in the name of the Lord Jesus Christ, that ye withdraw yourselves [as a

Church] from every brother that walketh disorderly, and not after the traditions [instructions] which he received of us."* "And if any man obey not our word by this epistle, note that man, and have no company with him, that he may be ashamed."—(2 Thess. iii: 6, 14.)

This withdrawing and having no company with the disobedient and disorderly, certainly involved exclusion from the Lord's table.

"But now I have written unto **you** not to keep company, if any man be a fornicator, or covetous, or an idolator, or a railer, or a drunkard, or an extortioner; **with such** a one, **no, not to eat.**"

The apostolic churches were peremptorily commanded to prohibit the table to all these, and such like characters—to allow no leaven to be mingled in the feast. For this purpose, each church is made the sole guardian of the Supper. It can not alienate the responsibility. It can not, under any plea, contravene the law. To execute it with fidelity, it must keep the feast within its jurisdiction; its permission to partake can not be extended beyond the limits of the Supper, since all who can be entitled to the Supper must be subject to its discipline.

It is conceded by all that members of other communities have no scriptural or any other right to eat the Supper in any church save their own. No one claims that it is the duty of any local church

* And what ingenuous mind will deny that this command equally excludes all such from the pulpit as well?

to offer the Supper to any but its own members. What, then, do I conclude?—

1. That Christ has not given me the right to commune in any church save the one which has the watch and care over me, and that my privileges are limited to my church.

2. That Christ has not made it the duty of any church to open the doors to this ordinance to any not subject to its discipline; but, by making it a church ordinance he has manifestly forbidden the practice, since, by the act, the participant declares he is a member of the church with which he communes—"we are one loaf," *i. e.*, one **church.**

3. And it may be safely affirmed that those churches that statedly offer and invite to their tables all the members of sister churches who may chance to be present in the congregation, openly violate the command of Paul—to allow no disqualified persons to participate in this ordinance—since it is morally certain that such are **often**, if not ever, present, and are the most certain to accept.

But the Lord's Supper is unquestionably a church ordinance, because—

4. It symbolizes church relations, *i. e.*, **that all who jointly partake are members of the one and self-same church.**

I only assert this fact here, and submit an eminent authority, that of Prof. Curtis, who has treated this subject with unsurpassed ability, and reserve the discussion and proof of it when I treat of the symbolism of the elements in the next Part. That the Supper is a church ordinance in the sense that it can be worthily celebrated by only one church and participated in by the members of only one church, Prof. Curtis argues most conclusively from the symbolism of the Supper, as well as from the fact that it is under the sole guardianship of the churches.

He says, in "Communion," page 85:

"We desire to show that this is the true view of the Lord's Supper, [*i. e.*, that it is a church ordinance, and a symbol of church relationship]. 'When ye come together therefore into one place,' says the apostle, 'this is not to eat the Lord's Supper. For in eating every one taketh before other, etc. . . Wherefore, my brethren, when ye come together to eat, tarry one for another.' (1 Cor. xi: 21–23.) The apostle here clearly alludes to it as the universally current opinion that the Lord's Supper was a church ordinance, so far as this, that it was completely celebrated in **one place**, by **one church**. . . . When he bids them 'tarry one for another' he clearly intimates that the regulation of the Supper, as far as time and place are concerned, is lodged in each particular church; **that it expresses the relations of the members of the church to each other, as such.**"

"That the Lord's Supper is a symbol of church relationship, subsisting between those who unite together in the participation of it, can be shown in various ways."

"Admission to the Lord's table, therefore, implies admission to it by a particular church, and this in fact settles the question that the Lord's Supper is a church ordinance."

The Lord's Supper, then, being a church ordinance, indicates church relations as subsisting between the parties who unite together in its celebration.

"It must be conceded that the Lord's Supper is ever the symbol of particular, visible church relations."—Page 138.

"It expresses the relations of the members of **that church** to each other, **as such.**"

"A fellowship in church relations, professed with those Christians with whom we visibly celebrate."

If the Lord's Supper is a **church** ordinance, as must be admitted, and a symbol, among other things, of our visible church relations in the same particular church with which we celebrate it, then it is a violation of the truth symbolized to invite members of other Baptist churches to participate in it.

When Baptists, in reasoning with affusionists, urge the symbolism of Baptism, *i. e.*, that it represents a burial—as conclusive that the **act** must be an **immersion**—they think candid Pedobaptists should see and admit so evident an argument. Will not all candid Baptists admit this?

4. **It was instituted by Christ to be observed as a church ordinance.**

I claim it as an—

AXIOM,

That a church ordinance must be instituted by Christ.

AND

That the symbolism of the ordinances was instituted by Christ.

Should we observe ordinances originated by man, our worship would be unacceptable to Christ, and as **vain** as it would be sinful.   Christ has said—

"In vain do they worship me who teach for doctrines the commandments of men."

Should we change the symbol of an ordinance by the slightest modification, we would vitiate it; and to vitiate the symbolism of an ordinance in the least, is to vitiate the ordinance.

" Ye do make the commandment of God of **none** effect through your traditions."—*Christ.*

That Christ did institute the Supper to be rigidly observed as a church ordinance, Prof. Curtis declares:

"So when our blessed Savior instituted the Supper, as he did, upon one of those Paschal occasions, it was, we say, as a **church ordinance** that he ordained it."

And he justly says, to claim the right to change it in the least, is to claim the right to **legislate.** If it is ever a symbol of particular church relations professed with those Christians with whom we visibly celebrate, as he declares, then to celebrate it with those not members of the same church, is to vitiate the symbol and change what Christ hath appointed.

5. The Lord's Supper was observed by the apostolic churches (A. D. 100) as a church ordinance ; *i. e.,* **as a symbol of church relations.**

Paul, we have seen, could not have delivered this ordinance unto the churches as he had received it from Christ, unless he had delivered it unto them as a church ordinance; for it is admitted that Christ ordained it as a church ordinance. (Curtis and others).

The apostolic churches could not have observed this ordinance as Paul delivered it unto them unless they had observed it as a church ordinance, *i. e.,* by one church only, and with the members of one church only.

But the churches did observe this, as well as the other ordinances, as Paul delivered them, because he praised them for so doing.

To the church at Corinth he wrote,—

"I praise you, brethren, because you keep the ordinances as I delivered them unto you." (1 Cor. xi : 2.)

To the church at Colosse he could say,—

"I rejoice, beholding your **order** and the stability of your faith."

The churches at Thessalonica he only exhorts:

"So, then, brethren, stand firm and hold fast the ordinances you were taught, whether by our word or letter."

Which clearly implies they had been, and still were faithful in their observance.

The church at Corinth for a season perverted the design of the Supper, and Paul promptly rebuked it [not its pastor or elders], and again set it in order, and we must believe that he corrected every departure from his instructions.

But suppose I grant that he did not deliver it to the churches as symbolizing the relations of all the participants to one and the same church, still I claim that the positive instructions Paul gave to the churches forbade them from inviting to their tables the members of all existing churches, without personal knowledge of their faith or character, as is the practice of this age. He placed the Supper under the **sole custody** of **each church,** and commanded it to purge away from its table all leaven of malice or wickedness. He taught them that **false doctrine** of all description, and all ungodly conduct (1 Cor. v.), and all works of the flesh (Gal. v.), was **leaven** that must not be allowed to defile the feast.

"Now we charge you, brethren, in the name of our Lord Jesus Christ, to withdraw from **every brother** who walks disorderly, and not according to the instruction which you have received from us." (2 Thess. iii : 6)

If it is said "that this was spoken to the church with reference to her own members," I will grant it, and demand if it does not equally teach that it should equally withdraw from those not members walking disorderly? That there might be no doubt, read the fourteenth verse: "But if **any one obey** not our word, signify that man by an epistle [the most approved rendering], and have no company with him, that he may be ashamed." All will admit that this command forbade them to invite all false teachers, as well as unsound and disorderly brethren, to the Lord's Supper.

Now false teachers and heretical brethren, abounded in Paul's day, all members of sister churches in good standing, and thousands of these belonged to the church at Jerusalem; and had it been the custom of the church at Corinth to invite "all members of sister churches" to its table, would it not have violated the instructions of Paul? But this feature will be more fully developed in a future Chapter. But finally—

For centuries after the ascension of Christ, the Lord's Supper was rigidly observed as a church ordinance.

I care little for the argument from post-apostolic history. It is enough for my purpose—and it must be quite enough for every conscientious Bible Christian—to learn that Christ appointed the Supper to be observed as a **church** ordinance, and that the apostles so delivered it to the churches, and the churches all observed it as such while they had the personal instructions of the apostles. Suppose, from the day the last apostle died, every church ceased to observe it as a church ordinance; how should that fact affect our present practice? Would it warrant a church to observe it, even once, in some other way, that would vitiate its symbolism? The fact granted would in no way vitiate the claim that there have been Baptist churches from the day of the defection. The church at Corinth had for years utterly perverted the Supper, and yet Paul addressed it as a church of Christ. It was disorderly in this respect, but a perversion of the Supper did not forfeit its existence.

My space does not allow me to treat this question historically. Let the statements of so cautious and eminent a scholar as Prof. Curtis suffice in support of my proposition. He says:

"There is sufficient proof to convince any close student of church history of the first three centuries, that in the very earliest ages, the Lord's Supper was regarded as strictly a church ordinance, as we have defined the phrase."—*Communion*, p. 88.

"The records of church history plainly show that originally the Lord's Supper was everywhere regarded as a church ordinance."—*Communion*, p. 137.

I will add the remarks of Dr. D. Spencer, in his treatise on "Invitations to the Supper," after showing that no invitations were given by the first churches, nor yet in the days of Justin Martyr, in the second century:

"How, then, did invitations originate? The answer is plain. **They originated with the perversion of the ordinance.** When the ordinance came to take the place of Christ, the churches began to invite to it, as they had formerly invited to Christ. Hence in Romish churches to-day you hear plenty of invitations to ordinances, but none to Christ."

I have not granted, in this discussion, that the unapostate churches, whom we account our ancestors, deflected at an early day into denominational Communion. It is my impression that this **laxity** is a late practice.

CONCLUSIONS FROM THIS ARGUMENT.

I think I have conclusively shown,—

1. That Christ appointed his Supper to be a church ordinance.

2. That any rational definition of church ordinance or privilege limits the enjoyment of it to the membership of, or to those approved for membership by a local church.

3. That when an ordinance or act symbolizes or implies **church relations,** it is pre-eminently a church ordinance, and must be confined to the members of a particular church only.

4. That the Lord's Supper, among other things, specially symbolizes church relations, as all standard writers admit, and, therefore, it can be scripturally observed by the members of one church only.

5. That for the members of various churches to participate in its joint observance, even though upon the invitation of a local church, as Associations and Conventions are wont in some places to do, would be to vitiate the symbolism, and consequently to render the ordinance, **null.**

The only issue now before Baptists is fairly stated by Dr. A. P. Williams:

"If he [a member of one church] ever has a right anywhere else, it must be either by a transfer of membership or by courtesy," etc.—*Lord's Supper*, p. 94.

In his "Tract on Communion," as though he would correct, in part, at least, the admission made in his book on Communion, he says:

"But this courtesy can not be exercised in violation of church discipline or of **divine authority.**"

It is demonstrable that it is in palpable violation of **both**:

1. It is always done at the expense of good **discipline**; for when a church invites to her table the members of all other Baptist churches present, she inevitably will invite those she would feel herself bound to exclude, if her own members; and she would often invite those whom she considers unbaptized, and would refuse their application for membership; and **oftentimes** she would invite back to her Communion persons she herself excluded, who are now members of other churches, in good standing. Can this be called good discipline?

2. Such a courtesy can never be extended and accepted, except in violation of divine authority, since Christ appointed the Supper to symbolize the organic unity of the body partaking—*i. e.*, partic-

ular church relations of all the participants with that one church.

It is claimed that the churches have the right to extend such invitations through courtesy. I answer that such a claim is not even supposable; for—

1. It can not be supposed that Christ would allow his churches to adopt any practice that would contravene any one of his own appointments—even if we can suppose he sometimes allows it to exercise legislative powers—by adding to, or modifying, the form of one of his ordinances.

2. But invitations to all Baptists present to partake of the Supper with the local church celebrating it, does manifestly contravene Christ's appointment of the Supper as a **church** ordinance.

3. Therefore it can not be supposed that Christ has allowed his churches to extend invitations to all Baptists present to partake of the Supper with them.

From the considerations submitted in this chapter, the reader will see that I have done what I have been called upon to do—proved that all those brethren who admit that the Supper is a church ordinance, do yield the question at issue between us, and, to be consistent, they must admit that Intercommunion of Baptists of different churches is unscriptural and inconsistent.

CHAPTER VI.

CHRISTIAN BAPTISM.

1 *Its Importance.*—2. *Its Acts.*—3. *Its Designs.*—4. *Its Effect.*—5. *Its Administrator.*—*Miscellaneous Matters.*

I. THE IMPORTANCE OF BAPTISM.

CHRISTIAN baptism is a positive duty enjoined upon each child of God by all the authority with which any law of God is enforced. Christ, when he commanded it, declared that he was clothed with all power in heaven and earth. In addition to his most emphatic **command**, he affectionately urges obedience to it upon his regenerated disciples by all the motives drawn from his love and death for their salvation—in fact, he makes it a **test** of the sincerity of their profession of friendship for him: "If a man love me he **will** keep my commandments." "Ye are my friends if ye do whatsoever I command you." "Why call ye me Lord, Lord, and do not the things I command you?" Of the "all things whatsoever" Christ singles out, he mentions but one act as representative of all, and that act is **baptism.** It was the first act of Christ's public ministry. He has made it **the** initial act of our Christian life and service. He has constituted it **the** act in which we confess to the world, in forceful symbolism, what Christ has done for us—**saved us;** and the act in which we profess before angels and men, our supreme allegiance to him with the Father and Holy Spirit, and obligate ourselves to cordially obey **all** things whatsoever he commands us.

Christ has also appointed baptism to be **the one** and **only rite** of initiation into his visible churches, and thereby into his kingdom, a duty he requires and enjoins upon every one who has received the grace of his salvation. Indeed, he implies that the professed disciple who refuses to unite with his people—with whom, and in the midst of whom, he declares he will always be—occupies the attitude of open hostility to him and his cause. "He that is not for me is **against me,** and he that gathereth not with me scattereth abroad." As certainly as we love Christ, or God, we will **love,** and love to **be with** the children of God. "If we love him that begot, we shall love them also who are begotten of him."

Christ positively requires his children to observe his Supper, in remembrance of him. "This do" is a command as inviolable as any specific law of the decalogue, and its violation involves us in equal guilt. If we are the recipients of his grace, we can not, with impunity, refuse or delay to obey the command to observe his Supper. To refuse to observe it is to **aggravate** the guilt of its violation.

Now the Lord's Supper is a church ordinance, and within the sacred inclosure of his churches, and we can not partake of it without being introduced into one of them. To attempt to eat the Supper outside, or in an organization not his church, is to eat and drink unworthily.

But no one ever was, is to-day, or ever can be, a member of an evangelical or Christian church, or of the kingdom of Christ, unless baptized as Christ was, and as he commands us to be, which will be fully shown in the closing section of this chapter.

All Christians, how widely soever they differ about other things, agree that no one can become a member of Christ's church without baptism. But let it be ever remembered that the act we submit to for baptism must be **baptism**, *i. e.*, must be the act which Christ commands, and it must be administered to us by the body he authorizes alone to administer it—one of his local churches; an organization not a church, though all its members were Christians, has no authority to administer the ordinances of Christ's house. Then as we would obey Christ, by observing his Supper, by uniting with his church, by confessing him as our Savior, by professing our hearty allegiance, it devolves upon us to be baptized as he was and as he commands us to be. It must be true that every true child of God has the mind and spirit of Christ, which was the spirit of **exact obedience**, and desires to know what that act is: and it is for such I write.

Why there is to-day the least doubt in the minds of the people about the appointed and primitive act, is—1. Because both the primitive **act** and **design** have been changed by the Romish church and the change adopted by Protestants to suit the tastes, feelings and convenience of the people; 2. Because the word Christ used to designate the act is not translated in our commonly received version; 3. Because other words used to describe the act are untranslated; and 4. Because there are large and influential denominations that teach that the word Christ selected is a word of generic signification, and denotes several different and even opposite acts; as to **pour** upon, to **sprinkle** upon a part of the body, and to **immerse** the whole body in water, and that we are at liberty to use any one of these. The flesh of course selects the one most convenient and popular, and for these reasons the primitive act is practically rejected.

It has been less than three hundred years past that there has been any serious doubt raised as to the act Christ commanded; and, indeed, among the best scholars of all denominations, there is no doubt entertained now, because, for thirteen hundred years, the primitive act was generally observed by all professed Christians. The real question among scholars and theologians since the days of Calvin has been, if a **modified** form of baptism, one more convenient and better suited to the refined feelings of the people will not answer just as well, and if the church has not the authority to change rites and ceremonies, so that the substance is retained? The thoughtful and reverent Christian can not believe that Christ empowered his churches to contravene his positive laws, or modify in the least his appointments. Moreover, the **form** is the substance of a ceremony, and the design of a rite determines its form, and one can not be changed without affecting the other, and the change vitiates the ordinance.

I again emphasize the fact that since Christ has not authorized his churches to modify in the least any one of his appointments, that unless we are baptized as Christ our great exemplar was, and commands us to be, we are not baptized at all, and we can not partake of his Supper without profaning the feast, and bring upon ourselves his condemnation.

Let it not, then, be said or thought that Christian baptism is a matter of little or no importance—that it is "a mere form" and "a non-essential." While not essential to our salvation, since we must be conscious of this before we are baptized, still it is essential to our obedience to Christ; it is essential to our acceptable worship of him; for he tells us this,

"In vain do they worship me who teach for doctrines the commandments of men," *i. e.*, the modified form, design, and subjects of baptism; it is essential to the maintenance and perpetuation of his truth; essential as an act of honor to him our Head; and it is quite essential as a test of the real state of our deceitful hearts and spiritual relation to him.

The importance of scriptural baptism is thus set forth by one of our most forcible writers in his Tract on the "Position of Baptism in the Christian System."

"1. It is a **fact,** that baptism was the initial of the ministry of Jesus Christ. 2. It is a **fact,** that he closed his ministry as he began it,—with baptism. 3. It is a **fact** that the record of his last conversation on earth shows specific mention of this duty and of no other. 4. It is a **fact,** that this is the only duty which we are required to perform in the name of the Trinity. 5. It is a **fact,** that once only was Godhead displayed to earth in triune character, and that this was done on the occasion of baptism. 6. It is a **fact,** that baptism is classed in the Scriptures with things of most tremendous import and of infinite dignity. 7. It is a **fact,** that the baptism of Christ was essential to the fulfillment of all righteousness. 8. It is a **fact** that baptism is the only duty of which one single moment in the life of an immortal being has a monopoly."—*Dr. H. H. Tucker.*

II. THE ACT OF BAPTISM.

1. It is admitted by all that Christ commanded John the Baptist, his Seventy disciples, and his

apostles, to baptize all who professed to repent and believed on him as their Savior—Messiah.

2. That he requires his churches, through their officers, now to baptize all who believe on him.

3. That this command will be in force until he comes again.

4. That it is our personal duty, who believe on him, to obey this command of Christ; therefore,

5. It must be evident to every intelligent mind, and is admitted by all jurists, that unless he used a word, when he commanded us to be baptized, the exact meaning of which we can undoubtedly understand, we are free from all obligation to obey the command, since we would not know what to do.

" A law that is hopelessly obscure, has no binding force, and no person can be held responsible for obedience."*

If Christ used a term of generic signification to indicate the rite of baptism, he did what he has nowhere else done, in either the Old or New Testament, when instituting a rite, civil or divine.

It is the form which constitutes, and is the essence of a rite, human or divine. We must conclude, therefore, that Christ did select a word of specific signification when he instituted the rite of baptism. It is agreed by scholars that the English word "baptize" in our version, is not a definition of the Greek term "**baptizo**," which Christ seected to indicate the act he wished performed.

* Pothier, "Smith's Law of Contracts."—p. 421.

Our present English Bible was translated—the Old Testament out of the **Hebrew** and the New Testament out of the **Greek**—by order of King James, over three hundred years ago, by a company of Episcopalian scholars. They did not translate "baptizo," but transferred it with a change of the last vowel. This is what Dr. Edward Beecher, an acknowledged Pedobaptist scholar, says:

> "At the time of the translation of the Bible, a controversy had arisen as regards the import of the word, so that although **it was conceded to have an import in the original**, yet it was impossible to assign it in English **any meaning** without seeming to take sides in the controversy then pending. Accordingly, in order to take neither side, they did not attempt to give the sense of the term in a significant English word, but merely transferred the word '**baptizo**,' with a slight alteration of termination to our language. The consequence was **that it does not exhibit its original significancy to the mind of the English reader, or, indeed, any significancy,** except what was derived from its application to designate an external, visible rite."—*Import of Baptism*, p. 5.

The reader can see the ignorance manifested by those who refer to Webster for a correct definition of **baptizo** by looking under this word "**baptize**," which is not the English synonym of the Greek word. Webster gives every act which the people call baptism. How, then, are we to ascertain, without a doubt, the literal, real, or true meaning of the word Christ used? Authorities on interpretation tell us that we have five sources of information. The first and highest is the—1. usage of standard writers in the age the author lived. The definitions we find in the lexicons are derived from this source; 2. The definitions given in standard lexicons; 3. The testimony of historians as to how the term was understood, and the rite performed at the time it was instituted; and, 4. The testimony of acknowledged scholars; 5. Internal evidence—*i. e.*, the manifest sense in which the term is used by the author.

Now let us briefly appeal to these sources of information, and inquire:

I. How did the ancient Greeks use it in the time of Christ and his apostles?

Dr. T. J. Conant, of New York, acknowledged to be one of the best Greek scholars in this continent, spent many years, with the assistance of eminent scholars on both continents, in collating and translating every instance of the use of **baptizo in every Greek author whose work is extant.** That every one can see the correctness of his translations he gives in his book the text of the authors. His work has been for years before the scholars of the world, and no one has objected to his translations. What is the result?

Every Greek author uses the term in every instance in the sense of to dip, to immerse, plunge, submerge; and in no instance in the sense of to sprinkle.

What must we conclude from this fact? That if Christ used baptizo in the sense the Greeks of his day used and understood it; he used it to signify to dip or immerse in water—this, and no other, meaning.

II. How do the lexicons define baptizo?

All the lexicons examined or quoted in the Carrollton debate* (some fifty in all) gave **to dip, to immerse** or **merse** as the **primary** or **literal** signification. We have nothing to do with the **figurative** which is based upon the real or primary, and can mean nothing different from it.

In the last few years three Greek and English lexicons have appeared; one in England, of the "Greek Language in General," by Liddell & Scott; and two Lexicons of New Testament Greek, in Germany, and all by Pedobaptist scholars, and the three works are acknowledged by all scholars as eminently authoritative. The testimony of these three recent lexicons, embodying as they do the results of the ablest scholarship and latest criticism, should settle the meaning of baptizo in the mind of every candid reader. I give them here.

1. Liddell & Scott, 6th Edition:

"To dip in or under water."

Giving but this one literal or real definition of baptizo, the few figurative meanings are built upon the idea of an immersion. Thus do they support the declaration of Dr. Chas. Anthon:

* See Graves-Ditzler Debate.

"Baptizo, means to dip, to immerse; pouring and sprinkling are out of the question."

2. Grimm's Wilke's Lexicon of New Testament Greek:

"'(1) To immerse, submerge;' '(2) to wash or bathe by immersing or submerging,' which he says is the meaning of Mark vii: 4, and in the cases of Naaman and Judith; **figuratively** to overwhelm as with debts, misfortunes, etc. In the New Testament rite, he says it denotes an immersion in water, intended as a sign of sins washed away, and received by those who wished to be admitted to the benefits of the Messiah's reign. No hint of its meaning any thing else."

Cremer's Biblico-Theological Lexicon of New Testament Greek:

He gives us the general meaning—"immerse, submerge"—and says in the peculiar New Testament and Christian use the word "**denotes immersion,** submersion, for a religious purpose." Not the shadow of the idea of sprinkling water upon an object is justified. According to the united testimony of all Greek lexicographers, Jesus commanded his apostles to **immerse** their disciples in water, and to-day commands his churches to immerse, thus forbidding them to sprinkle water upon them by his authority.

All scholars, all critics and lexicographers are agreed that in **classic Greek** baptizo means nothing else save to dip, to immerse, in or under water. But some few polemics claim that in New

Testament Greek, its sacred use took on a different meaning, as to purify by the application of water, to wash or bathe by applying water to a part of the body.

To show how groundless this theory is, I quote a canon of interpretation from Morus, indorsed by Ernesti and Stuart:

"The principles of interpretation are common to sacred and ordinary writings, and the Scriptures are to be investigated by the same rules as other books."

Moses Stuart (Pedobaptist) for thirty years professor in Andover Theological Seminary, upon this subject says,—and with his statement Bible readers and students can not be too familiar:

"If the sacred Scriptures be a **revelation** to men, then they are to be read and understood by men. If the same laws of language are not to be observed in this revelation, as are common to men, then they have no guide to the right understanding of the Scriptures, and our interpreter needs inspiration as much as the original writer. It follows, of course, that the sacred Scriptures would be no revelation in themselves, nor of any use except to those who are inspired. But such a book the sacred Scriptures are not, and nothing is more evident than that when God has spoken to men, he has spoken in the language of men, for he has spoken by men and for men."

Before quoting the definitions given in all the lexicons of the New Testament, I submit the statement of Dr. Geo. Campbell, president of Marischal College, Scotland, a Presbyterian:

"The word baptizein, both in sacred authors and in

classical, signifies to dip, to plunge, to immerse; and was rendered by Tertullian, and the old Latin fathers, **tingere,** the term used for dyeing cloth, which was by immersion It is always construed suitably to this meaning (Note on Matt. iii: 11). 'I should think the word **immersion** (which, though of Latin origin, is an English noun) a better English name than baptism, were we now at liberty to make choice.' 'On the Gospels,' vol. 2, p. 23, 'I have heard a disputant * * in defiance of etymology and use, maintain that the word rendered in the New Testament **baptize,** means more properly to sprinkle than to plunge, and, in defiance of all antiquity, that the former method was the earliest, and for many centuries the most general practice in baptizing. One who argues in this manner never fails with persons of knowledge to betray the cause he would defend; and, though with respect to the vulgar, bold assertions generally succeed as well as arguments—sometimes better—yet a candid mind will disdain to take the help of falsehood, even in support of truth."—*Lec. on Pul. Elo.,* p. 480.

THE TESTIMONY OF THE LEXICONS OF THE NEW TESTAMENT.

Schleusner's Lexicon of New Testament:

"**Baptizo**—Properly to immerse and dip in, to immerse into water, and it answers to the Hebrew, Taval."—2 k. v. 14.

"**Baptisma**—Properly immersion, dipping into water, washing. Hence it is transferred to the sacred rite, which is called baptism, in which those formerly baptized were immersed in water," etc.

Leigh:

"If we are willing to observe the import of the word, the term of baptism signifies immersion into water, or the act itself of immersing and washing off. Therefore, from the very name and etymology of the word, it appears what would, in the beginning, be the custom of administering baptism, whilst we now have for baptism rather rhantism—that is, sprinkling."

Stokius, an authority of great weight:

"Baptizo.—1. Generally, and by force of the original, it denotes immersion or dipping; 2. Specially, properly, it denotes the immersion or dipping of a thing in water, that it may be cleansed or washed. Hence, it is transferred to designate the first sacrament of the New Testament, which they call of initiation, namely, baptism, in which those to be baptized were formerly immersed into water, though, at this time, the water is only sprinkled upon them," etc.

Wahl's Clavis of New Testament (1829, Leipsic):

"Baptizo (from bapto, to immerse; often to immerse in New Testament)—1. To immerse (always in Joseph. Antiquities, 9, 10, 2 and 16, 3, 3, Polyb., 1, 51, 6), properly and truly concerning sacred immersion."

Dr. E. Robinson, American Presbyterian, in his Lexicon of New Testament:

"Baptizo—a frequentative in form, but not in fact; to immerse, to sink."

Prof. Sophocles (Professor in Harvard College), himself a native Greek. His Lexicon covers a period of 110 years before Christ to the year 1100 after:

"Baptizo—to dip, to immerse; sink, to be drowned (as the effect of sinking). **Trop** [figurative meaning], to afflict; soak in liquor; to be drunk, intoxicated. There is no evidence that Luke and Paul, and the other writers of the New Testament, put upon the verb meanings not recognized by the Greeks."

The latest editions of two of the great standard Lexicons of New Testament Greek, viz.: **Grimm's Wilkes'** and **Cremers'** "Biblico-Theological Lexicon," give **only** to dip, to immerse, as its literal and real sense everywhere in the New Testament (see their definition on page 6 of MS.).

So far as the authority of lexicographers and critics can determine the meaning of a word, they have settled the meaning of baptizo and its cognates—the only word Christ or the apostles used in commanding or speaking of Christian baptism; and the verdict I will give in the forceful language of Prof. Stuart, of Andover (Pedobaptist):

"Bapto and Baptizo mean to dip, plunge, or immerse into any liquid. All lexicographers and critics of any note are agreed on this. It is, says Augusti, 'a thing made out, viz.: The ancient practice of immersion. So, indeed, all the writers, who have thoroughly investigated the subject, conclude. I know of no usage of ancient times which seems to be more clearly made out. I can not see how it is possible for any candid man, who has examined the subject, to deny this."—pp. 55, 149, 150.

HOW DO STANDARD HISTORIANS SAY THE CHURCHES IN THE APOSTLES' TIME, AND FOR AGES AFTERWARD, BAPTIZED?

I will introduce a few of the representative historians, with a statement of Prof. L. L. Paine,

D. D., who occupies the chair of Ecclesiastical History in the Bangor Theological Seminary (Congregational), which is his defense against the charge of teaching the young ministers under his tuition Baptist sentiments, because he teaches them that immersion was the universal practice of the apostolic churches for thirteen centuries after Christ, and the prevailing practice of christendom—sprinkling being the exception:

"It may be honestly asked by some, Was immersion the primitive form of baptism? and, if so, what then? As to the question of fact, the testimony is ample and decisive. No matter of church history is clearer. The evidence is all one way, and all church historians of any repute agree in accepting it. We can not claim even originality in teaching it in a Congregational Seminary; and we really feel guilty of a kind of anachronism in writing an article to insist upon it. It is a point on which ancient, mediæval and modern historians alike, Catholics and Protestants, Lutherans and Calvinists, have no controversy; and the simple reason for this unanimity is, that the statements of the early fathers are so clear, and the light shed upon these statements from the early customs of the Church is so conclusive, that no historian, who cares for his reputation, would dare to deny it, and no historian who is worthy of the name would wish to. There are some historical questions concerning the early church on which the most learned writers disagree; * * but on this one—of the early practice of immersion—the most distinguished antiquarians—such as Bingham, Augusti, Coleman, Smith, and historians such as Mosheim, Gieseler, Hase, Neander, Millman, Schaff, and Alzog (Catholic)—hold a common language. The following extract from 'Coleman's Antiquities' very accurately expresses what all agree to:

"'In the primitive Church, **immersion was undeniably the common mode of baptism.** The utmost that can be said of **sprinkling** in that early period was, in case of necessity, permitted as **an exception** to a general rule. This fact is so well established that it is needless to adduce authorities in proof of it.'"

As further testimony that sprinkling is an innovation upon the primitive act, I quote a sentence from Dr. Schaff's "Apostolic Church." He is the highest **Presbyterian** authority in America:

"As to the outward mode of administering this ordinance, **immersion** and **not sprinkling** was unquestionably the original normal form. * * But while immersion was the universal custom, an abridgment of the rite was freely allowed and defended in cases of urgent necessity, such as sickness and approaching death [for which Christ made no provision]; and the peculiar form of sprinkling thus came to be known as 'clinical' baptism, or the baptism of the sick. * * And hence it is difficult to determine, with complete accuracy, just when **immersion gave way** to sprinkling as the common church practice. The two forms were employed—one as the rule, the other as the exception—until, as Christianity traveled northward into colder climates, the exception silently grew to be the rule."

I will now present two or three only of the representative historians and scholars of the leading Pedobaptist sects, commencing with—

ROMAN CATHOLIC HISTORIANS AND SCHOLARS.

It is well known to all scholars that the Catholics claim that their church has the **right** to change rites and ceremonies and determine doctrines, and that this Mother Church **did** substitute sprinkling for immersion, and infants for believers. History confirms this alleged fact.

Robinson, in his "History of Baptism," upon unquestioned authority, states this:

"In the spring of the next year (754) in answer to some Monks of Cressy, in Brittany, who privately consulted him—Pope Stephen III—he gave his opinion on nineteen questions, one of which is allowed to be the first authentic law for administering baptism by pouring, which, in time, was interpreted to signify sprinkling. The question proposed was:

"'**Whether, in case of necessity, occasioned by illness of an infant, it were lawful to baptize by pouring water, out of the hand or cup, on the head of the infant.**'

"Stephen answered: 'If such a baptism were performed, in such a case of **necessity**, in the name of the Holy Trinity, it should be held valid.''

Robinson says:

"The answer of Stephen is **the true origin of private baptism and of sprinkling.**"

NOTE.—For the remainder of the argument on this subject, see Tract by Author, "The Act of Baptism," price, **10** cts. Baptist Book House, Memphis, Tenn.

PART III.

THE LORD'S SUPPER.

"What, then, is th criptural doctrine of the Lord's Supper? This question is now **the great question** of our epoch; it will be the great question of the closing years of this century. Deprecate controversy around this precious feast of a Savior's love as much as we may, we can not escape the responsibility of the discussion. **We must set forth clearly and strongly the true nature of the Lord's Supper,** as set forth in the Scriptures—teach from the pulpit and by the press, in Bible-classes and in Sabbath-schools—so that the minds of our people shall be fortified against the entrance of grievous error."

BISHOP CUMMINGS.

OPINIONS OF DISTINGUISHED AUTHORS.

Dr. E. T. Hiscox, D.D., New York, Author of "Baptist Church Directory," an acknowledged and standard authority.

"I have read your book with unusual interest. It is fresh, vigorous, manly, and, for the most part, strongly logical. ** I am much pleased with your discussion of the wine question. ** Your statements on pages 317, 318, as to the church independency and the restless drift in certain directions to centralization meet my most hearty approbation. ** Allow me to express my own convictions as to the subject under discussion:—

"1. I hold the Supper to be in the strictest sense a Church Ordinance, to be observed **by a church** when assembled in one place for that purpose. 2. **The privileges of a church and its authority and discipline are coextensive.** No person not a member has any right to any privilege in a church. The Supper is the highest privilege of associated piety, and he who has a right to that can not consistently be denied any other. I should be heartily glad to see the plan adopted by general consent, **of confining the Supper strictly to the churches.**"

Rev. W. W. Gardner, D.D., Russellville, Ky., Author of "Church Communion," "Missiles of Truth," etc.

"I have examined your new book on 'Intercommunion, Unscriptural,' etc., with much care and interest. While I dissent from your exposition of some passages, I approve of the work in the main, and **hope it will tend to check intercommunion among our churches, which practice I regard as unscriptural and of evil tendency.**"

Rev. G. A. Lofton, Pastor 3d. Baptist Ch., St. Louis, and Author of "Bible Thoughts and Themes."

"I have read with some care Dr. Graves' work on 'Intercommunion, etc.,' and, while I do not see the necessity of some questions discussed, and while I do not agree with all the positions assumed, yet, upon the Communion question, this book **is the ablest and most logical I have ever read.** No true Baptist who has read it carefully will condemn it, or who will not **confess its ability** and consistency upon one of the most troublesome questions which afflict the Baptist denomination. ** I firmly believe the position impregnable, scripturally and logically; and I firmly believe **that it will bring peace and strength to the denomination, if adopted. It will effectually and rationally kill open communion among ourselves.**"

Hon. J. Harral, Miss.

"If I undestand what demonstrative proof is, the author of this book has demonstrated that the intercommunion of churches is forbidden by their Divine Constitution, and that according to the teachings of the apostles the N. T. Churches could not intercommune and that from history the practice was unknown in the first ages of Christianity. The Baptists, have therefore, in this respect swerved from the primitive order, and thereby brought odium upon themselves and a great loss of members. This book should be extensively circulated. It is the harbinger of a new and better day, touching the Communion Controversy, and must and will forever settle it, for all men can be made to see that institutes can only be observed by members of the institutions themselves."

Rev. Wm. Norton, D. D., England.

"I have been deeply interested by your work on the 'Intercommunion of Churches' and have admired most the **clearness**, and, as it seems to me, the **correctness** of your views on 'the kingdom of God,' and what is essential to constitute a divinely instituted **assembly of saints.** With these views I can express not only **admiration but concurrence.**"

CHAPTER I.

THE LORD'S SUPPER.

The Inspired Accounts of the Institution of the Lord's Supper Synchronized and Harmonized, and the question of the connection of Judas with the Lord's Supper determined.

BEFORE entering upon the discussion of the Lord's Supper, it will be proper to copy the inspired account of its institution.
 1. Institution.
 2. The circumstances attending it.
 3. The directions concerning its observance.

It must be understood by the reader, that, under the especial guidance of the Holy Spirit, the evangelists wrote each a different narrative of the life, teachings, and actions of the Messiah. No one writer related **all** that was said or done by Christ, in consecutive order, as would seem to us most fitting to be done; but one evangelist records a part, while another adds other occurrences. It is noticeable that the account given by John, written some time after the rest, contains very little that is found in the other three, and was evidently written to supply what was lacking, so that their united records might make a full and rounded life of Christ.

Then the evangelists manifestly differ more or less in their attention to **the order** of events. Says Dr. E. Robinson:

"On the one hand, it appears that Mark and John, who have little in common, follow, with few exceptions, the regular and true order of events and transactions recorded by them; on the other hand, Matthew and Luke manifestly have sometimes not so much regard to chronological order, as they have been guided by the principle of association, so that in them transactions having certain relations to each other are not seldom grouped together, though they may have happened at different times, and in various places."

This being the case, it follows that, in order to obtain a full and consecutive account of any particular transaction, we should take the most extended account given by the evangelist who most strictly observes chronological order, and the relation of events to each other, and fill up, **what it lacks in completeness**, from the relations of the others. Without such a procedure, our knowledge of all the great events of the life of Christ will be but **fragmentary and partial**.

The vast importance of the subject under consideration demands that we pursue such a course in order to obtain a clear comprehension of all that Jesus said and did in connection with the institution of the sacred Supper; the observance of which, as he appointed it, is so solemnly enjoined upon his churches until he comes, and the misobservance of which he threatens with such fearful consequences. Surely we may not dare to add aught to this ordinance with impunity, nor can we modify in the least, with respect to its form or symbolism, without perverting and profaning it.

It is conceded by all scholars that John, "the disciple whom Jesus loved," paid more attention to the **order** of events which he relates than do the other evangelists. It is true, he does not relate the facts in connection with the institution and administration of the Lord's Supper, because, perhaps, so minutely described by the other evangelists; yet, by describing the Paschal Supper, that preceded it, the washing of feet, and the exposure and expulsion of the traitor Judas, preparatory to the Supper, he furnishes the needed initial data to guide our investigations. I have, for this reason, adopted his narrative for the order of the text; and shall supply what is wanting for the full history from the statements of the other writers.

HISTORY OF THE INSTITUTION.

THE TIME.—The eve of the fourteenth day of Nisan, introducing Friday, corresponding to our Thursday eve, A. D. 30.

"Now, before the feast [*i. e.*, festival, which commenced the day after the Paschal Supper was eaten, and lasted seven days], Jesus, knowing that his hour had come that he should depart out of this world, having loved his own, he loved them to the end. The Supper [*i. e.*, Paschal Supper] being prepared [the devil having put it into the heart of Judas Iscariot, Simon's son, that he should betray him], Jesus, knowing that the Father had given all things into his hands"—(John xiii: 1-3)—

"He sat down, and the twelve apostles with him,—* * and there was also a strife among them, which of them should be accounted the greatest. And he said unto them, The kings of the Gentiles exercise lordship over them; and they that exercise authority upon them are called benefactors. But ye shall not be so; but he that is greatest among you, let him be as the younger; and he that is chief, as he that doth serve. For whether is greater, he that sitteth at meat, or he that serveth? is not he that sitteth at meat? but I am among you as he that serveth. Ye are they which have continued with me in my temptations. And I appoint unto you a kingdom, as my Father hath appointed unto me: that ye may eat and drink at my table, in my kingdom, and sit on thrones, judging the twelve tribes of Israel."—(Luke xxii: 14, 24-50.)

"He riseth from supper [*i. e.*, a table, not having yet eaten], and laid aside his garments, and took a towel and girded himself. After that, he poureth water into a basin, and began to wash the disciples' feet, and to wipe them with the towel wherewith he was girded. Then cometh he to Simon Peter; and Peter saith unto him, Lord, dost thou wash my feet? Jesus answered, and said unto him, What I do thou knowest not now; but thou shalt know hereafter. Peter saith unto him, Thou shalt never wash my feet. Jesus answered him, If I wash thee not, thou hast no part with me. Simon Peter saith unto him, Lord, not my feet only, but also my hands and my head. Jesus saith unto him, He that is washed needeth not save to wash his feet, but is clean every whit; **and ye are clean, but not all.** For he knew who should betray him; therefore, said he, Ye are not all clean. So after he had washed their feet, and had taken his garments, and was set down again, he said

UNSCRIPTURAL AND INCONSISTENT. 209

urto them, Know ye what I have done to you? Ye call me Master and Lord; and ye say well; for so I am. If I then, your Lord and Master, have washed your feet; ye also ought to wash one another's feet. For I have given you an example, that ye should do as I have done to you. Verily, verily, I say unto you, The servant is not greater than his lord; neither he that is sent greater than he that sent him. If ye know these things, happy are ye if ye do them. I speak not of you all; I know whom I have chosen; but that the Scripture may be fulfilled, he that eateth bread with me hath lifted up his heel against me. Now I tell you before it come, that, when it is come to pass, ye may believe that I am he. Verily, verily, I say unto you, he that receiveth whomsoever I send receiveth me; and he that receiveth me receiveth him that sent me. When Jesus had thus said, he was troubled in spirit, and testified, and said, Verily, verily, I say unto you, that one of you shall betray me. Then the disciples looked one on another, doubting of whom he spoke. Now there was leaning on Jesus' bosom one of his disciples, whom Jesus loved. Simon Peter therefore beckoned to him, that he should ask who it should be of whom he spake. He then lying on Jesus' breast saith unto him, Lord, who is it? Jesus answered, He it is to whom I shall give a sop, when I have dipped it."—(John xiii: 4–25.)

"The Son of man goeth as it is written of him; but woe unto that man by whom the Son of man is betrayed! it had been good for that man if he had not been born. Then Judas, which betrayed him, answered and said, Master, is it I? He said unto him, Thou hast said."—(Matt. xxvi: 24, 25.)

[Matthew does not mention the giving of the sop].

"And when he had dipped the sop, he gave it to Judas Iscariot, the son of Simon. And after the sop Satan en-

14

tered into him. Then said Jesus unto him, That thou doest, do quickly. Now no man at the table knew for what intent he spake this unto him. For some of them thought, because Judas had the bag, that Jesus had said unto him, Buy those things that we have need of against the feast; or, that he should give something to the poor. He then, having received the sop, went immediately out; and it was night. Therefore, when he was gone out, Jesus said, Now is the Son of man glorified, and God is glorified in him. If God be glorified in him, God shall also glorify him in himself, and shall straightway glorify him. Little children, yet a little while I am with you. Ye shall seek me; and as I said unto the Jews, Whither I go ye can not come; so now I say to you. A new commandment I give unto you, That ye love one another; as I have loved you, that ye also love one another. By this shall all men know that ye are my disciples, if ye have love one to another. Simon Peter said unto him, Lord, whither goest thou? Jesus answered him, Whither I go, thou canst not follow me now; but thou shalt follow me afterward. Peter said unto him, Lord, why can not I follow thee now? I will lay down my life for thy sake. Jesus answered him, Wilt thou lay down thy life for my sake? Verily, verily, I say unto thee, The cock shall not crow, till thou hast denied me thrice."—(John xiii: 26–38.)

"And he said unto them, When I sent you without purse, and scrip, and shoes, lacked ye any thing? And they said, Nothing. Then said he unto them, But now, he that hath a purse, let him take it, and likewise his scrip; and he that hath no sword, let him sell his garment, and buy one. For I say unto you, that this that is written must yet be accomplished in me, And he was reckoned among the transgressors; for the things concerning me have an end. And they said, Lord, behold, here are two swords. And he said unto them, It is enough."—(Luke xxii: 35-38.)

"And taking a loaf, (*i. e.*, one of the loaves of unleavened bread used at the Paschal Supper), he gave thanks, and brake it, and gave unto them, saying, This is my body which is given for you; this do in remembrance of me. Likewise also the cup after Supper, saying, This cup is the New Testament in my blood, which is shed for you. (Luke xxii: 19, 20.)

"And he took the cup, and gave thanks, and gave it to them, saying, Drink ye all of it: For this is my blood of the New Testament, which is shed for many for the remission of sins. But I say unto you, I will not drink henceforth of this fruit of the vine, until that day when I drink it new with you in my Father's kingdom."—(Luke xxvi: 27-29.)

Let the reader here turn and read the whole of the fourteenth chapter of John.

At the close, they all rose from the Supper, and, while standing, Jesus continued his discourse, as given by John in the 15th, 16th and 17th chapters, at the close of which they went out to the garden of Gethsemane, where he was arrested by a mob headed by Judas.

CONCLUSION FROM THE FOREGOING NARRATIVE.

From this harmony of the evangelists, we learn several important **facts** intimately connected with the institution of the Supper, about which there is no little difference of opinion.

First Fact.—That the Supper here referred

to by John and the other evangelists was, without question, the Paschal Supper, and it was at the close of the **Paschal** Supper that Christ instituted the Supper we call the Lord's Supper. Not a few deny this, for the want of the correct harmony of the accounts. It is held by many that the Lord's Supper comes in place of the Passover, the **antitype** and fulfillment of it, but this is to mistake the Supper. This Passover was a type of the **sacrifice** of Christ for us, "For even Christ our Passover is sacrificed for us." (1 Cor. v : 7). The Lord's Supper is purely **commemorative** of his sufferings and death. The Passover was **typical.** The Lord's Supper **emblematic** and symbolical. There are points of striking likeness in the form and symbolism of the two, which Paul points out, but no physical rite in the old is ever employed as a type of a physical rite in the new dispensation. The Supper was a new ordinance, instituted at the **close** of the Passover Supper—"Because the Passover night immediately preceding his sufferings was the best and fittest time for its institution."—*Dr. G. W. Clark, Notes on Mark.*

Second Fact.—We learn that Christ ate the Paschal lamb with his disciples upon the very night it was appointed by the law to be eaten, namely, on the 14th day of the first month, Nisan, at even, *i. e.*, Thursday evening, and that he was betrayed that night, and crucified on the day following, expiring at three o'clock in the afternoon, and that evening buried, and arose from the dead on the first day of the week, corresponding to the Monday of the Jews. He, therefore, rose on the **third day,** according to the Scriptures.

Third Fact.—That the Supper referred to by John ch. xiii, Luke xxii: 14, was the **Paschal** Supper, and not the Lord's Supper, which was instituted at the **close** of the former.

Fourth Fact.—We learn that the washing of the disciples' feet was in no sense whatever connected with the observance of the Lord's Supper, either as introducing or concluding it. That occurrence took place before the eating of the Paschal Supper, and most clearly to my mind as a reproof to the apostles, who, having failed to provide a servant to wash their soiled feet as they came in from the street, were unwilling each to volunteer to perform this menial act for the other, or even for the Master, since it might be construed into a confession of inferiority, for "a strife having arisen among them who should be the greatest." Christ did not institute the washing of feet here nor while on earth. It had been observed as a necessary act of hospitality from the days of Abraham, and was of universal observance in all Eastern countries where sandals were worn instead of close shoes and boots as now. The feet were soiled by traveling; and upon coming into a house, and especially reclining upon cushions to eat, it was not only cleanly, but **needful,** that the feet should be washed.

The apostles did not understand, as some of our brethren of this age do, that Christ intended feet-washing to be observed as a church or religious ordinance in connection with his churches, for **they never enjoined it upon any church;** they never rebuked any church for not observing it; they never praised any church for having observed it; they nowhere intimate that any church ever did observe it; nor can we find in church history any account of its observance by a church or by Christians, as a religious exercise, for seventeen hundred years after Christ. The most that can be made of the words of our Savior is that the apostles, who were ambitious for superiority, should wash each other's feet, or do what was equivalent to it—be the servants of each other—"in honor preferring one another." We have not the slightest intimation that they ever after that washed each other's feet; but, **provided** they did, **we** have nothing to do with it, since secret things belong to God, but things that are revealed alone belong to us and to our children. If the apostles did not wash each other's feet **literally,** they did what was equivalent to it—ministered to one another.

Fifth Fact.—That the Supper alluded to in John (xiii: 1), being the Paschal and not the Lord's Supper, it should not read **"ended"** as in our version; for,—

1. The context forbids this, for they continued to eat after this, and, indeed, had not eaten before

this (see v. 26 and Mark xiv: 18–21), for it was contrary to established usage to eat any meal, much less the sacred feast, without a bath, and washing the feet after the bath.

It should read—Supper being "prepared" or "ready"—*i. e.*, the Paschal Supper being prepared. All critics are agreed on this reading.

Sixth Fact.—That Judas went out at the command of Christ before the Paschal Supper was finished, even **before the lamb was eaten.**

This was the order of the Supper in the time of Christ—1. A blessing; 2. Wine (first cup); 3. Washing of hands; 4. Eating bitter herbs; 5. Wine (second cup); 6. The Feast explained; 7. Singing Ps. 113, 114; 8. Eating unleavened bread; 9. Eating the lamb; 10. Wine (third cup of blessing); 11. Singing Ps. 115, 118; 12. Wine (fourth cup); 13. Singing Ps. 120, 138.

They prepared a sauce of dates, figs, and seasoning, which was of brick color, representing the clay and brick of Egypt. Into this they dipped their bread and bitter herbs. This was the sop referred to in John xiii: 26. The reader can see it was at the very first part of the Supper (No. 4), while eating the bitter herbs, that Christ sent Judas away. But it was not until the close of the Passover Supper that Jesus took one of the loaves of unleavened bread prepared for the Paschal Supper, and instituted the new ordinance, which we call

The Lord's Supper. Judas was not for a moment therefore, at the Lord's Supper.

But had Judas remained and partaken of the Lord's Supper, the act would not have violated the letter of the laws governing the Supper; for, 1. Judas had been immersed; 2. He was in full fellowship with this **family** of Christ, this church of the apostles, as some call it, for he had committed no overt act of sin known to them. But Christ knew what was in his heart—knew him to be a **thief**—knew of his secret conference with the High Priests (Mark xiv: 10, 11), and, therefore, knew him to be in heart a **murderer**, and so he purged him out as "leaven" for an example to his churches in all future time, to put all improper persons away from the sacred feast.

OTHER ACCOUNTS OF ITS INSTITUTION.

Matthew.—"And as they were eating [the Paschal Supper at its close], Jesus took the loaf, and giving praise [*i. e.*, to God] he broke it and gave it to the disciples, and said, Take, eat; this is my body. And taking the cup, and giving thanks, he gave it to them, saying, Drink ye all out of this; for this is my blood of the New Testament, which is shed for many for the remission of sins. But I say unto you, I will not drink henceforth of the fruit of the vine, until the day when I drink it new with you in my Father's kingdom."—xxvi: 26–29.

Mark.—"And as they did eat—[*i. e.*, of the Paschal Supper], Jesus took a loaf, and giving praise [*i. e.*, God] he broke it, and gave it to them, and said, Take, eat; this is my body. And taking the cup, when he had given thanks [*i. e.*, to God], he gave it to them: and they all drank out of it. And he said unto them, This is my blood of the New Testament, which is shed for many. Verily I say unto you, I will drink no more of the fruit of the vine, until that day when I drink it new in the kingdom of God."—xiv: 22–25.

Luke.—" And taking a loaf, and having given thanks, **he** broke it and gave it to them, saying, This is my body which is given for you: this do in remembrance of me. In like manner [*i. e.*, after giving thanks] the cup, after the Supper, saying, This cup is the New Covenant in my blood, which on your behalf is being poured out."—xxii: 19, 20.

Paul's Account.—" For I received from the Lord, what I also delivered unto you. That the Lord Jesus the same night in which he was betrayed, took a loaf; and when he had given thanks he broke it, and said, Take, eat; this is my body which is broken for you; this do in rememberance of me. After the same manner also he took the cup after the supper [*i. e.*, the Paschal Supper], saying, This cup is the New Covenant in my blood; this do ye, as oft as ye drink it, in remembrance of me."

CONCLUSIONS FROM THESE NARRATIVES.

First Fact.—That Jesus took but **one** loaf—εισ αρτοσ—**one wheaten loaf**, with which to celebrate the Supper. His example is a command to his churches; they should use but **one** loaf.

Second Fact.—Christ took one loaf of **unleavened** bread for the observance of his Supper. There can be no doubt about this, for he took one of the loaves left from the Passover Supper, and no leavened bread, on pain of death, could be used in that Supper. Christ's example should be considered law unto us. It is a sad fact that a **plurality** of loaves and **leavened** bread is generally used by the churches on this continent. Why should the churches be so thoughtless and indifferent to the bread used at the Supper, while they are so particular to use water as the element in which to immerse? Has Christ anywhere commanded his churches to use water rather than any other liquid? What have we but the **examples** of John and of Christ to guide us in this?

Third Fact.—Christ did not **tran**-substantiate, nor **con**-substantiate, nor **consecrate**, nor **bless** the bread or the wine, as Romanists and Protestants affect to do; but he simply **gave thanks,** and his example should govern us, not that of Ritualists.

Fourth Fact.—Christ used the fruit of the vine—*i. e.*, "the blood of Grapes"—pure wine. In these days of fanaticism and infidelity, it is boldly asserted by the professed **friends,** but actually the worst **foes** of Temperance, that Christ never made, never drank, or warranted his disciples to drink the fermented juice of the grapes—*i. e.*, wine—any thing that would intoxicate. I shall discuss this question when I treat of the Symbolism of the Cup in a future chapter. Suffice it to say here, that the church at Corinth doubtless used the element that Paul taught them to use when he instituted the Supper, and that did intoxicate. (See 1 Cor. xi: 21.) Paul did not tell them they used the **wrong element,** but that they **drank too much.**

Fifth Fact.—We learn that Christ did not institute his Supper to be observed as a **sacrament** of remission of sins, or of regeneration, or sanctification, or salvation, but simply as a feast in **commemoration** of himself. His words are without the least ambiguity—"This do ye in **remembrance of me."** To use the Supper as a **sacrament,** as Catholics and all Protestants do, is to utterly pervert and profane it, to eat and drink unworthily, not discerning the Lord's body.

Sixth Fact.—We see that it was not designed that we should remember each other as friends or as Christians, when we partake of this feast, nor to extend it to our brethren through amity or **courtesy,** or as a mark of our **Christian** regard or fellowship for them. To use it for these selfish purposes is to disregard its grand design, and do violence to its whole spirit.

It is not a feast of communion with each other, but a feast in commemoration of Christ.

It is with Christ, his broken body and shed blood—as our Sin-bearer and Redeemer—that we are to commune, and not with each other. The specific symbolism of the elements used, and what is implied in the joint act of participation of but one loaf, will be considered, but let it be kept in mind that the grand end for which Christ appointed this Supper was for an "Holy Ordinance of Commemoration."

CHAPTER II.

The Lord's Supper first given to the apostles as the family of Christ.—This no evidence that it is a ministerial or social ordinance.—Christ instructed his apostles to commit both ordinances to the churches. —I. Accounts of the observances of the Supper. We learn from them the nature of the rite: (1.) Not a Sacrifice; (2.) Not a Sacrament; (3.) Not a Seal; (4.) Not a social rite; (5.) Not a mark of Christian fellowship; (6.) Not a token of church comity or Christian courtesy.—II. The scriptural names given it; (1.) Not Mass; (2.) Not Sacrament; (3.) Not Eucharist, but Communion—the Lord's Supper.—III. The essential qualification of the participants; (1.) Baptized believers; (2.) Members of a scriptural church, holding the faith and walking in gospel order; (3.) Can only be administered by a church to its own members.

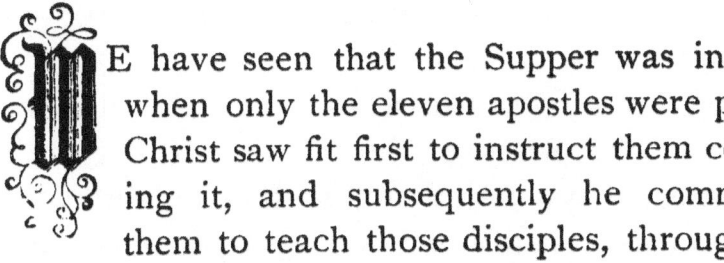E have seen that the Supper was instituted when only the eleven apostles were present. Christ saw fit first to instruct them concerning it, and subsequently he commanded them to teach those disciples, through their ministry, "to observe all things whatsoever he had commanded **them**;" and the Supper was among

those all things. If the apostles taught their disciples to observe the Supper as a church ordinance, and not as a social act, then we must believe that Christ so commanded them to do. Whether the apostles did so teach, we shall inquire in a chapter following.

The reasons that influenced Jesus to institute this ordinance, which he intended to be a **church** ordinance, with the apostles alone present, we may not apprehend, but it is evident that he did not institute it for a **social** rite, else he would have invited the seventy disciples he had commissioned, and some or all of their converts, and especially his own mother and brethren, the Marys, and noble women who had ministered unto him. His was certainly an act of very strict Communion. Had he designed it for a **ministerial ordinance,** *i. e.*, to be observed by his ministers only, Christ would have invited all his ministers and instructed them as such to observe it, but his apostles—not ordinary ministers of the word—alone were present, and they were afterward commanded to teach all their disciples to observe this ordinance, and we will see in what capacity.

This we know, that Christ, as a Jew, did observe the feast of the Passover during his ministry with his apostles **only,** and therefore that he did consider them as constituting, in a Jewish sense, his **family,** for (1.) They were intimately associated with him; (2.) Were wholly supported by him;

(3.) Recognized his supreme authority; and (4.) were constantly with him. The Passover was not a national or individual, nor a social, but strictly a **family** rite. It would have been in open violation of the divine law to have observed the Passover except **as a family.** For this reason he could not have eaten the Passover with his church, but only with his **family**—the eleven apostles—which we may consider here as actually representing his local church. It was peculiarly proper to institute this Supper at the close of the Passover, since it was designed to **symbolize** the great saving facts which that rite **typified,** and which, before another Passover, were to be fulfilled by Christ, and thus the type and symbol would evermore be associated in our minds, both teaching us that salvation is by the sole and sovereign grace of God.

Dr. Jones (T. G.), in his late work, seems to take this view of the case:

"The first Supper, we have seen, was celebrated in the church and by **its** members **alone**—not even the mother of Jesus or the other holy women who so loved and served him, or the seventy evangelists whom he had sent forth to propagate his gospel being invited to it."

Speaking of the Passover—

"They [the Jews] never so perverted it as to carry it out **of the family** (beautiful image of the church), or otherwise materially departed from its divinely appointed conditions."—*Misnomer*, pp. 143, 144.

Dr. Richard Fuller was impressed with the close analogy between the Passover and Supper. He says:

"As the Passover was a meal for each family only, **so the Supper is a family repast for the members of that particular church in which the table is spread.**"

Baptism, as well as the Supper, was first, so far as the written law is concerned, committed to the ministry, and finally to the apostles, but it is contrary to the teachings of God's word to say that it is under their control. Christ commanded his apostles to teach their disciples, whom they were instructed to organize into churches, to observe all things whatsoever he had commanded them—the apostles; and we find that they did to the very letter obey this injunction, for they delivered the ordinances, both of them, and all else Christ had taught and committed to them—the gospel of man's salvation—to the churches as soon as organized (1 Cor. xi: 1). Therefore we can not decide otherwise than that, though first delivered to the apostles, Christ designed it be observed by his **churches**, as such, and not by his ministers alone, or by his **disciples** as a social rite.

I will now place all the remaining accounts of the observance of the Supper, with the apostle's explanation of its design, before the eye of the reader (rather than to refer to them), so that he may see at a glance their obvious teachings concerning the **nature** and **design** of the rite, as well as its scriptural **name,** and the indispensable qualifications of its participants. The first allusion to it, after the ascension, is during the first Pentecost.

1. "Then they who gladly received this word were baptized, and the same day there were added"—*i. e.*, to the church, as many as—ὡσει—"three thousand souls. And they continued steadfast in the apostles' doctrine, and in fellowship, and in **the breaking** of **the loaf,** and in prayers." (Acts ii: 41, 42.)

We think there is no reference to the observance of the Supper in the forty-sixth verse, by "breaking bread at home" (lit. 7), as claimed by some who hold it as a social ordinance, because, had it been the expression in Greek, would doubtless have been identical with that in the forty-second verse—*i. e.*, κλασει του αρτου—where the Supper is undoubtedly referred to, while here it is the noun without the definite article, and the context also determines it to have been a common meal, "breaking bread at home they partook of **food** with gladness and singleness of heart."

Whether there was or was not a church at Troas at the time of Paul's last visit, and if the expression to "break bread," indicated an observance of the Lord's Supper, will be examined in a future chapter devoted to "Objections to Church Communion."

The next positive allusion to the Supper is found

in Paul's first letter to the church at Corinth, which he had planted some years before, and had instructed in the observance of the Supper:

2. "The cup of blessing which we bless, Is it not the Communion of the blood of Christ? The loaf which we break, Is it not the Communion of the body of Christ? Because there is **one loaf**, we—the many—are one body; for we all partake of the one loaf." (1 Cor. x: 16, 17.)

Again, in the eleventh chapter of this letter—

3. "And, brethren, I praise you, because you have remembered me in all my instructions, and you keep the ordinances as I delivered them unto you." . . "But in noticing this matter—*i. e.*, concerning the Lord's Supper—that you come together, not for the better but the worse, I do not praise you. For, indeed, in the first place, I hear that on your coming together in church, as a church, there are divisions among you, and as to a certain part, I believe it. . . Then, again, your coming together to the same place, is not to eat the Lord's Supper, for each one, in eating, takes first his own Supper, and one indeed is hungry, and another is drunken. Have ye not houses in which to eat and drink? Or despise you the church of God, and put to shame those who are poor? What shall I say to you? Shall I praise you? In this I praise you not." (Vs. 17–23)—**literally translated.**

Let us first determine from these and the previous accounts:

I. The nature of the Lord's Supper.

(1.) It was not designed to be a real sacrifice, as the Catholics hold and teach.

The Rt. Rev. Dr. Milner clearly sets forth what they believe:

> "We firmly believe, as an article of faith, that [after the consecration] there is no bread nor wine, but Christ alone, true God, as well as man, present in it," *i. e.*, the Eucharist.—*End of Controversy*, p. 223.

In proof of this theory they quote the language of Christ after he had given thanks, "This is my body," claiming that Christ used this language literally and not figuratively. This can not be the case; for—

(2.) It is contrary to reason. Almighty power can not bring into existence that which is already in existence. Christ is existing bodily in the heavens, and man nor God can not bring him into existence, or **re-create** him, which they claim to do, out of the wafers in the hands of a priest.

Again: Almighty power can not duplicate Christ. There never was, there is, there never can be but one Christ Jesus—the "only Son" of God. But according to the Catholics, whenever the words of consecration are pronounced by the priest, each wafer on the chalice, though there be a hundred, instantly becomes a perfect Jesus Christ, the very one who was born of the virgin Mary, in body, soul, divinity, and real presence. And more, according to the Council of Trent, if each wafer is separated into parts, each piece and particle is a perfect Christ, in his bodily presence. If the wafers, then, were grated into particles, the priest would hold in his hand millions of Christs, and at the next breath could eat them all!

Again: This theory compels us to believe that Christ, when he uttered these words, while in his real body, held, at the same time, his real body in his hands! Did Christ have two bodies? The neuter verb is here equivalent to "represents;" and every scholar knows the sentence is a **metaphor**, as are these phrases: "And the Rock was Christ" (1 Cor. x: 4); "The field is the world" (Matt. xiii: 38, 39); "It [the Paschal Lamb] is the Lord's Passover" (Ex. xii: 11); "I am the true vine, ye are the branches." Was Christ literally a vine, and his disciples literal branches? "I am the door!" Was Christ ever, for one moment, a real door? Christ evidently meant that he appointed the bread he held in his hands to represent, in this rite, his body, that was broken for us. But—

(3) **It is contrary to the testimony of our senses.**

Christ and his apostles appealed to the testimony of our senses as the highest possible evidence. When he appeared unto the eleven in a closed room, they were affrighted, and supposed they had seen a vision. Christ, to prove to them conclusively that he was there bodily, said:

Behold my hands and my feet; that it is I myself. **Handle** me, and see, for a spirit hath not flesh and bones, as ye **see** me have. He appealed to the testimony of their **sight** and **touch**, as in the case of doubting Thomas, to whom he said: "Reach hither thy finger, and behold my hands; reach hither thy hand, and thrust it into my side, and be not faithless but believing." Why did the Savior appeal to their senses, if they could not be implicitly relied on?

Now, try the bread and wine after the act of consecration. Does not the loaf still **look** like bread, and the wine like **wine**? Taste each. Does not the bread **taste** like bread, and the wine like wine? Did not the members of the church at Corinth become intoxicated upon the contents of the cup? Will blood intoxicate? Put the priest to the test—require him to drink a bottle of the wine he has consecrated, and see if it will not intoxicate him as soon as any other wine.

But, if the nature of the bread and wine is wholly changed, test him by putting prussic acid in the wine, and demand that he drink it, if he really believes he has changed the **nature** of the contents. The doctrine is as blasphemous as it is absurd. But—

(4) **It contradicts the teachings of the Scriptures.**

They expressly teach that Christ was but once offered; but, if the Lord's Supper is a sacrificial offering, then he has not ceased to be offered, but suffers, as a sacrifice for sin, tens of thousands of times daily—as often as any one of the thousands of Catholic priests, in any part of the world, performs mass. The inquirer can read the following passages upon this point: Rom. vi: 9-10—Christ died but once; Heb. vii: 26-27, and ix: 24-28, and x: 10-18—Christ is **offered but once**; ix: 11-12—Christ **shed and offered his blood** but once. Other reasons will occur to the thoughtful reader.

We also learn—

(5) **That the Lord's Supper is not a Sacrament, as the Catholics and all Protestants teach.**

A sacrament, in the ecclesiastical use of the term, is a physical medium, appointed by God, through, and in connection with which, he transmits all the benefits of Christ's death to our souls—as remission of sins, spiritual regeneration, sanctification; in a word—the salvation of souls.

Protestant sects, as well as the Catholics, teach that both baptism and the Supper are sacraments of salvation. To teach that baptism and the Supper are sacraments—*i. e.*, the ordained channel to convey grace to the soul through physical media, the application of water to the body, or by the receiving of bread through the mouth, even when the subject is unconscious—is a most absurd delusion. There is no dogma of Rome more unscriptural or shocking to our common sense, or more utterly subversive of Christianity, modifying the language of the Bishop of Cork. To teach that, in baptism, or the Lord's Supper, we are made one with Christ, clearly implies that we can not be one with Christ without it; whereas, the word of God teaches that we have no right to come to baptism, or the Lord's Supper, until we are, by personal faith, one with Christ. "For we are all the childen of God by faith," and not by sacraments, as baptism and the Lord's Supper. To teach that baptism and the Lord's Supper—purely physical acts—were appointed by our Savior as the **media** by which he comes to live in us, as if by no other means could he enter our hearts and live in us; whereas, he himself teaches us that we have no fitness to come to baptism or the Supper until he comes to us first and live in us, until we come to him and live in him. I emphasize it, that it is subversive of the whole plan of salvation, and an utter perversion of the ordinances, to teach that in and by baptism or the Supper Christ forgives our sins and releases us from their guilt; whereas, all this is done before we can rightly come to baptism, or the Lord's Supper. We come to Christ **for** forgiveness, and to baptism **with** forgiveness. We come to Christ **for** life, and we come to the Supper **with** life. The symbolism of the Supper proclaims that the one partaking is alive in Christ, and comes to it for the strengthening and refreshing of his soul by the body and blood of Christ, as our bodies are by literal bread and wine. A dead body can not receive nourishment—it must first have life. The sinner, by faith only, gets life from Christ, and lives in Christ, and Christ lives in him; and to refreshen and strengthen this life, by a lively remembrance of Christ, who is our Life, this Supper is eaten. The living soul, not a dead soul, is fed. To use the Lord's Supper as a sacrifice, or a sacrament, is evidently to eat and drink "unworthily."

(6) **The Supper was not appointed to be a " Seal of the Covenant of Grace."**

The Presbyterians teach that the Supper was appointed to be one of the two "**sealing ordinances.**" See "Confession of Faith." This implies that the Covenant of Grace has two seals—baptism and the Supper; and, if this be so, no one ever was or can be saved without **both**—one, at least, all will admit. But nowhere, save in the "Presbyterian Confession of Faith," do we learn that either ordinance was appointed to be a Seal of the Covenant of Grace, or any other covenant, or of any thing connected with Christianity. If either rite is a seal of covenanted blessings, who was ever saved without them? for **no unsealed** person ever was saved. But the **monstrousness** of this doctrine can be seen, not only by its consigning all the unbaptized, and "uncommunicated," of the ages past, to hopeless perdition, unless they can show that God had still another seal before these church rites were instituted, but the doctrine takes the sealing out of the hands of the Holy Spirit, and puts it into the hands of sinful men, who can not tell when the subject is prepared to be sealed, thus making ministers, priests and mediators between man and God! What saith the Scriptures? "In whom [Christ] **after that ye believed** ye were sealed **by the Holy Spirit,**" etc.—(Eph. i: 13; and iv: 30.)

(7) **Nor do we find the Lord's Supper observed as a social rite.**

Not as a mark or expression of Christian fellowship on the part of those who partake of it together. A moment's thought will convince any one that, if this was included in the design, it could never be celebrated again. For what pastor, who has an intimate acquaintance with his church, believes, in his heart, that all are Christians, and would be willing to declare it by his word or act? His saddest convictions are that many, very many, are strangers to "regenerating grace," love this present world, and have not the mind of Christ!

Is it better with the members of our churches? Would the membership of any church existing ever again assemble to observe the Supper if they understood that it was, on their part, a solemn declaration before God that they, in their hearts, regarded all members with whom they partook as Christians, and that they sincerely fellowshiped them as such? It is the thought or fear that this possibly may be implied by the joint participation in the rite that deters so many hundreds of our conscientious members from coming to the table. It was not observed by Christ as a social feast, for but eleven of his disciples were present; even his **mother**, and his own **brethren**, according to the flesh, were not invited. In all the other cases, we see it strictly limited to specific characters.

(8) **Nor was it appointed to be used as a mark or expression of "courtesy" and "comity" toward, or good feeling for, our brethren of other churches, or Christian friends.**

Let the reader read over every account of its observance, and every direction given, and see if he can gather the faintest idea that Christ instituted the rite, or the apostles delivered it, for any such purpose. The idea is utterly opposed to the very spirit of the institution.

Why did not Christ insist upon his mother's attendance, or his own family, according to the flesh? Why did Paul so severely rebuke the members of the church at Corinth, whose practice looked so strongly in the direction of "courtesy" and the social idea? To degrade the terms of the Sacred Supper to the conventionalities of the parlor and drawing-room, or the common feast, to which we invite our neighbors and special friends, as an expression of our courtesy and good-feeling toward them, is certainly to profane it. Well might the apostle remonstrate with those who advocate this use. "What! have ye not houses to eat and to drink in, parlors and drawing-rooms for such expressions of courtesy and friendship, or despise ye the Church of God?"

THE NAME GIVEN TO THIS ORDINANCE.

Mass. The Catholics, as we have seen, regard it as a real sacrifice for sin offered by the priest. The term is from the Latin **missa**, from the verb **mitto**—to send away. In the ancient **Catholic** churches, the public services, at which the catechumens were permitted to be present, were called **missa catechumenorum**, because, at the close of them, proclamation was made thus: "**Ite missa est ecclesia.**" Then followed the **communion service**, which was called **missa fidelium**, and which, under the name of **mass**, is still celebrated.

The reader can see that there is nothing in the appointment or observances of the Supper that warrants this name.

Sacrament. All Protestants, as well as Catholics, regard the rite as a sacrament, and hence the name. But, as we have seen, there is nothing in the Word of God to warrant the idea, and therefore the name is unwarranted and misleading. We have been pained, all our life, by hearing Baptist ministers speaking of this rite as "The sacrament," and "Sacramental occasion," and "Sacramental board," "Sacramental bread," and "Sacramental wine." It is aping the language of Ashdod. Such terms are not found in the Word of God, and should be unknown in a Baptist vocabulary. What have Baptists to do with any thing sacramental?

Eucharist. It has been called the Eucharist, because the Lord gave thanks—**eucharista** meaning thanksgiving. But it is nowhere spoken of as "the thanksgiving" in the Scriptures.

The Communion. It is quite generally called the "Communion," as Communion service, and partaking of the Communion, etc. This word is derived from the Greek **koinonia**, which signifies **fellowship, joint participation,** and also **communicating.** The Scriptures seem to justify the use of this term. Paul says: The cup of blessing for which we give praise, is it not the Communion, the **"fellowship"** of the blood of Christ? The loaf which we break, is it not the Communion—**fellowship**—of the body of Christ? (1 Cor. x: 16.) John says: "That which we have seen and heard declare we unto you, that ye also may have **fellowship** with us; and truly our

Communion—fellowship—is with the Father and with his Son Jesus Christ." **It is with Christ, and not each other that we commune "The Lord's Supper."** There can be no doubt about the scripturalness of this name, for Paul, by inspiration, called it "the Lord's Supper," (1 Cor. xi: 20.) These last titles will be the only ones I shall use in this book.

QUALIFICATIONS OF THE PARTICIPANTS.

Now let us examine the passages submitted, and learn the invariable qualifications of the participants of the Lord's Supper. We find:

1. That in every case those who partook of the Supper had been baptized.

In the first instance it is clear that all those who continued steadfastly in "breaking the loaf" had been previously baptized.

In the second account Paul addressed his letter to the members of the church at Corinth, and these had all been baptized; because there never was a church of unbaptized Christians. Dr. Rice (Presbyterian) says:

"I admit that we can not get into a visible church without baptism."

All denominations, save one,* are agreed that the Supper never was, and can not scripturally be given to any one before baptism.

*The Methodists, believing that the Supper, as well as baptism, is a sacrament of salvation offer it to the unbaptized impenitent to secure pardon, etc. (See future chapter.)

Without multiplying authorities let one suffice for all. Dr. Wall, in his "History on Infant Baptism," says:

"No church ever gave the Communion to any persons before they were baptized; among all the **absurdities** that ever were held, none ever maintained that any person should partake of the Communion before they were baptized."—Part 2, c. 9, p. 484.

We also learn from these accounts—

2. **That all who partook of the Supper were church members.**

They had, therefore, professed a change of heart, and been baptized. It is specifically stated that three thousand were **added**—*i. e.*, to the **church**, for it was into a church they were all baptized, (see 1 Cor. xii: 17, and last clause of v. 47), "and the Lord **added to the Church**—the saved."

In the third reference (1 Cor. xi) no one questions that all who ate the Supper were church members. From these accounts we are warranted in the conclusion that all who partook of the Lord's Supper in the apostolic age, were: 1. Professedly regenerate persons; 2. Scripturally baptized; and, therefore, 3. Members of scriptural churches; and 4. That the Supper was under the special and sole control of the local churches to whom it, with baptism, was delivered by the apostles. (For the discussion of which, see Chapter V, Part II.)

WE LEARN CONCLUSIVELY,

That the Lord's Supper is not like the worship of God by praise, or prayer, or a social service.

A company of missionaries on shipboard, bound for heathen lands, may not partake of the Supper; nor a company of ministers, though they should by chance meet some Sabbath morning on Mount Olivet or Calvary, celebrate the Supper,* for they are not a church. Neither may a pastor, though with a number of his church members, even with the permission of his church, attempt to celebrate the Supper in the room of a sick or dying Christian, although a member. That gathering would not be a church, and the church has no authority to allow such an act to change the rite from a church to a social ordinance.† How often do we hear of the ordinance administered in such like

* An account of a company of ministers of different denominations meeting on the top of Mount Olivet on Sunday morning, and the thought occurred to celebrate the Supper, which they did, with the bread of their lunch and a bottle of wine, recently appeared in American religious papers without condemnation. The Communion of outgoing missionaries on shipboard is often mentioned with pious favor.

† If the church can not delegate her authority to her pastors and deacons to administer the Supper without her presence, how can she delegate her pastor to baptize without her presence and approval of the Christian character of the subject?

circumstances, and spoken of as commendable and pious acts, when they are solemn profanations of the sacred Supper.

Let it be borne in mind, ever, that the rite is only the Lord's Supper when observed by one church, and as one church.

The divine symbolism of the Supper remains to be developed, the right understanding of which will determine all things not hitherto considered, and that solemn question, "What is it to eat and drink unworthily?"

CHAPTER III.

THE SYMBOLISM OF THE LORD'S SUPPER.

The fearful declaration, " eateth and drinketh damnation to himself," etc.—Its import.—The Symbolism of the bread; 1. One loaf; 2. The unbroken loaf; 3. The wheaten loaf; 4. The unleavened loaf; 5. The broken loaf; 6. The eating of the one loaf.

CHRIST has guarded no ordinance of his church with such solemn sanctions as he has his Supper. Notice the fearful words:

"Whosoever shall eat this bread and drink this cup of the Lord unworthily shall be **guilty of the body and blood of the Lord.**

"For he that eateth and drinketh unworthily, **eateth and drinketh damnation to himself,** not discerning the Lord's body."—(1 Cor. xi: 27, 29.)

They are sufficient to appall the stoutest heart! "Guilty of the body and blood of the Lord!" "Eateth and drinketh damnation to himself!" It seems that he has left **one** ordinance at least that he will not allow profaned with impunity. The least these words can imply is certainly fearful enough to influence a Christian to the most serious inquiry for the proper observances of this rite.

WHAT DO THEY MEAN?

Grotius renders it:

"He does the same thing as if he should slay Christ."

Bretschneider:

"Injuring by crime the body of Christ."

Bloomfield:

"He shall be guilty respecting the body—*i. e.*, guilty of profaning the symbols of the body and blood of Christ, and consequently amenable to the punishment due to such an abuse of the highest means of grace."

Rosenmuller:

"He shall be punished for such a deed as if he had rejected Christ himself with ignominy."

Barnes:

"The obvious and literal sense is evidently that they should, by such conduct, be involved in the sin of putting the Lord Jesus to death."—See *Barnes, in loco.*

I am satisfied that there is no expression in the Bible that has more troubled and distressed the most conscientious Christians than these. There are thousands who go to the Lord's Table with fear and trembling on account of them, and other thousands of pious Christians, who, through their misgivings, are deterred from approaching it. This ought not, and need not, so to be.

Christ having commanded his disciples to "do it," it is certain that we may know how to eat and drink **worthily**, so as to secure the divine approval and blessing, rather than the deserved displeasure of God.

To explain the Supper so that the weakest Christian may know how to eat and drink **worthily**, and to discern the Lord's body, is my object.

I see not well how this can be known unless the participant has some just knowledge of

THE SYMBOLISM OF THE SUPPER.

Prof. Harvey, in his late work on "The Church," has this:

> "The bread and wine are symbols divinely appointed to represent the body and blood of Christ, through which symbols the **sacrifice of Christ** is vividly presented to the mind, and by partaking of which the believer expresses in an outward and significant act, his **faith in that sacrifice**. The Supper is thus at once a symbol setting forth this central, vital fact, more distinctly than is possible in language; and a significant act, declaring the partaker's personal reliance on this fact as the ground of his salvation. **Christ** is present in the ordinance, as according to his promise; he is always present in his **truth**, but, as truth finds its clearest and strongest expression in the symbol, he is present in the Supper in a more marked manner than in the Word; for, as in the Supper, the believing soul more clearly apprehends Christ, and more fully yields itself to him; so in it Christ more clearly manifests himself to the soul, and more fully communicates to it the fullness **of his life**."

How important, then, that the expounders of the Word should clearly set forth and explain the symbolism of each act, so that the least intelligent and instructed member of the church can understand, and thereby be enabled to apprehend the great doctrines in connection with the sacrifice of Christ, and so more fully enjoy the blessings con-

flesh and this **bread** God designed to be types of Christ, whom he promised to give for the life of his people, and the Jews always understood that they were typical of their Messiah, who was to be to them **spiritually** what that flesh and bread was to their fathers. They well understood this in **theory;** and when Jesus, claiming to be their Messiah, declared himself the **true** bread that came down from heaven—*i. e.*, the antitype of the manna, they had no excuse for misunderstanding his meaning. They never for one moment believed that they were to **literally** eat the flesh and drink the blood of their Messiah when he came, in order to enjoy his promised blessings, but by receiving him, and believing him, and obeying him.

In the following passages Christ asserts himself the antitype and substance, of which the flesh and the manna were the shadows:

"I am that bread of life. Your fathers did eat manna in the wilderness, and are dead. This is the bread which cometh down from heaven, that a man may eat thereof and not die. **I am the living bread,** which came down from heaven. If any man eat of this bread, he shall live forever; and the bread that I will give him is **my flesh,**

When God would deliver his chosen people from their bondage in Egypt, he commanded them to sprinkle the blood of a lamb upon the door-posts of their houses, as a sign for the destroying angel to **pass over them;** and this sprinkling of blood was appointed to be a type of salvation through the blood of the Lamb of God. And the unleavened bread appointed for the children of Israel to eat for seven days, in connection with their Passover, was designed to typify the sole agency of God in their salvation. Now each of these—the **flesh,** the **bread**—supports of physical life, together with the *blood* of animals, which was their very life itself, were types of Christ, through whose sacrificial death we can alone receive the grace of spiritual life and nourishment. Christ applied these types to himself in his celebrated discourse recorded by John, sixth chapter:

"Except ye eat the **flesh** of the Son of man, and drink his **blood** ye have no life in you. Whoso eateth my flesh and drinketh my blood hath eternal life. For my flesh is meat indeed, and my blood is drink indeed. He that eateth my flesh and drinketh my blood dwelleth in me and I in him. As the living Father hath sent me, and I live by the Father; so he that **eateth me** shall live by me."

When God was leading his people through the desert by the hand of Moses, they hungered and longed for the flesh-pots of Egypt, and He sent the flesh of quails and manna from heaven, and thus supported them for forty years. Now this flesh and this **bread** God designed to be types of Christ, whom he promised to give for the life of his people, and the Jews always understood that they were typical of their Messiah, who was to be to them **spiritually** what that flesh and bread was to their fathers. They well understood this in **theory;** and when Jesus, claiming to be their Messiah, declared himself the **true** bread that came down from heaven—*i. e.*, the antitype of the manna, they had no excuse for misunderstanding his meaning. They never for one moment believed that they were to **literally** eat the flesh and drink the blood of their Messiah when he came, in order to enjoy his promised blessings, but by receiving him, and believing him, and obeying him.

In the following passages Christ asserts himself the antitype and substance, of which the flesh and the manna were the shadows:

"I am that bread of life. Your fathers did eat manna in the wilderness, and are dead. This is the bread which cometh down from heaven, that a man may eat thereof and not die. **I am the living bread,** which came down from heaven. If any man eat of this bread, he shall live forever; and the bread that I will give him is **my flesh,** which I will give for the life of the world. Moses gave you not **that** bread from heaven; but my Father giveth you the **true bread** from heaven. For the bread of God is **he** who cometh down from heaven, and giveth life to the world."

Nor did Jesus leave them uninstructed as to what he meant by his flesh **and blood,** or what the eating of his flesh and the drinking of his blood did signify:

"And Jesus said unto them, I am the bread of life; he that **cometh to me** shall never **hunger, and** he that **believeth on me** shall never **thirst**" (v. 35). "Verily, verily, I say unto you, He that believeth on me hath everlasting life" (v. 47). "What if ye shall see the Son of man ascend up where he was before? It is the **Spirit** that quickeneth; the **flesh** profiteth nothing; **the words that I speak unto you, they are spirit, and they are life**" (v. 63).

The reader should bear in mind that in all the passages in which Christ speaks of his **body, flesh,** and **blood**, given for the **life** of the world, he does not mean his literal body, flesh, and blood, but the **"words"**—doctrine—he taught them; in a word, the plan of salvation consummated by his vicarious sufferings in that body of our flesh, and by his blood shed for the remission of sins. It is by apprehending and cordially receiving the great truths represented to our minds by these expressive symbols that we eat the flesh and drink the blood of Christ, so that he becomes life eternal to us. A few passages will make this very clear to every mind:

"Whoso abideth not in the **doctrine** of Christ hath not God. He that abideth in the **doctrine** of Christ hath both the Father and the Son" (2 Jno. 9). "For that life which I now live in the flesh I am living by that **faith** of that God and Christ who loved me even, to the delivering himself up on my behalf" (literal)—Gal. ii: 20.

This, then, was "the bread of life" on which Paul lived. The **bread** of the Lord's Supper, then, is not a symbol of the literal body or person of Christ, but of **life through the sacrificial death of Christ**—it is our fellowship, our participation of that which we symbolize in partaking of the bread.

§ 1. THE ONE LOAF.

Here are the passages that refer to the first element:

"He took **a loaf,** and, having given thanks, he brake it, and said, This is **my body** that on your behalf is **offered** or **given**" (literal). "As often as ye eat **this** loaf * * ye do show the Lord's death until he come."

"Because there is **one loaf**, we the many are **one body** [organization], for we all partake of the **one loaf**."—(1 Cor. x: 17.)

"The **loaf** we break, Is it not the communion—*i. e.*, participation—of the **body** of Christ?"

In determining the symbolism of the elements, we should avoid the error most commentators have fallen into—*i. e.*, making the bread and wine, which are symbols, symbolize the literal "body" and "blood" of Christ, which, he teaches us, are but **figures**—figures of life through his sacrificial death—"the doctrine of Christ"—"the Gospel of our salvation." Symbols in no language symbolize symbols. Types never typify types in the spiritual world, any more than shadows cast shadows in the natural world.*

The **bread** of the Supper, then, symbolizes just what Christ taught the Jews his flesh and blood represented to them, viz., the "**words**" he spoke, "his **doctrine**," "the **faith** of the Gospel."

If I have rightly apprehended the symbol, the **one loaf** symbolizes the "one faith" of the Gospel—the one plan of salvation through Christ. There was but one Divine Savior, and it is not supposable that he would originate but one system of doctrine, and it is therefore expressly stated that there is but "**one** faith," as there is but one Lord and Savior, who is the Author and the Finisher of "**the faith**"—not our act of faith, but **the** faith of the Gospel. †

When we look upon "the **one loaf**" upon the the table, we are symbolically taught that there is but one Savior, who is our bread of life, and but one Gospel—**one saving faith** or "doctrine of Christ," one "plan of salvation," one name given under heaven whereby we may be saved, and that one is **Christ**.

But the symbolism of the Supper, like that of baptism, has a complex application. As each loaf

---

* Not a few of our most scholarly writers and preachers speak of the Lord's Supper as the **antitype** of the Passover. If I have done so, it has not been through ignorance, but inadvertance.

† There is no "our," but a **definite** article in the original.

represents the body of Christ, so it is designed to represent each church as "**a body of Christ.**" Paul said to the church at Corinth: "Ye are a body of Christ." And, as the loaf is one—an organic unity, complete in itself—so the participants eating of the loaf must be "**one body,**" one organic unity; and, if so, only the members of one church can jointly partake of it together.

§ 2. THE UNBROKEN LOAF,

Then, symbolizes the **unity** of the faith of which Christ is the Author and Finisher, the Beginner and Perfecter; and that nothing less than a whole Gospel—the whole work of Christ—will save a soul. It required all he did to save one soul from death, so that all he did must constitute the ground of our trust. We may not accept a part and reject a part: accept a part of his "all righteousness," and supplement it with our own; accept a **partial** salvation by grace, and complete it by our works. No one ever was saved by such a faith.

As respects the Church, the symbolism of the **unbroken loaf** demands that the church, celebrating the rite, should be unbroken by schisms or factious parties. It is recorded of the church at Jerusalem, during the first great revival, that all that believed were of **one accord**; and, in the case of that church, the thing signified agreed with the symbol—**unbroken unity.** But Paul severely rebuked the church at Corinth because of its **divided** state; rent, as it was, by heresies and factions, it was wholly disqualified to eat the Supper.

§ 3. THE WHEATEN LOAF.

The kind of flour of which the bread was to be made for the typical sacrifices, under the law, was by no means an unimportant matter. Flour from **any** grain used for food was not permissible. Only **one kind** of flour was allowed. God specifically commanded that the bread that was offered upon his altars should **be wheaten bread,** and we must believe that God had a design in this particularity— that it had some reference to its typical teaching. This we know, that it was the most **costly** bread that was used—that it was the only kind deemed fit for the table of **kings** or persons of dignity. We can see that this fitly symbolized the costliness of the sacrifice requisite for our redemption; the exceeding preciousness of the Gospel—the **faith** that alone can save a lost race.

"For the **redemption** of their soul is **precious,** and ceaseth forever."—(Ps. xlix: 8.)

"For the merchandise of it [wisdom] is better than the merchandise of silver, and the gain thereof than fine gold."—(Prov. iii: 14.)

"Thanks be to God for his **unspeakable gift.**"—(2 Cor. ix: 15.)

"Whereby are given unto us exceeding great and **precious** promises."—(2 Peter i: 4.)

§ 4. THE FINE WHEATEN LOAF.

It must not merely be bread of **wheat** flour, but it must be **fine flour** of wheat. In his specifications concerning the quality of the flour allowed in the sacrifices, God specified **fine** flour nineteen times. There must have been a sufficent reason for this, though we may not apprehend it. If it pointed to the purity—the immaculateness—of the person of Christ, it certainly was an appropriate type, for he was holy and undefiled; if to the "doctrine of Christ"—the unadulterated **faith** of the Gospel, of which Christ was the Author and Perfecter, as I understand it—then it is most strikingly appropriate, and in harmony with the symbolism of the types. Nothing can be **purer** and **sweeter** than **superfine flour of wheat**. There is no deleterious **foreign** matter in it, and it can be safely trusted to support life. So it is a **pure Gospel** alone that saves us; mixed with error, it is a savor of death.

"The **words** of the Lord are **pure words**; as silver tried in a furnace of earth, purified seven times."—(Ps. xii: 6.)

The **words** of the Lord constitute the **faith** of the gospel.

"The **words** that I speak unto you, are spirit and are life."—(Jno. vi: 63; Prov. xxx: 5.)

So should the body—church—partaking of the pure bread, be correspondingly pure and healthy in all its influences; the **faith** of its members unadulterated; its doctrine pure, free from the least poison or defilement of error. Paul especially refers to the importance of **wholesome words** and **sound doctrine**, etc.;

> "If thou put the brethren in remembrance of these things, thou shalt be a good minister of Jesus Christ, nourished up in **words of faith** and of **sound doctrine**, etc. (1 Tim. iv: 6; also i: 10, vi: 3 and 14.

§ 5. THE UNLEAVENED LOAF.

We are not left in the least doubt as to the **kind** of bread Christ used when he instituted the Supper. He took one of the loaves, or cakes, that had been scrupulously prepared for the Passover. To meet the plea of those who claim that "the **kind of bread**" **we** use at the Lord's Supper is a matter of indifference, and that Jesus doubtless used the unleavened loaf because "it was the most convenient" and therefore we may use the most convenient, article of bread. I submit the **fact,** that Christ designed the bread of his Supper to symbolize the self-same truth, fundamental to the plan of salvation, that the **unleavened** bread of the Passover, and of the burnt offerings under the law, was appointed to typify; namely, the great doctrine that our salvation is alone of grace through the sacrificial death of Christ, that we "are saved by **grace** through faith, and that not of ourselves." This fact determines the kind of bread the churches must use at the Supper, if they would not vitiate its symbolism. **Leaven** is dough in a state of partial fermentation and decomposition—**rottenness;**

and placed in a mass of sweet dough speedily excites fermentation, and, if left, the whole mass is speedily corrupted and made unfit for use. It is therefore most befittingly used as a type and a symbol of any doctrine or principle that **depraves** and **corrupts.** When God instituted the Passover he commanded, on pain of death or excision from his people, that no one should eat it with **leavened** bread. (Ex. xii: 15.) No Christian will charge God with capriciousness in the selection of unleavened bread. He explained to the Jews **why** he instituted the unleavened bread of the Passover. It was to teach them and their children, in the generations following, that he, their Sovereign Lord, alone and unassisted, had delivered them and brought them up out of Egypt: "Remember this day, in which ye came out from Egypt, out of the house of bondage; for by strength of hand the Lord brought you out from this place; there shall no leavened bread be eaten." Their salvation was of the Lord **alone.** To symbolize this fact, all leaven of every sort was to be diligently sought for in all their coasts for seven days, and burned with fire; and by this they were given to understand that God was jealous of his honor, and that no part of their salvation was ever to be ascribed to their self-help, to man or idol.

In all the sacrifices of the Jewish worship, which typified salvation through the coming Messiah, no leaven was allowed to be used. **Unleavened**

wheaten bread of fine flour was alone permitted. It typified the central doctrine of the gospel, salvation only by the grace of God through Christ. To add any thing of self-help, or any created assistance, vitiated and effectually destroyed the whole plan,—would be like adding **leaven** to a mass of pure dough. The least reliance upon works renders **null** the grace of God. The apostle says: "If it is of works it is no more grace, else works are no more works; and if of grace it is no more works, else grace is no more grace." This is the pure unadulterated doctrine of the gospel—salvation by grace. Understanding this enables us to see the force of the Savior's warnings against "leaven"—how that a little **leaven** of **false doctrine**, surreptitiously hid away in the churches, and left unpurged, would, like leaven hid in measures of meal, soon corrupt the whole mass of them. It should be immediately purged out. Paul seems to allude to this when he said, "A little leaven leaveneth the whole lump."

Christ also warned his disciples to beware of the "**leaven** of the Pharisees and Sadducees." It was not their leavened bread, as he himself explained, but their leavened doctrine—comparable to modern Arminianism, legalism, and Ritualism—a dependence on **self-righteousness** and deeds of law, moral or ceremonial, for salvation. There can be no doubt that Christ symbolized the false doctrines of self-righteousness for salvation as leaven, and this is what it typified; while the pure **unleavened** bread of the sacrifices and the Passover typified, as we have seen, the doctrine of salvation by grace only, through the sacrificial death and mediation of Christ.

Paul uses leaven in the same sense, as a symbol of a corrupted faith—any thing in heart or life foreign and opposed to the teachings of the gospel of Christ. He evidently alludes to the symbolism of the Supper when he instructed the church at Corinth to exclude from its fellowship an ungodly man. The influence of this man in the church, Paul compared to **leaven**: "Know ye not that a little leaven leaveneth the whole lump;" "Be not deceived, evil associations corrupt good manners;" "Purge out, therefore, the old leaven—vice and sin—that ye—the church at Corinth—may be a new lump, as ye are **unleavened.**" Christians, by their profession, are holy, pure in heart, and therefore ought to be in their faith and their lives. Paul invariably uses "leaven" as a symbol of a corrupt doctrine, of a mixed, and therefore unsaving faith. He declared to the churches of Galatia that the doctrine taught by the Judaizing teachers, who were generally members of the church at Jerusalem, was "**leaven.**" It was in principle that self-same doctrine of the Pharisees, which Christ called "leaven," and of which he warned his disciples to beware—*i. e.*, Judaism—dependence on deeds of law, self-righteousness for salvation it whole or in part. Its name with us is Arminianism, which teaches that only so long as a Christian works is he saved. Let the reader study the whole fifth chapter of Galatians, and especially the second, third and fourth verses:

"Behold, I, Paul, say unto you, that if ye be circumcised, Christ shall profit you nothing. Christ is become of non-effect unto you: whosoever of you are justified [literally who are justifying yourselves by law] are separated from Christ; ye are fallen off from the grace. This persuasion cometh not of him who calleth you. A little **leaven** leaveneth the whole lump."*

False doctrine is leaven, and unleavened bread, without question, symbolized the fundamental doctrine of **salvation by grace only.**

But Paul, in his first letter to the church at Corinth, likens all ungodliness of heart and life to leaven—every thing in the daily conduct of its members contrary to the spirit of the gospel, and destructive of its influence, to **leaven,**—and commands the church to purge out all such members

---

* With this explanation the reader can the better understand the parable of the leaven, and of the mustard seed, for both teach the same thing. A little false doctrine hidden, and surreptitiously introduced into a church, if left to work out its natural result, will leaven the whole body, as a little leaven will corrupt a whole mass of dough. It should be purged out. The church of Christ, though small in his day, he foretold would become large, so that "the fowls of the air"—wicked persons, would **lodge** in it. What is the effect of a multitude of birds lodging in forest trees?

before celebrating the Supper, as the head of a Jewish family was required to carefully remove all leaven from his house and burn it with fire before the Passover could be eaten. "Purge out therefore the old leaven, that ye—the church at Corinth—may be a new—pure—lump, as ye are unleavened—pure. For Christ our Passover is sacrificed for us; let us keep the feast—the Supper—not with the old leaven of **malice** and **wickedness,** but with the **unleavened bread** of sincerity and truth" (1 Cor. v: 8). With a loaf of **leavened** bread upon the table, Paul's allusion here would be without meaning, as his allusions to a burial in baptism would be if sprinkling or pouring was the act.

As the thing symbolized must agree with the symbol, all those members whose lives are **leavened** with such conduct, and "walk" as Paul specifies in this epistle, as well as in that to the churches of Galatia, must be put away, "purged out" of the church, else the feast is kept with **"old leaven."**

"But now I have written unto you **not to keep company,** if any man that is called a brother be a fornicator, or covetous, or an idolater, or a railer, or a drunkard, or an extortioner; with such an one, **no, not to eat.**"

To these characters in his letter to the churches of Galatia, he adds these works of the flesh:

"Adultery, fornication, uncleanness, lasciviousness, witchcraft, murders, **revelings** (or **dancings of all sorts, for this is** the literal import of the term, **komoi,** translated revelings in our version) **and such like;** of the which I tell you before as I have also told you in time past, that they who do such things shall not inherit the kingdom of God."—Gal. v: 19-22.

The one unleavened loaf, therefore, symbolizes two things:

1. The one, pure unadulterated faith of the gospel—the uncorrupted doctrine of Christ—viz., that salvation is solely by the grace of God in Christ Jesus.

2. That the body—the church—should, like the loaf of which it partakes, be unleavened, *i. e.*, before God and man a **pure** body.

From this it is demonstrably clear that an Arminian in faith can not eat the Lord's Supper worthily,—I mean one who believes in "falling from grace," as it is called, because he believes that **some deed of some law,** though it be the "law of pardon" or good works of some sort, must be added to God's grace, and continued on the part of the Christian, or he can not be saved. The symbol of the unleavened loaf forbids his approach on peril of eating and drinking damnation to himself.

Such being the symbolic significancy of the bread used in the Supper—which I think no intelligent Christian will deny—it can not be a question but that the bread must be an **unleavened** loaf. A church that is so regardless of the symbolic teachings of the Supper as to use any **kind of** bread,* can not scripturally discipline her members, should they decline to become **particeps criminis** in her violation of the divine law of the Supper.

Suppose my church should adopt a fruit-cake for the bread, and molasses and water, or rasin-water for the "fruit of the **vine**," would it be right for me to partake in **violation** of the law of Christ? Could the church discipline me for refusing to come to **her** table, for it would not be the **Lord's**? For the violation of what law would she try me? She can make no law. She can not modify any appointment of Christ. She might as well discipline and exclude a member for refusing to attend a **Saturday** conference which Christ never required at his hands.

§ 6. THE BROKEN LOAF.

"Christ took the loaf and broke it, saying, This is my body that is broken for you."

He could not have meant that his breaking of the loaf should symbolize his literal broken body,

---

* A church in this State, of which the writer was a member, used a **silver cake** bought at the confectioners, to make a nice table. He wrapped the piece he took from the plate in his handkerchief, and on going out threw it into the gutter. Many of our churches use **baker's bread**, a compound of **Irish potatoes**, flour, **alum** and **leaven**. Very many use the common light bread from the table. Why not **corn bread**, or **Graham**, or **Buckwheat bread** as well?

because it is written, "not a bone of him was broken;" but he explains (John vi : 5) "the bread that I will give him is my **flesh,** which I will give for the life of the world." "For my flesh is meat **indeed**"—*i. e.*, represents in the Supper what the flesh, bread, and blood of all the atonement sacrifices under the law typified; viz., **salvation through the sacrificial death of Christ.**

The breaking of the loaf, then, symbolized the grace of God, which is unto life, **provided** and made **accessible** by the voluntary offering up of Christ for his people. The loaf broken before our eyes symbolically teaches and assures us that all the covenant obligations Christ assumed for his people have been fully discharged; that the infinite satisfaction, justly due to the divine government from us, which demanded the sufferings of the Infinite Redeemer, have been made, so that the free gift of eternal life through Christ can be offered to a lost race.

Christ himself broke the loaf—prepared it to be eaten ; so he himself provided bread of life for his people. No man took his life from him, he himself laid down his own life. While he, the Lord of glory, veiled in our **flesh and form,** was the offering—**bread**—he himself was the only **priest** in the universe who could offer it up for us—he **freely offered up himself.** He furnished and **offered** the offering, and thus became the **author and finisher** of the **faith.** Glorious symbolism!

Salvation's feast prepared by Christ at infinite expense and graciously offered to the perishing famine-stricken millions of earth! Christ has broken the bread—nothing of it remains to be done. All things are now ready! He has fulfilled the all-righteousness the violated law demanded!

> "Nothing, either great or small,
>   Remains for me to do;
> Jesus died and paid it all,
>   All the **debt** I owe."

§ 7. THE EATING OF THE ONE LOAF.

"He took a loaf, and when he had given thanks, he brake it, and said, **Take, eat**; this is my body, which is broken for you [to eat.]

"The bread which we break, is it not the Communion—fellowship—of the body or church of Christ?"—1 Cor. xi.

The first thing that strikes us in these Scriptures is the fact that Christ did nothing more than to **"give thanks."** He did not use a word that indicated transubstantiation—any change wrought upon the bread; nor did he **"consecrate** it," impart to it a mystic, supernatural efficacy, but he simply gave thanks. And we should effect to do nothing more, and leave transubstantiation with the Catholics, who would make a sacrifice; and **consecration** with the Protestants, who would make a **sacrament** of it. We can all join with the pastor in giving hearty thanks for these speaking symbols of his love. The **bread** Christ held in his hand was not by him intended to symbolize his "mystical body," if any one knows what that is; nor his literal body, but just what the flesh and blood of all the atonement sacrifices typified—just what the bread and flesh God sent from heaven to preserve the lives of the children of Israel typified—the offer of eternal life through the sacrificial sufferings of Christ in literal flesh. This doctrine of Christ is the flesh, the **body** of Christ by which we became dead to the law. (See Rom. vii: 4.)

Let Christ explain this:

"I am that **bread** of life. I am the **living bread** which came down from heaven; if any man eat of **this** bread he shall live forever. Except ye eat the flesh . . of the Son of God ye have no life in you. . . He that **eateth** me, even he shall live by me."

The command of Christ to his children to "take and eat of the loaf" of his Supper, implies vastly more than to masticate a piece of unleavened bread in historical commemoration of the fact that Jesus of Nazareth, the son of Mary, was crucified. If this is all that is meant by "discerning the Lord's body," the unregenerate could discern it as well as the Christian. It is **to eat Christ himself** in the sense he meant when he said above, "He that **eateth me** shall live by me."

It means, then, that while we perform the **physical** act of eating material bread, we should, by faith, gratefully review Christ's gracious work of redemption, the living sacrifice of himself for our sins, realizing in our hearts a conscious participation in the benefits of his death, and thus renew our faith, and confirm our trust in, and quicken our love for Him as our divine Redeemer. With such an exercise of faith and heart we should leave the table refreshened like a strong man with an abundance of meat.

Thus we symbolize our personal relations to Christ our Life.

But by eating of the one loaf with our brethren, we symbolize that we are **fellow-members of the same particular church with them**—members one of another of **the self-same body.** While the act only **implies** that all who partake are professed Christians, it is **appointed** by Christ to symbolize **church relations**—*i. e.*, that all who partake are incorporated in the same local church—one body. A correct translation of 1 Cor. xvii will make this clear. The allusion to the symbolism of the Supper here is only by way of illustration, as is the apostle's allusion to baptism in Rom. vi.

"Because there is one loaf, we the many [members of the church at Corinth] are one body: for we all partake of the one loaf."

That is, we use but one loaf to symbolize the fact that we are all members of but one visible church, which the term body evidently refers to. The idea of **organic unity**—one body—rules the expression. The many particles of flour were, **by chemical affinity,** incorporated into oneness—

one loaf; so the members of each local church, by spiritual affinity, and **one act of profession,** are incorporated into **one** organism.

"For in one spirit we are all baptized into **one body** * * and all have been made to drink into one spirit."—(1 Cor. xii: 13.)

Paul's instruction to the church at Corinth (1 Cor. xi: 2) corroborates the above interpretation—*i. e.*, that the Supper was placed under the guardianship of each local church, and symbolizes **church relations**; they were to "tarry one for the other"—**observe it as a church.** So important is the right understanding of this subject, so generally overlooked and misunderstood, that I submit the opinions of several standard authorities:

Macknight:

"The Greek word **artos**, especially, when joined with words of number, **always** signifies a **loaf**, and is so translated in our Bibles: Matt. xvi: 9—'Do ye not understand, neither remember the five—**artous**—**loaves** of the five thousand?' Matt. iv: 3—'Command that these stones be made—**artous**—**loaves.**'"

Olshausen:

"As all who constitute the Church (hoi pantes) eat of one and the same bread * * so this common participation converts their plurality (hoi polloi) into a higher unity—a "body of Christ" in a comprehensive sense—so that the Church itself may be called Christ" (xii: 12).

Dr. Knapp:

V. 17. "While we all eat of one and the same bread (a portion of which is broken for each), we profess to be all members of one body—*i. e.*, **of one church.**"—*Christian Theology*.

Dr. Adam Clark, the standard Methodist commentator, says:

"The original would be better translated thus: **Because there is one bread or loaf, we who are many are one body.** As only one loaf was used at the passover, and those who partook of it were considered **one religious body** [family], so we who partake of the eucharistical bread and wine in commemoration of the sacrificial death of Christ are one spiritual **society,**" etc.

Albert Barnes:

1 Cor. x: 17. **Are one bread.** "One loaf, one cake. That is, we are united, or are one. There is evident allusion here to the fact, that the loaf or cake was composed of many separate grains of wheat, or portions of flour united in one; or, that, as one loaf was broken and partaken by all, it was implied that they were all one. We are all **one society,** * * and one body, one society."

JESSE MERCER'S VIEWS OF THE LIMITATIONS OF THE LORD'S SUPPER.

If the analogies drawn in this essay be sound, then the churches of Jesus Christ are charged with the faithful and holy keeping of his ordinances, and made responsible for their purity and perpetuity. They are instructed who to receive into their union and how to right-order them for their communion. For the discharge of the duties of this, and every other ecclesiastical obligation, they have received power from on high. This is sustained by the apostolic requisitions, reprehension, and approvals of the churches, connected with the repentance and reformation, which followed in the Corinthian church.—See 2 Cor. ii: 9; vii: 11. Compared with text and context. The appeal to the church, 1 Cor. v: 12, in regard to her judicial power, and the requisition made thereon, put the subject at rest. Paul asks, "Do not ye judge them that are within?" and then adds, "therefore put away from among yourselves that wicked person." Here the apostle asserts the power to govern, and requires its use in purging out the old and corrupting leaven, in order to a pure and holy communion. *If, then, the church, in her judicial capacity, is charged with the holy keeping of the feast of the Lord's Supper, of consequence it must be restricted to those who are under her power; as, without controversy, it would be arbitrary and oppressive to charge her beyond her power, or right of control."*

Speaking on the necessity of *love* in *unity* and *fellowship*, in order to a proper observance of the Supper, he says:

"No set of believers can be practically brought to this state of Christian unity and fellowship, without the pious use of a godly discipline, and therefore, *none can sit together, with gospel propriety, at the table of the Lord, but those who are subject to its control;* for if discipline guards the table of the Lord, then *none can gospelly sit around it, but those who are under its banner."—Geo. Pulpit,* vol. 1, pp. 60, 61.

In both these extracts he teaches that the authority of the church and the privileges of the Supper are exactly co-extensive and coterminal, and confines the Supper to the membership of each church.

The thoughtful reader will see that Jesse Mercer, in 1811, advocated the self-same principle which I have only developed in this book. How say some that I have originated it?

Prof. Curtis, whose work was endorsed and published by the American Baptist Publishing Society, says:

"Thus, then, it is **clear** [*i. e.*, from 1 Cor. xi] that the Lord's Supper is given in charge to those visible churches of Christ, in the midst of which he has promised to walk and dwell (Rev. ii: 2). To each of these it belongs to celebrate it as **one family**. [Then certainly not as parts of different families or bodies.] The members of that particular church are to be tarried for, and it is to be a symbol of their relations, as members, to each other."—*Progress of Baptist Principles,* p. 307.

If this be so, then is intercommunion impossible.

Dr. Richard Fuller, in his work on "Baptism and Communion," says:

"As the passover was a **meal for each family only,** so the Supper is a family repast, **for the members of that particular church in which the table is spread.** This is so plain to our minds, hearts, and conciences, that there is never any discussion about it."

Dr. A. P. Williams, in his work on the "Lord's Supper," says:

"Now here (1 Cor. x: 16, 17) **it is plainly** argued that this joint participation in the one cup, and the one bread, is designed to show that the participants are but **one body,** and, as such, they share this joint participation."

Dr. Harvey, Prof. of Theology in Hamilton Seminary, N. Y., in his late work, "The Church," p. 221, says:

"It is a symbol of church fellowship.

"When a man eats of that 'one bread,' and drinks of that 'one cup,' he, in this act, professes himself a member of that 'one body,' in hearty, holy sympathy with its doctrines and life, and freely and fully **subjecting himself to its watch-care and government** (1 Cor. x: 17). Hence, in 1 Cor. v: 11, the Church is forbidden to eat (in the Lord's Supper, as the context clearly shows) with immoral persons, thus distinctly making the ordinance a symbol of church-fellowship."

That Dr. Harvey clearly apprehends the "one body," in this passage, as referring to the **one local** church at Corinth, he leaves us in no doubt, for an invisible church has neither watch-care nor government, and there can be no reasonable doubt that this is the apostle's meaning, despite the efforts of the advocates of the Universal Church theory. He is also clear that the eating of the "one loaf" symbolizes the fact that each member eating professes himself a member of **that one church, and in hearty subjection to its government, which a member of another church could not do.** The reader can see that intercommunion with members of other churches **is as certainly forbidden** as it is with immoral persons, for the one as certainly vitiates the symbolism as the other.

Dr. Wm. C. Buck, D. D., in his great work, "The Philosophy of Religion," has these strong comments on 1 Cor. x: 17:

"That it was the design of the Lord to signify, in the

use of this ordinance, **the unity of each church as one body**, is distinctly asserted by the apostle; for he assures us that 'one bread' is the symbol of 'one body;' and he further teaches us that 'we,' the apostles, break **the** 'one bread'—loaf—and bless the 'one cup,' and we have proof, as clear as a ray of light from heaven, that they copied, with punctilious exactitude, the pattern set them by the Messiah. We may therefore consider this a **settled principle** in the practical philosophy of this rite."—p. 456.

While I might add other distinguished authorities, I will conclude in the language of Prof. Curtis:

"That the Lord's Supper is a symbol of **church relations**, subsisting between those who unite together in the participation of it, * * can be shown in many ways."—p. 136.

CONCLUSIONS.

The following axiom will assist us in drawing our conclusions from the above exegesis of the passages:

AXIOM.

The rite is vitiated and null when the thing symbolized does not exist.

Two things are symbolized when a church celebrates the Supper:

1. That a spiritual relationship exists between the participants and Christ, effected through his sacrificial death and atonement.

2. That visible church relations exist between all those who jointly partake of the "one loaf;" that though many individual Christians, yet all

constitute one organic unity—"one body"—**one particular church.**

1. We conclude, therefore, that the Supper can be celebrated only as a **church** ordinance—*i. e.*, by a particular church; and, as such, a church can not invite other than her own members to a joint Communion, without vitiating the symbolism of the one loaf, since the thing signified would not exist—viz., church relationship of all the communicants.

2. We conclude, that, since the Supper was divinely appointed to be observed as a **church** ordinance, it would be a profanation of the ordinance for a Christian to attempt to observe it **privately**; or for a company of such to observe it **socially,** since the symbolism would be vitiated.

3. We conclude that should you go to the table of a church, of which you are not a member, and partake, not being a member, you would to all intents and purposes be eating as an **individual,** and would eat and drink unworthily. The invitation of the pastor or of the church would not change your relation to that church or its ordinance, for two reasons: 1. The **invitation** of the pastor or church to partake, does not make you a member of that church, and you can not partake of the Supper scripturally or **worthily** with any church of which you are not a member; and, 2. The pastor nor the church has any authority to give such an invitation, and therefore the invitation gives

you no warrant to disobey Christ, by violating the laws he has appointed for the observance of his ordinance. **You can only eat it worthily in the church of which you are a member.**

Prof. Curtis says:

> "It [the joint participation of the Supper] therefore **unquestionably** indicates **visible church relations as subsisting among all who, by right, unite together in its celebration.** Occasional communion, by invitation, must follow therefore the principles established for the regular celebration of this ordinance. We may not bend the rule to the exception, but the exception to the rule."—*Prog. Bap. Prin.*, p. 303, 304.

This means that those visitors wishing to Commune, must first unite with the church—**actual church relationship must exist between all the communicants and the church** to preserve the divine symbolism.

4. We have good reasons to conclude that Infinite Wisdom appointed the symbolism of the one loaf, to impress his people by keeping the fact constantly before their eyes, **that the churches of Christ are each complete and independent bodies, and that he never designed a national or universal church,** such as Catholics and Protestants have originated. It may have been for this, as well as other reasons, that he guarded its perversion with such appalling sanctions. It is certain that had this ordinance always been observed as delivered, there never would, for

there never could, have been a national or universal church originated. The divine directions are that all the members of each church **assemble at one place**, and for the church to tarry until the members are assembled, and **to all eat and drink together.** But national, provincial, or universal churches (?) like those of the Catholics and Protestants never did, never **can**, assemble to eat the Lord's Supper.

From the second century there has been a strong tendency to church **confederation** and **centralization.** It is a noticeable fact that all who have apostatized from the true churches, both Catholics and Protestants, have adopted the national or universal church theory!

JESSE MERCER'S ADVICE.

Speaking of the symbolism of the one loaf he says:

"That he [Paul] also uses it as a figure of the *unity* of the church, in order to show what she ought to be, to hold a *meet* communion, *one body;* which can only be represented *properly by one loaf or cake.*"

" I would respectfully suggest to all the churches, the propriety of henceforth, having at all our communions, *only one loaf* or cake, as the more appropriate figure of the body of Christ, broken for our sins, and also of the *unity* and *fellowship* of the *church,* when in communing order."—*Geo. Pulpit*, vol. 1, pp. 62, 63.

I especially call the attention of my brethren to the statements of the venerated Jesse Mercer on the gospel restrictions of the Lord's Supper, and the symbolism of the "one loaf," to refute the charges of those unfriendly critics who charge me with inventing the idea of *Church Communion.* I teach no different from Mercer in insisting that the symbolism of the Supper demands that its celebration should be restricted to the discipline of the particular church celebrating it. Let Mercer and Curtis, Gardner and Harvey, then be charged with what my opposers so rashly charge upon me—*i. e.*, the sin of being a heretic and a disorganizer of the denomination. In principle I differ not from these; but only in this—if they say the church can grant the right by *invitation,* I deny it. If they say that they must be members for the time being if they wish to commune, and the invitation makes them so, I deny it, and every Baptist knows it is not so; they can not be members of two churches at the same time—and the invitation to the communion table never did and never can make an alien a member. This is the head and front of my heresy.

CHAPTER IV.

THE WINE.

1. The Fruit of the Vine; 2. The unleavened Fruit of the Vine; 3. The One Cup; 4. The drinking of the One Cup.

CHRIST used and enjoined the use of the fruit of the vine.

This proposition all will **admit**, for it is the very language of Christ.

"But I say unto you, I will no more drink of the fruit of the vine," etc. And he gave it to them, and said: "Take, drink ye all of it." —Matt. xxvi: 27–29.

It was, then, the fruit of the vine, not of the tree, or of corn, and much less of the brier, that Jesus had drank with his disciples, and here commands them to drink. To use the fruit of any thing, save of the vine, is to violate the positive command of Christ. It well becomes us, then, to impartially ascertain what this "fruit of the vine" signified.

It will not be denied, that throughout the Bible, this phrase is used to denote one definite kind of drink—"the blood of the **grape**" (Deut. xxxii:

4)—**wine**. The Jews designated it by several words, as **yani, tirosh, asis, chamer,** but all meaning the same thing—the expressed juice of the grape. This leads to another question:

Was this "fruit of the vine" the fermented or unfermented juice of the grape—unleavened or leavened?

This is only asking whether it was **real wine** at all, or something else. I do not understand that there ever was, or can be, a drop of **real wine** made without fermentation. The technical name of the mass of crushed grapes, or juice, before fermentation, is "**must.**" If it is ever called wine before fermentation, which is the process by which all leaven is purged out, it is by **anticipation;** as it is said of the cook, "she has just put her bread into the oven to bake." The cook never bakes bread, but the dough to make it bread. The dough is sometimes called bread by anticipation.

It will be conceded by all that the wine Jesus used at the passover was identical with that the Jews were, in that age, wont to use in its observance, whatever they may use now.

It has been absurdly argued that fermented wine could not have been used at the passover, because leaven was expressly forbidden. For this very reason fermented wine should be used. That which causes fermentation in wine is comparable to **leaven**—foreign to the nature of wine; and fermentation is but the latent energy of nature to throw this matter off, or settle it to the bottom of the vessel, so as to leave the wine pure and clear, and fitted to drink. Before this clarifying process takes place, it is unfit to drink, and will produce powerful cathartic effects. The corn and wine of Palestine were valuable products of trade and commerce, but unfermented wine was not known in their consumption or commerce.

(1) **Yayin** is the usual term for their wine. It is used one hundred and thirty-six times in the Hebrew of the Old Testament. That it was fermented, and, therefore, if used to excess, intoxicating, read Gen. ix: 21–24, and Prov. xx: 1, and Ps. civ: 15. In itself, rightly used, it was valuable; but, abused, a curse.

(2) **Tirosh**, new wine, or wine of the first year, unmellowed by age, and heady. In Hosea iv: 11, we are told that "whoredom and wine (**yani**, and new wine, **tirosh**) take away the heart." Not if **tirosh** was insipited and unpalatable "**must**." Improperly used, **tirosh** can excite men to evil.

(3) **Asis** is used in four places, and capable of intoxicating (Isa. xlix: 29).

(4) **Chamer** was the fermented juice of the grape (Deut. xxxii: 14, Isa. xxvii: 2). In both cases spoken of as a valuable product of the soil. One of the distinguished blessings God promised to his obedient people (Prov. iii: 10).

The Holy Spirit selected but one Greek word to indicate the wine Christ was charged with **drinking,** which he **made** at Cana, which the Jews used at their passover, which Paul instructed the churches he organized to use at the Lord's Supper, and Timothy to drink medicinally. That word is **oinos.** It is used twenty-seven times in the New Testament to indicate the fermented juice of the grape, twice as wine drinker, and five times figuratively. There is not the slightest ground for the most captious to question the well-established fact that **oinos** means the fermented juice of the grape. Think of the Jews charging Christ with being a bibber of something wholly unintoxicating! And Christ's comparison founded upon men putting new grape-jelly, or conserves of grapes, into old skins, and they bursting per consequence! Or the members of the church at Corinth getting drunk on canned grape juice and sugar! But seriously, this latter case settles the question with all who bow to the authority of inspiration. This church used the kind of wine Paul instructed them to use when he instituted the ordinance. It was the fermented juice of the grape, and intoxicating when used to excess. He charged them with getting drunk at the communion table; but, in correcting their abuses, he did not tell them they used the wrong kind of wine, but only that they drank too much of the kind he appointed.

So much has been said and written of late by

fanatical men under the plea of "temperance," and yet much against the cause of temperance, to drive the wine from the Lord's Supper which Christ used and commanded us to use till he comes again, that I submit a few authorities conclusive of the question.

The claim is that **fermented** wine was not used by the Jews, in their passover, in the days of Christ; but the unfermented juice, preserved by boiling, or the water of dried raisins, or conserves of grapes, etc., and, therefore, we may, and should, use such slop; or even molasses and water, or water only, rather than **real** wine.

Rev. J. W. Willmarth, of Philadelphia, in an exhaustive article in reply to one of these raisin-water advocates, says:

"Evidence in regard to what modern Jews practiced, in the passover, is not decisive. It requires much credulity to believe that the ancient passover cup, and the 'cup of blessings,' were filled with 'an infusion of raisins in water,' which Dr. Cunningham says Jews now use. If **true wine** was the only wine known to the Jews, and to the writers of the Bible, who can doubt that the same is meant in the Mishna, and was used at the passover, and so at the communion?

"I feel justified, therefore, in reaffirming them; and in exhorting my brethren not to **mutilate the Lord's ordinance**, in accordance with the demands of ultraists, whose exegesis is worthless, and whose projects would annul the commandment of Christ, without doing a particle of good to any human interest."

A. Van Dyck, D. D., for twenty-five years missionary in Syria, and a philologist of great renown, says (*Bibliotheca Sacra*, Vol. 26, p. 170):

"There is not, and, as far as I can find out, there never was, in Syria, any thing like what has been called 'unfermented wine.' The thing is not known in the East * * They could not keep grape or raisin-water unfermented, if they would. It would become either wine or vinegar in a few days, or go into putrefactive fermentation. The native churches—Evangelical, Maronite, Greek, Coptic, and Arminian—all use fermented wine at the communion. They have no other, and have no idea of any other.

"The evidence goes to confirm my views of 'Bible wine,' and of the wine of the Lord's Supper. If any one wishes to examine further, the sources of information are open; the verdict of Christian scholarship is decisive."

If the reader will refer to "Hackett's Smith's Bible Dictionary," Art. WINE, he will find this:

"In the condemnatory passages, no exception is made in favor of any other kind of liquid, passing under the same name, but not invested with the same dangerous qualities.

"Nor again, in these passages, is there any decisive condemnation of the substance itself, which would enforce the conclusion, that elsewhere an unfermented liquid must be understood. The condemnation must be understood of **excessive use** in any case; for even when this is not expressed, it is implied; and, therefore, the instances of wine being drunk without any reproof of the act, may, with as great improbability, imply the moderate use of an intoxicating beverage, as the use of an unintoxicating one."

The editor of the *Congregational Review*, No. 54, in reviewing a book of Mr. Thayer's on "Communion Wine and Bible Temperance," published by the National Temperance Society, in which he attempts to show that there are **two kinds** of wine mentioned in the Bible, one intoxicating and the other not, uses this language:

"We have gone over the arguments he has produced; we have considered his so-called evidence, which has so often done duty in its narrow range; we have pondered the discussions of Lee, Nott, Ritchie, and Duffield before him; what is more, we have gone over the Greek and Hebrew Scriptures carefully for ourselves; have sifted testimony of travelers who know, and those who did not know; have corresponded with missionaries and Jewish Rabbis on this subject; and, if there is any thing in Biblical literature on which we can speak confidently, we have no doubt that Dr. Lawrie is right, and that Rev. Mr. Thayer is wrong. In these views we are thoroughly supported. If we mistake not, the Biblical scholarship of Andover, Princeton, Newton, Chicago, and New Haven, as well as 'Smith's Bible Dictionary,' and ' Kitto's Bible Cyclopædia,' is with us. One of the most learned and devout scholars of this country recently said to us: '**None but a third-rate scholar adopts the view that the Bible describes two kinds of wine.**'"

Gavazzi, the most learned and eloquent Protestant preacher of Italy, says:

"I have indulged in the expression 'unfermented wine' for the sake of argument, * * although, to me, as an Italian, the expression imparts downright nonsense. In fact, wine is only wine by fermentation, and to speak of unfermented wine, is to speak of dry water, of nightly sun, of unelectric lightning."—*Belfast Witness.*

Such a cloud of witnesses, representing the

highest scholarship of America, ought to forever settle this wine question with every Christian man and woman.

The fruit of the vine, **purged of all its leaven**, cleansed of all impurities by nature's own energy, was used by Christ, instead of blood, to symbolize the great fundamental doctrine of his vicarious sufferings and death for his people—the laying down of his own life. It was none other than the Lord of glory, the Lawmaker himself, who so pitied and loved us that he gave himself, and not another, for us; who alone, without the partnership aid of man or angel, endured all the penalty due our sins. It is this great fact we should discern, that it was the Lord's—our Lord's—body, and not the body of a mere human being, that was lacerated and torn, and writhed in pain, every pang of which reached the Divinity that inhabited it: that it was our Lord's blood which the wine symbolized, even the blood of the Everlasting Covenant, every drop of which cost him a pain; and not the blood of a man, the sufferings of a mortal being, in the slightest conceivable degree, that is symbolized by the wine of the Supper.* What had mortal, finite man

* Since the fifth century there have been dialecticians who claim that it is impossible for Divinity to suffer, and that the mere human part of Christ alone endured all the suffering, while the divine part of the Christ, the Lord of glory, suffered not the slightest inconvenience! If this be so, then the wine symbolizes the blood of a **human** being, and not the blood of God, our divine Redeemer, and we

to do in assisting Christ to pay our penalty, much less to have paid it all! Christ surely had no helper in this infinite transaction. The name he ever wishes to be known to us is the "Lord our Righteousness." He himself, unassisted and alone, fulfilled all righteousness for us; and it was none other than the blood of our Divine Redeemer that was the purchase price of our redemption. Paul emphasizes this fact in the strongest language possible, when he declares that God purchased his Church **with his own blood** (Acts xx: 28), **his own sufferings,** and the offering up of himself as a sacrifice for our sins.

THE ONE CUP.

There should be but "one cup" or **measure** of wine upon the table, not several bottles or measures, and this, after thanks, can be poured into as many glasses or cups as is necessary to distribute it readily.

" 'The loaf which we break, is it not Communion in the body of Christ? Because [as there is] one loaf, we the many are one body, for we are all partakers of the one loaf.' Such seems to us most probably the translation of this confessedly difficult passage . . . **There should be only one loaf** and *one vessel of wine*, to symbolize the one body."—*Religious Herald*, September 30, 1880.

While in one aspect it has respect to the one-

find ourselves **idolaters!** But Christ said: 'This is my blood,' it symbolizes my sufferings and death in your own stead.

ness of the local body celebrating, in another it symbolizes the one sacrificial offering of Christ for us. We have heretofore seen that whatever was used to typify—**point forward to**—the salvation provided through the sacrifice and mediation of Christ, is selected to symbolize—**point back to** the same saving truths. By referring to the twenty-ninth of Exodus we find the law of the daily sacrifices. **One** lamb was appointed to be offered for the morning and **one** for the evening sacrifice continually, and in this way: "And with the one lamb a tenth deal of flour mingled with a fourth part of a hin of beaten oil, and a fourth part of **a hin of wine** for **a drink** offering." This offering was a representative of all the atonement sacrifices, because general in its application and continually offered. It was precisely at the hour when the evening atonement sacrifice was to be offered that Christ on the cross cried out with a loud voice, "It is finished;" and yielded up his spirit—**offered up himself.** This cry signified that all the types that pointed to the Great Sacrifice for sin **once** to be offered, were in him fulfilled; in visible attestation of which—"Behold! the veil of the temple was rent in twain from the top to the bottom," and the mercy-seat, now sprinkled with the blood of the everlasting covenant, and thus made accessible to sinful man, was thrown open to the approach of a lost race through the mediation of Jesus Christ.

So, in this ordinance, **wine** instead of blood is employed to symbolize the great saving truth, that a complete satisfaction of the infinite claims of violated law had been made by the **blood**—the precious **blood**—of our Divine Redeemer. Christ said of the wine, this is—represents—the new covenant in my blood which was shed for you. The doctrine, the saving truth symbolized, is **salvation only through the sufferings and death of Christ.** The **one** cup or measure of **wine**, therefore, evidently signifies the **one suffering** Redeemer, not two, a God and a man, but **one victim**, the **one** offering for sin, not **two**, the one human and the one divine; and that but **once** offered for our sins, which forever takes the place of those continual offerings which could not take away sin. Paul explains it thus: "By the which will or covenant, ratified by the blood of Christ, we are sanctified through the offering of the body of Jesus Christ **once.**" Here Paul refers to the daily sacrifices above described: "And every priest standeth daily ministering and offering **oftentimes** the same sacrifices, which can never take away sins; but this man, after he had offered **one sacrifice** for sins forever, sat down on the right hand of God. For by **one offering** he **hath perfected forever** them that are sanctified."

By the light of this teaching we can the better understand Paul's reasoning with the Jewish Christians upon this **one** offering, once for all offered for each one that comes to God by it has had all its divine efficacy applied to his cleansing and sanctification. If such an one should fall away from this, lose the efficacy of this, he must necessarily be lost forever, since there remaineth no more sacrifice for sin. Christ can not again suffer and die as his sacrifice, and no other blood is more availing, and this can not be applied the **second** time, and, therefore, it must be impossible to renew such an one to repentance, to save one who has exhausted the efficacy of the **one** and **only** offering for sin. The reader will see that it is only a **supposition,** doubtless used to emphasize the infinite superiority of the blood of Christ over that of the blood of the bestial sacrifices under the law. Paul leaves his brethren in no doubt as to the value of the blood of Christ, for he declares that, by its application **once,** "**it forever perfected** those sanctified by it," so that there was no necessity for Christ to be offered again, or for any other atoning blood to be applied, since **the efficacy of the blood of Christ can never be lost.** Bless God for this symbol of deepest significance! **One cup—one blood.** Enough for me—for all, and **one application** of it! Enough, since it forever perfects, saves, all who receive its gracious cleansing!

CHAPTER V.

THE PRACTICE OF THE APOSTOLIC CHURCHES.

They observed the ordinances as they were delivered to them.—The Supper was delivered to be observed as a church ordinance.—They had no authority to change any rite in the least respect.—They were commanded to judge all whom they allowed to eat with them, and they can not judge the members of sister churches.—Intercommunion was unknown among the apostolic churches in the earliest ages of Christianity.

THE **invariable practice** of the apostolic churches, and the **specific instructions** delivered them by the apostles, will have a **conclusive** bearing upon the right settlement of the question before us. If we find that these are in accord with the nature and symbolism of the ordinance as developed in the previous chapters, it will certainly be the part of Christian candor to admit that the practice of Intercommunion was unknown among the apostolic churches, and is, therefore, unscriptural. Baptists indorse this as logical reasoning when opposing infant baptism and feet washing; **the practices were unknown to the apostolic churches**, and, therefore, must be unscriptural. To place the subject fully before the reader, I will submit this

AXIOM.

Any practice or theory which vitiates or contravenes what Christ has appointed must be unscriptural, and fraught with evil.

Now there are **two principles** fundamental to the New Testament and Baptist church polity, viz. :

1. **That each church of Christ is an absolutely independent organization, complete in itself, and clothed with executive functions only.**
2. **That to the churches, as such, Christ delivered the ordinances, and constituted** each one responsible for the purity of its administrations.

I mean by fundamental, that a scriptural church can not be constituted without them. An organization may possess every other feature; but not possessing these two, it is not a Christian or evangelical church, and should not be so called. I refer the reader back to Bishop Doggett's position (p. 21). Any theory or practice, therefore, that antagonizes or contravenes either of these principles, must be unscriptural, and of evil tendency.

1. The theory of some that the rights, ordi-

nances. and privileges of one church belong in common to the members of all churches, is both unscriptural and pernicious. For,

(1.) **It is destructive of the polity Christ appointed for his churches, abrogating as it does the principle of Church independency.**

Once establish this theory, and no church could discipline its own members, administer its own government: for the members of surrounding churches could command majorities, and control the business meetings of a local church; dismiss its pastor and elect another; determine his salary; arraign, try, and exclude members; receive and administer her ordinances. The reader who can not see how utterly this theory annihilates the last vestige of church independency is simply unreasonable. The theory must, therefore, be unscriptural and pernicious.

(2.) It is equally manifest that the above theory as utterly ignores and abrogates the second fundamental principle, viz.; the **guardianship** of the ordinances by the local churches. If the members of one church have equal privileges in all churches, it follows, of course, that no church has the **right** to refuse them the exercise of any church privileges—as of voting and coming to its table— and consequently can have **no control of the Supper** any more than of **baptism** or of **its discipline.** The most obnoxious characters, retained as they are in the fellowship of so many sister churches,—drunkards, fornicators, adulterers, revelers, and even those unbaptized, and those excluded from her own fellowship,—can come to the table of any church without let or hinderance on its part. This is the monstrous theory set forth by some who propose to teach Baptists the right observance of the ordinances. It utterly **annihilates** both the **independency** of the churches and their control of, and responsibility for the right observance of the ordinances, and is therefore unscriptural and pernicious, and fraught with evil only.

We are therefore compelled to conclude that no member has a scriptural right to any church act, privilege, or the Supper, in a church of which he is not a member. All standard Baptist authors are agreed in this.

Dr. A. P. Williams, D. D., says:

"He [a regular Baptist] has a right to the Communion in the church of which he has been added; **but nowhere else.** As he had no general right when running at large, so he has no general right now."—*Lord's Supper*, p. 93.

Dr. Arnold, of Madison University, N. Y., says:

"Such a principle is in our judgment incompatible, alike with the **independence** and the **responsibility** of churches—with their independence, because it takes from them the right to judge of the qualifications of those whom they receive to their highest privileges; and with their responsibility, because it deprives them of the power to guard the table of the Lord against the approach of the unworthy."—*Prerequisites to Com.*, p. 62.

Dr. Gardner says

"A member of one Baptist church has no more **right** to claim the privilege of voting in another Baptist church, than has a Campbellite, Methodist, or Presbyterian. The same is equally true of Communion at the Lord's Table, which is a **church act,** and the appointed **token,** not of Christian or denominational, but of the **church fellowship** subsisting between **communicants at the same table.** Hence it follows that a member of one Baptist church has no more right, **as a right,** to claim Communion in another Baptist church, than he has to claim the right of **voting,** for both are equally **church acts and church privileges.** The Lord's Supper being a **church** ordinance, as all admit,* and every church **being required to exercise discipline over all its communicants,** it necessarily follows that **no church can scripturally,** [and it is certain that it can not **unscripturally!**] **extend its communion beyond the limits of its discipline.** And this, in fact, settles the question of church Communion, **and restricts the Lord's Supper to the members of each particular church as such.**"—*Com.*, pp. 18, 19.

Now if this be true—and who will presume to doubt it?—can we for a moment suppose that the apostolic churches habitually contravened those fundamental principles, and the express instructions of the apostles without their remonstrance or reproof? If not, we can not believe that the apostolic churches practiced Intercommunion.

I now propose still further to demonstrate that—

* That Christ has not given the members of one church a right to the table spread in another church, see **Curtis, Paxton, Adkins, Harvey, Pendleton,** and **Hovey.**

THE APOSTOLIC CHURCHES DID NOT PRACTICE INTERCOMMUNION.

My first argument is:

1. There is not a precept for, nor an example of, Intercommunion in the New Testament.

If Baptists really believe that this is a valid argument against infant baptism and feet-washing being **church** ordinances, or even **Christian** duties, they must admit its equal force against Intercommunion. It is inferred to have taken place at Troas, but no one ever has, or can prove, that there was any church at Troas in the first century at the period of Paul's last visit;* and, therefore, the expression "when we come together to break bread," refers to a common repast, and not to the Lord's Supper.

My second argument is:

That the apostolic churches did observe this ordinance, as well as baptism, as the apostles delivered them unto them.

The churches were especially praised for this. (1 Cor. xi: 2; Col. ii: 5.)

In whatever respect any church departed from the traditions of the apostles, for this they were reproved (1 Cor. xi: 17, 22; Rev. ii: 3). But we have no intimation throughout the New Testament that any church had transgressed in **this re-**

---

* This case will be treated in a future chapter.

spect. (See letters to the seven churches.) But I have shown, what is generally admitted, that Christ did appoint the Supper to be observed as a **church** ordinance, and among other things, to symbolize "church relations"—*i, e.*, that all who unite in partaking of it are fellow-members of the same church.

So Prof. Curtis:

"So when our blessed Savior instituted the Supper, as he did upon one of these Paschal occasions, it was, we say, as a **church** ordinance that He **ordained it.**"—*Com.*, p. 87.

He therefore committed it to his churches to be so observed to the end of time. **Therefore, the apostolic churches did observe** the Lord's Supper as a **church** ordinance, and **Intercommunion was unknown among them.** But, strange to say, there are good Baptists who believe that in virtue of the independence of Baptist churches, they can invite members of other churches to participate in their church acts.*

* Is it in violation of the Scriptures for a member in good standing in a church of Christ, to partake of the Lord's Supper, with another church of the same faith and order?

"ANSWER.—The Lord's Supper is strictly a church ordinance; yet, by virtue of the independence of a church, she may, or may not, invite to her Communion, members of sister churches of the same faith and order, who she knows to be in good standing, and we advise the brethren to moderation and forbearance."—*Ans. of The Suwanee Bap. Ass'n, Fla.,* 1881.

Now, it is evident that, if Christ did appoint the Supper to be observed as a **church** ordinance, as these brethren all admit, and as a symbol of **church relations**, then it is certain that he forbade the intercommunion of members of different churches. This must be as evident to a Baptist as that Christ forbade the sprinkling of water on the head for Christian baptism, by appointing the act to symbolize his death, burial, and resurrection.* Let not Baptists use the arguments they do to disprove sprinkling, unless willing to admit their force with reference to the Lord's Supper. For a Baptist Church, then, to grant a right which Christ has withheld, it must be authorized by Christ to modify his appointments—in a word, to **legislate**. But scriptural churches are executive bodies only, and therefore have no authority to enact or abolish rites or ceremonies, or modify, in the least, any ordinance or appointment of Christ. For a church to presume to do

---

* It would not be strange for Protestants and Catholics to believe that a **church** may change Christ's appointments, for the right is incorporated in the very creeds of those sects—

"Each particular church may ordain, change, or abolish rites and ceremonies, so that all things may be done to edification."—Acts xxii ; *Methodist Discipline.*

And they have changed both the subjects and the acts which Christ commanded, for their convenience; but this doctrine has always been, and should be, peculiarly repugnant **to all Baptists.**

this, would be to forfeit its claims to be considered a Church of Christ.

This fact should be indelibly impressed upon the mind and heart of every Baptist—**a church of Christ has no authority to enact laws or to change, in the slightest respect, what Christ has appointed.** It can not be true, therefore, that a church may grant a privilege which Christ has withheld, and much less to so modify an ordinance of his Church as to change its entire character. This would be equivalent to enacting a new law. If a church can enact one law, she can a thousand; if she can **change** one law or ordinance of Christ, she can abolish all his laws, and enact those suited to her tastes, feelings, and convenience. By granting a church the authority to modify the **least** appointment of Christ **in the least,** is to concede all the powers claimed by the Papacy. **A principle can not be divided.**

2. But suppose it is conceded that Christ did authorize his churches to **legislate, in some things,** in some peculiar circumstances, can we for a moment suppose that he authorized them to make changes, or do that which would **contravene** his own appointments, or vitiate the very symbolism of his ordinances, and thus render them **null?** But it has been shown that it inheres in the very nature of a church act or privilege, that its participation is limited to the members of the **one**

church; that it can not be extended beyond the jurisdiction of the church celebrating it; that Christ appointed the Supper to be such an ordinance, as to symbolize **church relations**, and therefore we can not suppose that he has authorized his churches to change his appointment at their pleasure; and therefore we can not suppose that the apostolic churches ever changed this ordinance, or extended the right to eat, any more than the right to vote, beyond the limits of their discipline.

3. My second argument is:

(1) If Christ appointed the eating of the "one loaf" to symbolize **church relations** subsisting between all those who jointly partake of it, then we must conclude that all the apostolic churches, **which observed the ordinances as delivered,** did symbolize the fact that all who ate together were members of the one self-same church, and they did not therefore extend the Supper to the members of sister churches.

(2) But it is admitted by all our authors, who have thoroughly examined the subject, that the symbolism of the "one loaf" is the organic unity of all the participants—*i. e.*, that they are members of the same local church (See Symbolism of the "One Loaf," Chap. III).

(3) We are thus forced to the conclusion that the apostolic churches observed it, among other things, as a symbol of church relations, and **therefore did not practice intercommunion.**

My third argument is:

From the fact that the guardianship of the Supper is strictly enjoined upon the local churches, she is to judge all with whom she is authorized to commune.

The apostolic churches were required to allow no one, whose faith or practice was "**leavened**," to come to their table. They were not only authorized, but commanded, **to judge** all with whom they ate. They were strictly required to **know**, so far as they were able to judge by their observation, or reliable information, that they were "**unleavened**" as respects their Christian faith and conduct.

"But now I have written unto you not to keep company, if any man that is **called a brother** be a fornicator, or covetous, or an idolater, or a railer, or a drunkard, or an extortioner; with such a one, no, **not to eat. For what have I to do to judge them also that are without? do not ye judge them that are within?**"

Each church, then, has not only the right, but is commanded, to **judge** all she permits to eat with her—judge of their **baptism**, and be assured that they have indeed received Christian baptism; judge of their **faith**, and decide if they are heretical; judge of their Christian **conduct**, and decide and declare openly by the act whether they are qualified or disqualified to partake of the Lord's Supper. Is there a church in all this broad land that will grant that a sister church has the right to sit in judgment upon the faith and conduct of her members? Is there a Baptist who will acknowledge the right of a church, of which he is not a member, to sit in judgment upon his faith and Christian walk, and discipline him according to her judgment? Not one, who has any regard for the appointments of Christ, or self-respect. But by **partaking of the Supper with another church, he does symbolically declare that he subjects himself fully to its government and discipline**.

Dr. Harvey, of Hamilton Theological Seminary, in his late work, "The Church," says:

"When a man eats of that 'one bread,' and drinks of that 'one cup,' he, in this act, **professes himself a member of that 'one body,'** in hearty, holy sympathy with its doctrines and life, and **freely and fully subjecting himself to its watch-care and government**."—(1 Cor. x: 17.)

"Hence, in 1 Cor. v: 11, the church is forbidden to eat (in the Lord's Supper, as the context clearly shows) with immoral persons, thus distinctly making the ordinance **a symbol of church fellowship**."—p. 221.

There is not a Baptist in the whole land who could be influenced to go to the table of a sister church if he was required to acknowledge himself a member for the time being, and subjected to its discipline. The church could arraign him before the Conference closed, try and expel him for conduct not fellowshiped by her.

Rev. G. M. Savage, President of the Masonic College, Henderson, Tenn., in a treatise lately put forth on "Communion," thus comments upon 1 Cor. v: 11, showing that Paul, in this letter, was establishing the doctrine that the Supper was a **church** ordinance, and symbolized **church relations** between those communicating:

"Again, there is a man in the Corinth church who was living with his father's wife, whether married to her or not, can not be determined. Paul, in giving orders to the church to exclude him, added: 'But now I have written unto you not to keep company, if any brother be a fornicator, or covetous, or an idolater, or a railer, or a drunkard, or an extortioner, **with such an one, no, not to eat.**'—(1 Cor. v: 11.)

"The first deduction I make from this passage is, that the celebration of the Lord's Supper **can not extend beyond the limits of church discipline.** Suppose it does. Then the offender, without a satisfactory reformation, may go and join some organization, claiming to be a follower of Christ; and, at the very next communion season, when the usual general invitation is given, present himself, and the church thus having to eat with him would violate the command of Christ. The only way to avoid such guilt, such trouble (for cases of this kind sometimes occur), is carefully to restrict the communicants to those within the limits of church discipline. From this deduction it follows, that **communion is a sign of church fellowship;** and, consequently, **intercommunion is unscriptural.**"

Dr. Gardner says:

"If another Baptist church thinks proper to invite him to its communion, then he may partake as an invited **guest** and as a **temporary member.** Such intercommunion [*i. e.*, without membership] among Baptists is not **only without Scripture** warrant, but does **much harm, and no** real good. The practice, therefore, is **unscriptural and of evil tendency;** and, doubtless, will be abandoned by all our churches as soon as they reflect properly upon the subject, and can overcome the force of **habit and prejudice.**"—p. 204.

If the above positions, indorsed by such authorities, are conceded, then it follows—

That the apostolic churches did not practice intercommunion, for it can not be conceded that they, unreproved by the apostles, habitually practiced what was unscriptural and of evil tendency.

My fourth argument is:

Let it be granted that the character and symbolism of the rite itself does not necessarily forbid the church extending it beyond her jurisdiction, nevertheless the special directions of the apostles to the churches, to refuse the Supper to the factious and heretical of that age, made it impossible for intercommunion to be practiced by them.

In the later years of Paul's ministry a multitude of false religious teachers infested the churches he had planted, and taught doctrines that subverted the souls of men, and corrupted the faith of many. The churches of Galatia seem to have been influenced largely by these false teachers, and turned away from the true faith (Gal. iii: 1). Paul called the doctrine of these Judaizing teachers "leaven," and all **persons** who embraced it would be called "leaven;" and he commanded the churches to purge **out** and away all "leaven" from the feast.

Now it is a fact that all these heretical ministers and false teachers were members, in good standing, of sister churches, which means not under discipline, many of whom belonged to the church at Jerusalem; and there were "many thousands" of the members of that church who held this doctrine of the "Concision."

"And certain men, who came down from Judea, taught the brethren, and said: Except ye be circumcised, after the manner of Moses, ye can not be saved."—(Acts xv: 1.)

These were members of the church at Jerusalem, as we learn from the letter of that church to that at Antioch, to which it sent up messengers to learn from the apostles of this church, it being their mother church, if the doctrine taught by these teachers was true.

During the discussion in the church at Jerusalem we read (v. 5):

"But there rose up certain of the sects of the Pharisees which believed [*i. e.*, were members of that church], saying: That it was needful to circumcise them, and to command them to keep the law of Moses."

Paul thus describes these brethren in his letter to the Galatians:

"And because of **false brethren**, unawares brought in, who came privily to spy out our liberty, which we have in Christ Jesus, that they might bring us into bondage, to whom we gave place by subjection, no, not for an hour, that the truth of the gospel might continue with you. But of these, who seemed to be somewhat [of influence in the church], whatsoever they were, it maketh no matter to me. God accepteth no man's person, for they who seemed to be somewhat in conference added nothing to me, but contrariwise," etc.

In the letter sent to the church at Antioch, the pastor, James the apostle, and the church, write thus:

"Forasmuch as we have heard, that certain who went out from us have troubled you with words subverting your souls."—(Acts xv: 24.)

When Paul visited Jerusalem, eight years after, and had recounted his missionary labors and successes to James and the elders, we hear them warning Paul of his imminent personal danger from these zealots of the law in that church:

"Thou seest, brother, **how many thousands of Jews there are who believe**, and they are all zealous of the law."—(Acts xx: 20.)

How did Paul regard these ministers, church members though they were?

"As many as desire to make a **fair show in the flesh**, they constrain you to be circumcised; **only lest they should suffer persecution for the cross of Christ.** And I, brethren, if I yet preach circumcision, why do I yet suffer persecution? Then is the offense of the cross ceased.

"For such are false apostles, deceitful workers, transforming themselves into apostles of Christ. And no marvel; for Satan himself is transformed into an angel of light.

Therefore it is no great thing if his ministers [these Judaizing teachers and brethren] be transformed as ministers of righteousness; whose end shall be according to their works.

"For many walk, of whom I told you before, and now tell you, even weaping, that they are the enemies of the cross of Christ, whose end is destruction."—(Phil. iii: 18.)

What does Paul say of their doctrine?

"I marvel that you are so soon removed from Him who called you into another gospel, which is not another; but there be some who trouble you, and would pervert the gospel of Christ. But though we, or an angel from heaven, preach another gospel unto you than that we have preached unto you, **let him be accursed**. . . I would they were cut off who trouble you* [*i. e.*, excluded from the church of which they were members, which it was not in Paul's power to accomplish, and, I suppose, not in the power of the pastor at Jerusalem; but he could advise it].

"Behold, I Paul, say unto you, that if ye be circumcised Christ shall profit you nothing. . . Christ is become of none effect unto you. . . Ye did run well; who did hinder, that ye should not obey the truth? This persuasion cometh not of him who calleth you. A little **leaven** leaveneth the whole lump."

How did Paul instruct the churches to treat these Judaizing brethren?

* Paul's wish that the false teachers of his day "were cut off"—**excluded**—should satisfy those brethren who call for proof that these false teachers, false apostles, and false **brethren** were church members. If church members, then Baptists, since all the apostolic churches were Baptist churches.—(See Chap. V, Part II.)

"Beware of dogs, beware of evil-workers, beware of the concision."—(Phil. iii: 2.)

"Now, I entreat you, brethren, to watch those who are making **factions** and laying snares contrary to the teachings which you have learned, and **turn away from them;** for such like ones as they are not in subjection to our Anointed Lord, but to their own appetites; and by **kind and complimentary words** they deceive the hearts of the unsuspecting."—(Rom. xvii: 18.)

To the Thessalonians he wrote this:

"Now, we charge you, brethren, in the name of our Lord Jesus Christ, to **withdraw** from every brother who walks disorderly, and not according to the instructions which you received from us. . . But if any one obey not our word by this letter, point him out, and do **not associate** with him, so that he may be put to shame."

These **brethren,** whom Paul called "false brethren," "false apostles," "false teachers," "dogs," "ministers of Satan," and the multitudes of brethren, in many of the churches, corrupted by their teaching, with the many thousands in the church at Jerusalem, were all members of sister churches in good standing—*i. e.*, in their own churches. The question I ask is, Could the church at Corinth, or any other, give the usual intercommunion invitation to all members of sister churches, in good standing in their churches, to come and eat, without openly violating the above instructions of Paul? I have no further argument with any one who will say that it could.

But such like characters, **leavened** with the ungodliness Paul specifies (in 1 Cor. v, and Gal. v), abound in all our churches, and our **general** invitations are therefore unscriptural, and most inconsistent; and, since they are in violation of the apostle's injunctions, and vitiate the ordinance of the Supper, they are of evil tendency.

I will take it for granted that all Christians will admit that **such** characters ought not to paricipate in the Supper. But the question arises, How are all such to be debarred the Supper, and the orderly of other churches admitted? Certainly not by "considering" (?) them all members for the time being, for these are **leaven**, and must be rejected as members; and no church has the right to receive applicants without a rigid examination both as to their faith and practice, for those received must be "unleavened," and no one can be received to membership without the unanimous consent of a church expressed in some way. This is universal Baptist practice, and founded on correct principles. To ascertan who, of a company of brethren present, are leaven as to **faith** or practice, it is evident that an examination before the **church** must be had, that all the members may be able to judge of their soundness, so as to receive the fellowship of all the church. But we have seen that no church has the authority to "judge" others, save its own members. It is quite as evident that no church would allow a sister church to sit in judgment upon her members, and decide by public vote which ones ought to be excluded from the Lord's Supper and the Church, and which ones retained, for those unfit for the Supper are unfit for the Church. Every one can see, that to invite the members of all sister churches, would have been to invite all the above characters to the Supper; but to have singled out these characters, and rejected them, would have been passing a sentence of judgment, by the church, upon members of those **without** its jurisdiction, which is strictly forbidden.

Now it seems that every candid Baptist, who wants no shadow of practice not warranted from the Word of God, must perceive that, by observing the Supper as a church ordinance, as it was delivered, all the above difficulties are solved, and all the Scriptures harmonized, and the admitted symbolism of the Supper preserved. I therefore claim, with the utmost confidence, that I have established it as a fact—

That both the teachings of the apostles, and the practice of the apostolic churches, were opposed to the practice of intercommunion.

THE PRACTICE OF THE EARLIEST AGES.

Touching the practice of the churches in the earliest centuries, I will only add the statement of so careful a scholar as Prof. Curtis:

"The records of church history plainly show that **originally the Lord's Supper was every-where regarded as a church** ordinance [observed by the members of one church only]; for, after centuries of gradual corruption had altered the **forms** of church government in many other respects, and many separate congregations were united under the care of one bishop, and were considered as only **one church**, there was ever one, and but one, altar to each bishoprick, at which alone the elements of the eucharist were consecrated. To set up another altar, or communion table, was considered a violation of unity, or a declaration of church independence. Each bishoprick had the absolute power of receiving to, or excommunicating from, the Lord's table. The whole of this shows how contrary to all the centralizing tendencies, and amid **many corruptions** on all sides, this truth remained, embalmed and preserved, that—

"**THE LORD'S SUPPER WAS A CHURCH ORDINANCE.**"

Dr. E. T. Hiscox, D. D., New York, Author of "Baptist Church Directory," etc., in a letter to the author expressly states his views upon this subject in these words:

"1. I hold the Supper to be in the strictest sense a church ordinance, to be observed **by a Church**, when assembled in one place for that purpose. [It can not then be observed by parts of several.]

"2. **The privileges of a church and its authority and discipline are coextensive.** [Therefore the privileges can not be extended beyond the church's discipline.] No person not a member has any right to any privilege in a church. The Supper is the highest privilege of associated piety, and he who has a right to that can not consistently be denied any other.

I should be heartily glad to see the plan adopted by general consent, of confining the Supper strictly to the **church.**" [*i. e.*, each local church.]

CHAPTER VI.

The inconsistencies, and the evils of Intercommunion among Baptists.

I WILL introduce this chapter with an unquestioned

AXIOM—

Truth is never inconsistent with itself.

When we examine the **workings,** and see the **results** of a given practice to be inconsistent and productive of evil, we may **know** that it is not of, but against the truth, as it is in Jesus; and if we are honest we will be willing to give up the practice, however consecrated as a denominational **usage.** Baptist churches, with all their rights, have no right to be **inconsistent,** nor to favor a practice unwarranted by the word of God, and productive of **evils.** Under the inflexible law of "usage," which compels the pastor to invite "all members of sister churches present" to the Lord's Supper, the following **inconsistencies** and evils, exceedingly prejudicial to our denominational influence and growth, are practiced and fostered.

THE INCONSISTENCIES OF INTERCOMMUNION.

1. Baptist churches, that practice Intercommunion, have practically no Communion of **their own.** They have **church** members, **church** conferences, **church** discipline, but no **church** Communion; and, therefore, no scripturally observed Lord's Supper. The Communion of such churches is **denominational,** and not **church** Communion.

2. Baptist churches that practice Intercommunion have no guardianship over the Lord's Supper, which is divinely enjoined upon them to exercise. They have control of their own members to exclude them from the table if unworthy, but none whatever of others more unworthy who may come. Such churches can exclude heretics, drunkards, revelers, and "every one that walketh disorderly" from their membership, that **they** may not defile the feast; but they **can not** protect the table from **such,** belonging to sister churches, so long as they do not limit it to their own membership.

3. There are Baptist churches that very properly exclude from their own membership all drunkards, theater-goers, dancers, horse-racers, and visitors of the race course, because they can not fellowship such practices as godly walking or becoming a Christian, and, therefore, believe that they are commanded to purge the feast of all such characters as **"leaven;"** not to eat with them,

and, yet, by the invitation to the members of all sister churches, they receive the very same characters to their table every time they spread it.

"ILLUSTRATION 1.—The church at C——— excluded a member for '**general hard drinking** and occasional drunkenness,' because it could not eat with such. He united with the church at W——— the next month, for he was wealthy and family influential; and on the next Communion at C———, he accepted the urgent invitation of 'courtesy,' and sat down by the side of the brother who preferred the charge of drunkenness against him!

"2. The church at M———, excluded two members on the charge of adultery, for marrying contrary to the law of Christ; the one having a living wife, and the other a living husband; they had both been legally divorced, not for the one cause specified, but it was generally believed that they deserted their respective companions that they might obtain an excuse for marrying. Three months after they both united with a church ten miles distant, and now never fail to accept the affectionate invitations of the former church to commune with it!"

4. There are multitudes—I rejoice to say nearly all our Southern churches outside the cities—who will not receive persons immersed by Catholics or Campbellites, Protestants or Mormons, because they do not regard them as baptized at all; yet by their open **denominational** invitations they receive all such—and there are many of them in the churches—to their table, as duly qualified.

"ILLUSTRATION 1.—The church at S——— refused to receive two Campbellites on their baptism. They offered themselves to the Sixth Street church, which received alien immersions, and whose pastor was an immersed Campbellite; were received, and they make it a point to accept the very pressing invitation of the church at L——— to commune with it!

"2. The church at H——— has several members received on their Mormon immersions. Her sister church at P——— repudiates such immersions as null and void, yet these very members never fail to accept her liberal denominational invitations. From **principle** and solemn duty she forbids all such as her **members**, but from **courtesy** invites all such, as **foreigners**, to commune with her!

"3. The church at A———, La., excluded two brethren for unchristian conduct, which disqualified them to eat with it. They joined neighboring churches, and that church, every time it communes and gives the usual invitation, invites those very brethren back to the table from whence it had so recently expelled them!"

Illustrations of the **inconsistencies** of this unscriptural practice could be multiplied, and many will suggest themselves to the reader. But any one of the above is quite enough for all who desire to be altogether right. The thoughtful reader knows that the Scriptures do not sustain a practice that is productive of such **inconsistencies** and destructive of church discipline.

THE EVILS OF INTERCOMMUNION.

Notwithstanding so many—the fast friends of Intercommunion—profess to see no evils attending the practice, still there are both **many** and grave ones, **which I can prove to those who grant that there are evils in open Communion**

with other denominations. I propose to try the practice, in the first place, by the self-same arguments these brethren oppose to unrestricted Communion with other denominations. They will, perhaps, admit the force of their own arguments. Dr. Howell asserts, and he is indorsed by English Baptists, that open Communion involves the entire subversion of the divine constitution of the churches. I assert that:

1. **Intercommunion involves the entire subversion of the divine constitution of a church of Christ.**

The practice is based upon one of two theories; 1. That the members of one church are entitled to all the privileges and rights of all other churches; or, 2. That a church may, if it sees fit, grant members of sister churches the right to commune with it—a right that Christ, for wise purposes, has withheld. The first of these theories entirely subverts the divine constitution of the churches, completely destroying, as it does, their **independency,** which is a fundamental principle, since no church would have the direction of its own government or discipline, or the control of its own ordinances [see last chapter]. The second theory would equally abrogate a fundamental principle of the constitution of a Christian church, which principle is that **a scriptural church is an executive body only,** and can not change **the least thing in the least respect.**

Dr. Howell and Dr. Jeter also urge this argument against open Communion, viz.:

2. That it subverts the discipline of Baptist churches.

I urge the self-same reason against Intercommunion—it utterly subverts the discipline of the churches.

I will adopt the very language of Dr. Jeter in his "Tract" (p. 51), using Intercommunion in the place of open Communion.

"This practice must proceed on one of two theories—either that every person [Baptist] is the sole judge of his qualifications for Communion, or that all the members of the intercommuning churches are entitled to come to the Lord's Table. The first of these theories entirely abrogates church authority and discipline. Suppose a church adopting it should be so inconsistent as to **excommunicate** a refractory member, of what avail would be its action? The excluded member, differing from the church in judgment, and having the sole right to decide on his own qualifications for communing, would come to the Lord's Table, and have a perfect right to come in defiance of the act of excommunication. . . If this theory is correct, church government is a farce and a folly. . . Suppose the other theory be adopted, and none but the members of evangelical [Baptist] churches be invited to the Supper, then what follows? . . One church tolerates dancing among its members, and another does not. A member excluded from a given church for dancing may be consistently received into fellowship by a church tolerating the amusement. Now, could this member of a more lax church be received to the Communion in the church from which he had been expelled, without enfeebling its authority and discipline?

It would be placed in the attitude of admitting to its Communion table members of other churches guilty of offenses for which it would excommunicate its own memmers. So long as [Baptist] churches insist on different conditions of membership, they can not practice open Communion [Intercommunion] without inconsistency, and a partial abandonment of discipline."—*Tract*, pp. 51, 52.

I submit this argumentation for the benefit of all those who **can** see that open Communion with other denominations is destructive of church discipline, since precisely the same result follow; viz., those excluded from one Baptist church can unite with another, because our churches are independent, and can receive into, as well as exclude from their fellowship, whom they please, without consulting another church; and at the next Communion season of the excluding church, come right back to the table from which, as leaven, he had been excluded! This is a matter of constant occurrence among us.

How a candid Baptist can resist, or why he should wish to resist this argument, I can not understand.

If the argument is valid and of conclusive force against open Communion, which all our writers and all Baptists for ages have declared it to be, why is it not equally valid and conclusive against Intercommunion and must be so long as Baptist churches are independent organizations? This is a mountain evil, and its operations disastrous.

3. Intercommunion is productive of bitter strifes, discords, and alienations between Baptist churches.

It has ever been, and still is, continued at the expense of peace, good feeling, and fellowship of the churches. It has in every state of this Union, where the independency of the churches has been rigidly observed, alienated churches, distracted and divided the brethren, and seriously paralyzed the influence of the cause of Christ. During the past year alone, two churches in Middle Tennessee, and two also in West Tennessee, with all the surrounding sister churches that could be drawn in to take sides, have been distracted and alienated, and forced into hostilities, because one church in each case, in the exercise of its scriptural independence, received into its fellowship a worthy brother, unjustly, in its opinion, excluded from the other. In each instance the excluding church is aggrieved, and protests at the act, since it compels it to observe its Supper as a **church** ordinance, or invite the excluded person back to its table, from which it had just expelled him as unworthy; and, rather than do this, the case is carried up to agitate and distract the association. The year before, the peace of three churches in Louisiana was destroyed, and the churches alienated for a like cause—one church having excluded two brethren, and these had joined two neighboring churches, and, with both of these, the excluding church was aggrieved, because, by their act, they enabled those excluded persons to return to its table. Was it not, in fact, Intercommunion, and not independency, that produced these evils? For years past two churches in Talladega county, Alabama, have been alienated, and the association disturbed and divided for the same cause. In every case church independency is surrendered by the churches, and the association acknowledged as having ecclesiastical jurisdiction over them, rather than to give up Intercommunion, at best but an **usage** of the churches. * Like difficulties are occurring all over the land, and have been ever since Intercommunion, stealing in unawares, became the practice of the churches. Who will say it has not been, and is not productive of evils—when, in so many places, the cause has for years been measurably paralyzed by it?

4. To Intercommunion may be traced a majority of all the Councils called to settle difficulties between churches, and of all the disturbances in our district associations, during the last fifty years. The difficulties have in one form or another, grown out of this practice, and would not have been, had our churches observed only **church** communion.

The Concord and the Central Associations of Tennessee were shaken to their centers by the discussion of the question that springs from this practice, viz: the right of one church to receive to membership a member excluded from another, because it **renders abortive the discipline** of the excluding church, since it can not invite the members of all sister churches to commune with it without often inviting her own excluded members. In the above cases the associations were called upon by the aggrieved churches to require the offending churches to exclude those members on pain of expulsion from membership in the Association. The trouble between those churches in Alabama distracted the Association for years, and disturbed the peace of its churches to the serious injury of Baptist influence and progress throughout the bounds of the body. Hundreds of brethren in that one Association can testify that the evils growing out of Intercommunion are not only many but grievous.

But these are not all or the worst evils of the practice.

5. Intercommunion is perceptibly influencing our churches to surrender their independency itself, in order to protect their Communion tables.

This is a portentous evil which is seriously threatening a speedy change in the polity of Baptist churches. During and from the apostolic period, potent influences, both from within and without, have been antagonizing and seeking to contravene the fundamental principle of absolute church independency. Ministers, ambitious of power and authority, have, from the beginning, antagonized it from within, and will to the end of time. The influence of powerful centralized religious organizations from without operate upon our leaders to desire similar power; as the kingly forms of government, of the nations, did upon God's people of old, causing them to desire a king to lead them forth to battle.

Able advocates are now using the pulpit, press, and pen in the plausible advocacy of a "modified independency," which they denominate the Inter**de**pendency of the churches, which means that the churches must consent not only to be bound by the acts of ministerial councils and associations, thus making them virtually appellate Courts, but also consent that the disciplinary decisions of **one** church, however unscriptural or unrighteous shall bind every other church. We are startled almost weekly of late at hearing southern editors and writers deprecating absolute church independency, and indorsing the specious pleas for interdependency, which, to the knowing ones, means nothing less than the total abrogation of local church independency, and the substitution of a centralized form of government, which floats in their conceptions as "the denomination," controlled by conventions, associations, and councils, the last analysis of which is hierarchism.

A Baptist minister was appointed recently by the Pastor's conference of Philadelphia to prepare and read an essay on "Denominational Centralization," which was adopted, I believe. He suggested the use of the word "Unification," as less likely to arouse the watch-dogs of the churches. I will quote a paragraph from that essay, which now lies before me:

"The tendency of our denominational **thinking and working** is towards **centralization;** or, if you will suffer me to substitute a word which is less liable to be perverted, less **likely to arouse prejudice,** and which also more completely expresses the meaning of current movements, I will say that the tendency of present thought and work is towards **unification.**"

We are given to understand that these pleas for inter**dependence and unification** mean nothing less than the utter subversion and abrogation of true church independency, and the substitution of a **centralized denominationalism** in its place, which is but another word for hierarchism—for the clergy invariably govern and control all centralized forms of ecclesiasticism. Now no more influential argument can be brought to bear upon the churches, one they can see and **feel,** than that by adopting the theory of church inter**dependency** they can effectually guard their communion tables from the approach of their own excluded members!

Thus to support a manifestly unscriptural practice the divine constitution of the churches of Christ is coolly proposed to be abrogated! The sad fact is, that in many and large sections of our country especially in the northern states, this interdependency is already so generally and so practically accepted by the churches that, Baptists excluded from one church, however unscripturally and unrighteously, no other church will restore him to his church rights until the excluding church restores and commends him, thus indorsing the theory that the acts of one church binds every other church. Who will deny that a practice, the support of which demands not only the violation of the appointments of Christ but the abrogation of the divine constitution of his churches, is not a fearful evil?

6. Intercommunion opens wide the door to all the ministerial tramps and impostors that pervade the land.

They never fail to accept the invitations to commune, nor does the pastor fail to call upon them to administer one element, and thus introduce them into the fellowship of the church. It is needless to say that the church is disgraced in its own eyes and the eyes of the community when the exposure of these too numerously married impostors takes place. This is a crying evil.

7. It has encouraged tens of thousands of Baptists, on moving away from the churches to which they belong, to go without transferring their membership to a church where they were going, since they can have all church privileges—preaching and communion—without uniting with, and bearing church burdens. If Baptists could have no such privileges without membership, they would keep

their membership with them, if, indeed, Christians and loving the church of their God; and if not it is more than well that they should not be members.

8. All the scandal heaped upon us as "close-communion Baptists," with much of the prejudice produced in the public mind and fostered against us, has come from **Intercommunion.** Had our churches, one and all, limited their communion, as they have their discipline, to their own members, we should no more have heard of "close-communion Baptists" than we now do of "close-membership Baptists," or "close-discipline Baptists." We are suffering all this by our own inconsistency and departure from the primitive practice.

9. We annually lose thousands and tens of thousands of worthy persons who would have united with us, but for what they understand as our unwarranted close-communion. Our practice can never be satisfactorily explained to them as consistent, so long as we practice a partial, and not a general, open communion. Our denominational growth is very materially retarded by our present inconsistent practice of Intercommunion. If we practiced strict church communion, these, and all Christians, could understand the matter at once; and no one would presume to blame us for not inviting members of **other** denominations to our table, when we refuse, from principle, to invite

members of other Baptist churches—our own brethren.

It is freely admitted by reliable brethren, who enjoy the widest outlook over the denomination in America, that for the last few decade of years the general drift has been, and now is, setting towards "open communion"—it is boasted of as a "broadening liberalism." There are numbers in all our churches—and the number is increasing, especially in our fashionable city and wealthy town churches —who are impatient of the present restrictions imposed upon the table; because, not being able to divide a principle, they can not see the consistency of inviting members of **sister** churches, and rejecting those whom we admit to be **evangelical** churches, as though all **evangelical** churches are not **sister**; nor can they divine why Pedobaptist ministers are authorized to preach the gospel and to **immerse**; are invited to occupy our pulpits, and even to serve our churches as supply pastors for a season—all their ministrations recognized as valid, and yet they are debarred from our table. "They **work** for us, and we refuse to allow them to **eat**." The only ground upon which we can successfully meet and counteract the liberalizing influences, which are imperceptibly bearing the Baptists of America into the slough of open communion, is strict local church communion, and the firm and energetic setting forth of our distinctive principles, as taught in God's Word.

Consistency.—If each Baptist church had its own communion, with its own members, independent of all others, then each church could receive into membership, or exclude from membership, whoever it pleased, and no other church would have the shadow of a right to complain, or would be affected by it. On the one hand, the church excluding a person would have no power to prevent his uniting with another church that could fellowship him; and, on the other hand, the church receiving the excluded person would not, in so doing, restore him to the communion from which he had been cast out.

CONCLUSION.

Now let the thoughtful, candid reader, in weighing all these specifications, especially consider the following before rendering his verdict:

1. If Christ originated his churches to be independent bodies, as all admit, would it not be reasonable to conclude that he appointed a symbolism, in some permanent and oft repeated ordinance, that would set this fact forth; that, so long as the churches rightly observed the ordinance, the centralization, interdependence, unification, or consolidation of his churches could never be effected? Have we not seen that the divine symbolism of the Supper does teach the absolute independency of the local churches, *i. e.*, that each church is complete in itself—has sole control of its ordinance—is alone responsible for its right observance, and, since it symbolizes church relations, that none but its own members can unite in its joint participation? I can but think that to preserve his

churches from centralizing tendencies and inevitable hierarchism, was one of the reasons why he guarded this ordinance with such fearful sanctions.

2. Is it not evident that the practice of Intercommunion involves the implied right, on the part of the churches, to change Christ's appointments, thus assuming legislative powers, and even assuming the right to abrogate and abolish Christ's own appointments? For, if Christ did appoint the Supper to be observed by each church alone, and, as such, the eating of one loaf to symbolize that all the participants are fellow-members of the one and self-same church, then to extend this privilege to others than its members, is to contravene Christ's appointment and to make void one of his ordinances by its traditions.

3. Let the thoughtful reader mark this fact, that Intercommunion must be abandoned if church discipline is to be sustained, or the independency of the churches given up and an interdependency adopted, practically at least, by which the acts of one church, however unrighteous, bind every other—thus precluding the possibility of an excluded person joining another church—and councils, associations, and conventions practically made courts of appeal, and the churches inevitably controlled by their decisions. But ministers control these bodies, ever have and ever will, and hence Intercommunion is the legislative parent of the hierarchy. If any one of these inconsistencies or evils is admitted, then

INTERCOMMUNION IS UNSCRIPTURAL.

CHAPTER VII.

FALSE PRETENSIONS EXPOSED.

Pedobaptists, the most rigid of Close Communionists, by their own Statutes, Standards, and Practice.—The Presbyterians are so.—The Methodist's, the Episcopalian's, the Campbellite's Open Communion a sham and fraud.

PEDOBAPTISTS and Campbellites make a great boast of their superior Christian liberality, and appeal to their open communion principles and practice in proof of it; and the world, and most Baptists, even, believe their pretensions are really valid, and Baptists alone unscripturally rigid and "close," and, therefore, illiberal and "bigoted." Now, the real fact is, that all Pedobaptist denominations are, by their very **principles** and their statutes, their standards and their **practice, more strict** than even those Baptist churches who observe the Supper as a strictly **church** ordinance, as set forth in this book—for they never give an open-communion invitation to Baptists and Campbellites, or to each other, except in open violation of those principles and laws which they have, by solemn oath or pledge before God, bound themselves to observe; and, more than this, in their **practice**, they do, and dare not, commune with half the members of their own societies—their baptized infants and children—while Baptist churches do commune with all of their own members.

Presbyterians, by their decisions and the practice of their judicatures, are close communionists.

The most eminent expounders of their ecclesiastical statutes tell us that only those who hold the self-same faith can unite in "Sealing Ordinances," without doing violence to the teachings of God's Word and the Presbyterian standards. Since this will be established in examining the discussions of their Assemblies and Synods, to be submitted, I shall devote no space to its proof here.

According to the Pan-Presbyterian Assembly, that met in Edinburgh, in 1877, there are, in the world, forty-nine different sects of Presbyterians.*

Now, it is a fact, that only two or three of these will commune with each other. Their divergence

---

* The First General Council convened in Edinburgh, July, 1877, at which twenty-two Presbyterian denominations were represented. Twenty-seven other Presbyterian "branches" expressed a desire to be represented.—*Ex. Proceedings Second Pan Council.*

from the old Presbyterian faith consistently separates them from each other's tables, since the Lord's Supper is, among other things, a symbol of a common faith held by all the participants.

In that Assembly a resolution was offered to unite in an open-communion service, as they all belonged to the same great Presbyterian family. A grave and reverent doctor of divinity is reported to have used these sentiments in opposing it:

"*Mr. President:*—Why are we to-day divided into different and distinct churches? Because we **could** not scripturally or consistently commune together. And why could we not commune together? Because, having embraced diverse **faiths**, separating from a common faith, we were compelled to separate from a common communion table. If we can scripturally or consistently commune together on the morrow, we can always do so; and all come together, and live henceforth in **one** church, and dissolve forty-eight of our organizations as **schisms**.

"*Mr. President:*—What would we proclaim by uniting in a common communion of this body? That we the many are all **one church**, and all hold and teach **one faith**, one doctrine; and would we not act a great untruth before the whole world—for the eyes of the whole world are upon us—when we know, and the whole world knows, that we are **forty-nine** distinct churches, holding and teaching **forty-nine different faiths?**"

The resolution was voted down with great emphasis. When the second session of this assembly was held, in New York, in 1880, a similar motion was rejected, and for the same reasons. Thus, by the highest Presbyterian authority in the world, is open communion pronounced unscriptural and **fraudulent**—a solemn acting of a palpable **untruth** before the world!

It is worthy of special note that this last Pan-Presbyterian Council would not admit the Cumberland Presbyterians to a seat, even so unorthodox did it consider them; and how much less could they consistently commune with them!

But this is not all the proof.

In 1845, the two Presbyterian General Assemblies, the Old School and the New School, met, the same week, in Philadelphia. The latter resolved to celebrate the Lord's Supper on the coming Sunday, and adopted a resolution inviting the Old School to unite with them in a joint celebration. A most courteous and fraternal invitation was drawn up and sent to the Old School Assembly by the hands of venerable ministers. How was that invitation received? A leading member of the Old School Assembly took the floor, and, with flushed cheek, and closed teeth, asked:

"Had we a right to expect this public insult from the body meeting in another part of this city, calling itself a "Presbyterian Assembly?" What is it, Mr. President, but an **insult**, openly cast into our teeth before the eyes of the whole world? What does it ask us to do? To unite with them in celebrating the Lord's Supper—a Sealing Ordinance—and thereby, in the presence of God and men, proclaim our **fellowship** for them in respect to their **faith and practice.** Have they not manifestly departed from our standard of **faith**—the Confession? and was it not for this that this body felt in duty bound to excommunicate them for **heresy**? What, then, do they ask us to do by this invitation? They ask us to stultify ourselves, and act a lie in the face of Christendom! Why did we separate? Because we hold different faiths, and, therefore, could not commune together. And now they ask us to say to the world, by our act, that we are **one body**, and hold **one** and the **self-same faith,** which we know, and they know, is not true."

The invitation was unanimously and indignantly rejected as an **insult.**

Is not this practical **close communion?** If two Presbyterian churches, constructively adopting the same Confession of Faith, can not consistently commune together, how can Presbyterians commune with Methodists and Campbellites! If it is accounted **an insult** for one sister Presbyterian church to invite another sister Presbyterian church to commune, how much more an insult must it be considered for Baptists to invite Presbyterians to commune with them? That grave doctor was right, though his language sounds severe. What insult more stinging could be offered a man, than to ask him to forswear himself for your benefit? And this very thing Presbyterians and Methodists do when they ask Baptists to say to the world, by the most solemn acts, that they cordially indorse the faith and the practice of Presbyterians or Methodists, and that they are all one and the **self-same Church of Christ**—"one body!" And this "**great untruth**" the various denominations, when they intercommune, do constantly act before the world and before God; and thereby eat and drink unworthily, profaning the sacred ordinance, and making themselves guilty of the body and blood of the Lord Jesus.

I will further prove my statement from the **Synodical Enactments** of a Synod in a neighboring State:

"The Committee on Bills and Overtures, to whom was referred the question: 'Is it proper that there should be intercommunion between Presbyterians and those denominations (Methodists and Campbellites) who hold **Arminian sentiments?**' presented the following report, **which was adopted:**

"'That, after giving it all the attention which the importance of the subject demands, they are of opinion, that, for Presbyterians to hold communion, in **Sealing Ordinances**, with those who deny the doctrines of Grace through the blood of Christ, etc., is highly prejudicial to the truth as it is in Jesus. Nor can such intercommunion answer any valuable purpose to those who practice it, as **two can not walk together except they be agreed.'"***

Now, not to incur the odium of "close communion," "bigotry," etc., this committee insert the provision, that, if any should greatly desire to commune with them, "after having conversed with them, and received **satisfaction** as to their **soundness in the faith**"—Presbyterian, of course, on the points of doctrine, etc.—"on which their church and ours differ," with **evi-**

* Quoted by Dr. Howell from Records. See *Com.*, ch. 16.

dence of their **piety,** as an act of charity, such can be admitted to **OCCASIONAL** communion!! This means that a Methodist or Campbellite, or Cumberland Presbyterian, can **occasionally**—and then only as an **act of charity**—come to the table of the Presbyterians, **provided** they will submit to an **examination** as to their **personal piety,** and will satisfy the session that they **fully indorse the doctrine of eternal personal election and reprobation**; and that Baptists, even, may **occasionally** come, if, in **addition** to the above doctrines, they avow their cordial delight with the doctrine of **federal holiness** of the seed of believers, **sacramental grace, infant baptism, and affusion.** Can Methodists and Campbellites, and, much less, Baptists, do this even **once?** If once, can they not one thousand times? Can they not unite, and be Presbyterians forever?

I quote one more Enactment from the same source:

"The committee on a former resolution of synod on the subject of Intercommunion, reported. The report **was** adopted, viz.:

"The committee are of opinion that for Presbyterians to hold Communion in sealing ordinances with those who belong to churches holding doctrines contrary to our **standards** [thus sweep out every other denomination under the whole heavens, together with forty-eight of the forty-nine Presbyterian 'churches' that hold contrary to the Old School Presbyterians!] is incompatible with the purity and peace of the church [*i. e.*, the Old School Presbyterian], and highly prejudicial to the truth as it is in Jesus. Nor can such Communions answer any valuable purpose [unless to prejudice the world against the Baptists], etc. In accordance with these views, your committee are of opinion that the practice of inviting to the Communion all who are in good standing in their own churches, **is calculated to do much evil and should not be continued!** while every church session is, however, left at liberty to admit to **occasional** Communion members of other denominations, **after having conversed with them, and received satisfaction of their soundness in the faith and Christian practice."** *

Rev. J. N. McLeod, R. Presbyterian, says:

"On the subject of sacramental communion the principles of the church are that such communion is the most solemn, intimate and perfect fellowship that Christians can enjoy with God and with one another; that when Christians are associated together in a church state, under a definite creed, **communion in the sacraments involves an approbation of that creed;** and that as the church is invested with authority which she is bound to exercise to keep the ordinances pure and entire, **sacramental communion is not extended to those who do not approve the principles of the particular church, or submit themselves to her authority."** * * * "She does not feel at liberty to allow every man to be judge of his own qualifications for sealing ordinances, **or to dispense those ordinances to such as do not assent to her religious principles, or whom she could not submit to her discipline were they found violating their Christian obligations."**

D. Monfort, D. D., a distinguished Presbyterian, in his letters to Dr. Rice on Intercommun-

---

* Synodical Records, 1832, vol. iii, p. 240.—*Howell.*

ion, after suggesting that the members of one denomination, if thrown into a community in which there was no church of their preference, should unite with one there, and so in an **orderly** manner come to the Communion, says:

"And it does seem to me that this would be a much **purer** and vastly more **consistent** charity in all denominations, than that of throwing open the **doors** (to the ordinance of the Lord's Supper) to some **half dozen** different **sects hostile to each other's peculiarities, and irresponsible to each other;** some making a profession of piety and baptism a condition, and others not; some enforcing infant baptism by discipline, as other Christian duties, others not; or really denying the duty [as do the Baptists]. Against this, I do **protest** with heart and voice, and uplifted hands. I deny it to be Christian fellowship at all. It is handling in the sight of God, angels, and men, the sacraments as **emblems of what does not exist.** It was never contemplated by the Westminster divines, and it has nothing, in my opinion, to support it but the **false charity** of the age. . . On a question so plain, I can not suppress my astonishment that there should be a difference of opinion and practice in any denomination."

We take the hand of Dr. Monfort in both of ours in heartiest indorsement of these plain truths. This absurd and hypocritical practice is not only opposed to the plainest teachings of God's word, and subversive of the very design of the ordinance, but in flagrant violation of the fundamental principles and standard authorities of the very denominations that practice it!

Another distinguished Pedobaptist writer (in *Prot. and Herald*) thus expresses himself:

"For the last twenty years or more, I do not recollect having entertained a doubt that the opening of the doors of our Communion to all, of what are denominated 'evangelical' churches is **erroneous,** that it will either **be changed,** or lead to errors of a still more serious nature, containing in itself essentially an **indifference** to **sound religious principle** and **practice,** though slow in its development."

The reader can see from the above **facts** and statements of representative Presbyterian doctors—

1. That the Presbyterians, so far from being able to offer their fellowship through the Lord's Supper to members of other denominations, can not even offer it to the different branches of **their own family** or "church," without a flagrant violation of their Confession, and the decisions of their Pan and General Assemblies and Synods.

2. That when they do practice open Communion with other denominations in token of fellowship and unity, the profession is a **heartless sham,** for the fellowship and the unity do not exist.

3. That Presbyterians can not, except in violation of their confession, which they are solemnly pledged to hold, commune with those whose doctrines they consider unscriptural, or with the unbaptized; and yet they commune with Methodists whose **Arminianism** they regard as subversive of

the whole plan of salvation, and who invite all unbaptized and unregenerate sinners, as such, to their tables as a means of pardon and regeneration!

4. The reader also notices that their most distinguished writers commend the closer Communion of the Baptists to the absurd practice of the day that passes under the name of "open Communion."

5. The reader can also see that according to the ruling of the General Presbyterian Assembly itself, it is a most **bitter insult** for Presbyterians to invite Baptists to commune with them; for it is asking us to fellowship their doctrines and practice, including **federal holiness, infant baptism,** and sacramental grace; which no honest Baptists can do without the renunciation of his own faith and principles. This is so. **A grosser insult could not be offered to a man than to ask him to act a flagrant untruth,** and this open communionists do.

THE EPISCOPALIANS CONSISTENTLY CLOSE.

Here is the decision of the Rt. Rev. Dr. Williams, Bishop of Connecticut, which must satisfy all:

"No member of any religious society outside of the church can receive her holy communion without a violation of a fundamental law of the liturgy; and **no clergyman can administer it to such a person without a** violation of his ordination vows. The Rubric commands that no person shall be admitted to the holy Communion until they have been, or are ready to be, confirmed."

What is true of Episcopal ministers is equally true of Presbyterian and Methodist preachers.

The Methodists are Close Communionists. Any one the least familiar with the Methodist Discipline and Bishop Hedding's work on the administration of it, knows that by the laws laid down there for the observance of the Supper, no Methodist preacher, elder, or bishop, can invite Baptists, Presbyterians, or Campbellites to the Methodist Communion table without openly violating the laws of his society, which, in his ordination, he vowed before God and man to strictly observe. I will give the teachings of the Discipline and the rulings of the Methodist bishop in the same connection, that no one can cavil.

Bishop Hedding, Methodist, in his work on the administration of the Discipline, asks:

"Is it proper for a preacher to give out a general invitation in the congregation to members in good standing in other churches to come to the Lord's Supper?

"No; for the most unworthy persons are apt to think themselves in good standing, etc."

And again:

"There are some communities, called churches, which, from heretical doctrines or immoral practices, have no claim to the privileges of Christians, and ought not to be admitted to the Communion of any Christian people."— pp. 72, 73.

He instructs the preachers to do what the Discipline enjoins, and it enjoins thus:

"But **no person shall** be admitted to the Lord's Supper among us who is guilty of any practice for which we would exclude a member of our church."

"**Inveighing against our doctrines or discipline**" are the capital charges mentioned in section 5; and what Presbyterian, or Baptist, or Campbellite does not oppose both the doctrine and discipline of Methodism as unscriptural and evil? Therefore, how can a Methodist preacher in palpable violation of his Discipline, the explicit instructions of his bishop, his vows to his God and his church, invite Baptists, Presbyterians, or Campbellites to his table? It is, on his part, **a most daring act,** and, on those members of these bodies who accept, the acting of a great untruth, as well as a **profanation of the ordinance.**

Then there is another fact that should make Baptists stand aghast when invited to a Methodist Communion table. It is by them made and administered as one of the sacraments of salvation; and the vilest sinners on the earth—without baptism, of course—are deemed qualified to come to it and partake for the purpose of securing the pardon of their sins and the regeneration of their hearts, and the overwhelming majority of their own members are exhorted to eat the Supper in order to obtain pardon and regeneration! I quote the language of Wesley himself:

UNSCRIPTURAL AND INCONSISTENT. 337

"To come to the Supper of the Lord, no fitness is required at the time of communicating, but a sense of our state of utter sinfulness and helplessness. **Every one who knows he is fit for** hell being just fit to come to Christ in this as well as all other ways of his appointment. . . In latter times many [*i. e.*, Baptists] have affirmed that the Lord's Supper is not a **converting ordinance** . . The falsehood of this objection appears both from Scripture precept and example."—*Wesleyanna*, pp. 283, 284.

Adam Clark, in his notes on 1 Cor. xi: says:

"Every minister of Christ **is bound** to administer it to **every man who is seeking the salvation of his soul,** as well as to believers."

Who can doubt that all those who eat with this intent, "**eat and drink unworthily,**" failing to discern the Lord's body, mistaking altogether as they do the true **design** of the ordinance? But what is truly amazing is the fact that most Campbellite ministers, though holding and teaching that no one can be a Christian unless immersed for the remission of sins, and that none can be church members or scripturally entitled to partake of the Lord's Supper unless immersed, do constantly invite Pedobaptists as well as Baptists, whom they declare unbaptized and unsaved, to come to their tables, and commune with them in token of church and Christian fellowship!

This was Mr. A. Campbell's opinion of their course—the man who originated the religious system justly called Campbellism—and we think it should be respected, unless they are willing to be regarded as supremely **hypocritical,** believing and teaching one thing and practicing the opposite!

"But I object to making it a rule in **any** case, to receive unimmersed persons to church ordinances; 1. Because it is nowhere commanded; 2. Because it is nowhere precedented in the New Testament; 3. Because it necessarily **corrupts** the simplicity and uniformity of **the whole genius of the New Testament;** 4. Because it not only deranges the order of the kingdom, but **makes void** one of the most important institutions given to man. It necessarily makes immersion of **non-effect;** 5. Because in making a canon to dispense with a divine institution of momentary import, they, who do so assume the very same dispensing power which issued in that tremendous apostasy which we, and all Christians, are laboring to destroy."— *Ch. Bapt.,* vol. vi.

I have not space to continue this exposure of the unscripturalness and **supreme absurdity** of open Communion. If Baptists, and all friends of truth and consistency, will but take these facts and arguments, and **boldly** and **vigorously** impress them upon the people, the days of open Communion would speedily be numbered. The most effective arms, the most powerful and destructive cannon, can effect nothing without brave and skilled men to use them, and this is what the Baptist cause now so greatly needs—**more brave and faithful men to use the weapons drawn from the divine armory upon bold, arro-**

gant error, that is rampant all around us, and only a few daring to strike a blow!

The humblest member, even a sister whom love of Christ and his truth makes bold, could reply when reproached, because her church does not invite all denominations to its table.

We believe, in common with your own denomination, that the Lord's Supper is a **church** ordinance, and, therefore, none but its own members have a right to partake together, as they alone have the right to vote in the same church.

But were this **not** the case, **we Baptists do not wish to insult you** by inviting you to **our** table, thus asking you to indorse, before God and man, our faith and order as scriptural, and thereby repudiating your own.

Nor can I understand, if your feelings are as kind towards us as you profess, why **you** should wish **to insult us** by inviting us to **your** tables **to renounce our own doctrine** and **principles** as false, and openly **proclaim our indorsement of yours.**

I have too much respect for you to make you such an insulting proposition, and too much sincerity and **respect** for truth to act the hypocrite to gain your favor.

CHAPTER VII.

OBJECTIONS TO CHURCH COMMUNION REVIEWED.

1. "*Paul and his eight companions, belonging to different churches, communed with the church at Troas.*" 2. *A local church has the* RIGHT *to invite members of other churches to her table.* 3. *It tends to destroy fellowship between the churches, and creates an extreme independency.*

THE only Scripture adduced to justify the intercommunion of the members of different churches, is the claimed example of Paul and his eight attendants communing with the church at Troas (Acts xx: 7). This is a most serviceable passage, being used by theorists to sustain diverse and **opposite** practices.

1. It was first forced into service against the Sabbatarians, or Seven-Day Christians, as a proof that the apostles and the churches they planted observed the first day of the week as the Christian Sabbath, which day they spent in preaching, **and** hearing the Word, and observing the Supper.

But this coming together at Troas was at the **close** of the day, and not in the morning.

(1) It is the main reliance of the advocates of **weekly communion.** The church at Troas communed weekly, and, therefore, all churches should now.

(2) It is the chief and only authority of the advocates of **Intercommunion.** They argue: Paul and his eight companions, belonging to different churches, communed with the church at Troas, and, therefore, it is right, and the duty of the members of different churches, to intercommune now.

(3) It is the only passage quoted in support of **social communion.** They argue that, since there was no church at Troas in the first century—which they prove—Paul and his brethren celebrated the Supper **socially,** without the presence of a church, and so may Christians now.

It is evident that these opposite theories can not be sustained by this one passage; and I confidently affirm that they are all equally unsupported by this passage, since they rest upon one or both of these two bald assumptions, viz.:

1. **That there was a church at Troas.**
2. **That the Lord's Supper was celebrated by Paul and his traveling companions.**

I am satisfied, after a patient examination, that—

There was no church at Troas in the lifetime of Paul—

Because, 1. There is no intimation in the New

Testament that Paul, or any apostle, or missionary, ever preached a sermon in Troas before Paul's last visit. If they did visit and preach there, 2. There is no evidence a church was ever organized or existed there; nor, 3, Mention of any brother residing there, or belonging to it; while the proof, both from the New Testament and the earliest ecclesiastical writers, seems conclusive that there was no church there in the first century, at least. Those who contend for a church believe that it was gathered by Paul in one of his missionary tours, which the Holy Spirit did not prompt Luke to record; and a tour of which Luke either never heard, or regarded too unimportant to describe! I have no theory or exegetical difficulty that requires what the Holy Spirit has not revealed. Luke nowhere intimates that Paul ever visited Troas but **twice**.

1. In his first missionary journey (Acts 13 and 14) he did not go west so far as Troas.

2. In his second, he visited Troas with the intent to preach, but the Holy Spirit forbade him to preach in "Asia," of which Mysia was a province, and Troas its chief city. Here, in his perplexity, being straitly shut up, the Lord opened a door for him into Macedonia; and, leaving Troas, and the friends he had made there, he entered that door **immediately**, and departed to Philippi, and there planted a church. For this account, see Acts xvi: 6–12.

3. The next intimation we have of Paul's visit to

Troas is in Acts xx: 3-6, at which visit no one claims that he, or his fellow ministers, organized a church.

4. But it is confidently asserted and contended that Paul made a missionary journey intermediate between these two, during which he visited Troas, and remained some time, and planted a prosperous church. This is purely **inferential**. If the Acts of the Apostles is the Word of God, I do not presume to add to it; nor am I prepared to charge Luke—who, if the Acts are Holy Scriptures, wrote under the infallible guidance of the Holy Spirit—with gross unfaithfulness. All that is important and useful for us to know, we must believe that the Spirit indited. The discussion of this question, and the important questions connected with it, show that it is more **important** for us to know that there was, or was not, a church at Troas, than at any other place, or all other places, in proconsular Asia.

It is mainly upon Paul's reference to a door being once opened to him, when he was in Troas (2 Cor. ii: 12), that this whole theory of an intermediate unrecorded missionary visit is based, and the intimation contained in Acts xx: 2. But this passage is quite fatal to a missionary tour in Asia, since it expressly states that he departed to go into **Macedonia**, and spent his time going over "those parts." My space does not allow me a further suggestion concerning that opened door, and into what place it opened, than the one above. It is enough for me that the Scriptures are silent as the grave touching a church, or a disciple, being at Troas, and I leave speculations to speculators. Some thirty-eight years after this, Christ commanded John, then on Patmos, to write letters to **the seven** churches that were in Asia, which clearly implies that there were seven there, and only seven in Asia at that time. From the earliest ecclesiastical writers we learn that, though there had been others, as the one at Colosse and at Hierapolis, they had been destroyed by earthquakes—fourteen cities having been destroyed in fourteen successive years in the reign of Nero (see App. B); and that there was not a church at Troas in the first century. I have no theory that requires me to **infer** a church at that place against the teachings of both the Word of God and ecclesiastical history.

The second assumption of a communion service held at Paul's last visit (Acts xx) is equally destitute of support from the narrative, and in violation of Paul's own teachings, as set forth in this book. (See p. 111, Chap. III.)

Let us, without prejudice, examine Luke's narrative—using the Bible Union version:

"And there accompanied him unto Asia, Sopater, son of Pyrrhus, a Berean; and of the Thessalonians, Aristarchus and Secundus; and Gaius of Derbe, and Timothy; and of Asia, Tychicus and Trophimus. These, having gone forward, were waiting for us [Paul and Luke] at

UNSCRIPTURAL AND INCONSISTENT. 345

Troas. But we [Paul and Luke] sailed forth from Philippi after the days of unleavened bread, and came to **them** [the above-named brethren] to Troas in five days; where we [Paul and his company] abode seven days. And on the first day of the week, **we** [Paul and all his companions], having come together to break bread, Paul discoursed to **them** [the self-same persons—the last "them" refers to Paul's companions], being about to depart on the morrow, and continued his discourse until midnight. * * And he [Paul] having come up, and had broken the bread, and eaten, he talked a long while, even till break of day, and so he departed."—(Acts xx: 4-12).

There is not the slightest intimation that Paul's disciples at Troas met Paul on his arrival, or brethren received him into their houses; not the slightest, that on that Saturday or Sunday night, when Paul and his companions gathered for their last meal and discourse from Paul, that any person, save that company of fellow-travelers, came together. The "we" of the seventh verse relates to the same persons that the "we" of the sixth verse does; and the "them" of the seventh verse refers to the self-same persons that the "them" of the sixth verse does. It was with these fellow-travelers that Paul and Luke assembled, and it was specifically for the instruction of these young ministers, as they were, that he discoursed, expounded the Scriptures and reasoned with them through that long night. There is not the least intimation that a single soul was present in that **third** story—the most unlikely place for a public meeting—save

Paul and his fellow-travelers, for the "we" of the eighth verse logically embraces no more than Paul and his companions. "But a young man, Eutychus, was in the window." Certainly; and it is singular that he is not claimed as one of the members of the church at Troas, as Carpus is for its pastor. It is far more probable that Carpus was the innkeeper, with whom these travelers lodged; and Eutychus the servant appointed to wait upon them. Heinricks and Rosenmüller hold that it was a common name, belonging to servants and slaves. Paul, it seems, did not seek an introduction to him after his resuscitation.

Another item that supports the above, is the verb translated, in the seventh and ninth verses, "to preach," which is nowhere else, in the New Testament, so translated, but "to reason with" (Acts xvii: 2; xviii: 4, 19; xxiv: 12); and "to dispute" (Mark ix: 34; Acts xvii: 17; xix: 8, 9; xxiv: 12; Jude 9); and it is significant that, later on, Luke says, "he **talked** on, even until daybreak."

It is my conviction if the Holy Spirit designed to use an expression that would not have misled, he would have employed the same one used in every other place where **arton**, bread, is the direct object of **klan**—to break; in every such case we find (in the Greek), the definite article before **arton**, "**ton arton**"—the loaf—a particular kind of bread, and not simply **arton**, a loaf, or bread, the bread of a common meal. It seems reasonable that a distinction should be made between a common supper or meal and the Lord's Supper, else there will be uncertainty in the minds of even scholars, as there is touching Acts ii: 42 and 46. With those who recognize no distinguishing phrase, I think the distinction is marked in those passages. In v. 42 we read, "and in the breaking of **the** loaf," as artos should be rendered with the definite article—**"tee klasei ton arton."** Here we have **the** before bread—where the Lord's Supper is undoubtedly meant. In v. 46, "And they continuing daily with one accord in the temple, and **breaking bread** from house to house, did eat their meat with gladness," etc. Here where a common meal is referred to, **arton,** bread, is without the definite article.

In Acts xx: 11, where Paul undoubtedly took a common meal, we have **"klasas arton,"** without the definite article.

In 1 Cor. x: 16, we have **"ton arton hon kloomen," "the** loaf which we break," the definite article before bread. In the next verse we find **"ex tou henos artou,"** we all partake of **the** one **loaf**—the definite article before bread, and the supper is undoubtedly referred to.

In the next chapter, v. 26, Paul, referring to the bread of the Lord's Supper, says: "As often as ye eat this bread (in the Greek) **"ton arton toutou,"** this **the** loaf, etc. In v. 27: "Whosoever shall eat **this** bread," "**ton arton—the** loaf." In the next verse, "And so let a man eat of **that** bread," "ex **tou** artou," "of **the** loaf." This, to my mind, means something, *i. e.*, the designation of a particular kind of bread used for a specific purpose—the Lord's Supper. Had the inditing Spirit used the phrase, klasai **ton** arton, in verse 7, and **klasas arton,** as he did in verse 11, every mind would have been satisfied, but he used the self-same phrase, klasai arton, that he uses in Acts ii: 4, and xx: 11, where a common meal is designated. I feel justified in believing that a common meal—Alford suggests a **love feast,** which was a full meal—is intended to be designated in verse 7, as well as in 11. Can any one conceive why the same phrase should be used in these two verses of the same chapter, if one is the Lord's Supper and the other a common meal? From the above induction of facts, I conclude that **klan** (infinitive), **arton** is never used to designate the Lord's Supper, but **klan ton arton** is always used when **arton** is the **direct** object of **klan,** where the Supper is undoubtedly alluded to.

There is no proof that there was a church at Troas. There is no proof that Paul and his companions observed the Lord's Supper at Troas.

2. It is objected that should the Supper be observed as a **church** ordinance, a majority of our preachers could not commune with the churches

they preach to, since they serve three, four, and sometimes five.

But this comes of our departure from apostolic appointment and practice. In their day there was then a pastor to **every** church, and elders in them all, and these belonged to the churches they served, and it **should** be so **now,** and then this objection would fall. But shall we bend the scriptures to our bad practice, or conform our practice to the scriptures? Is there a minister pastor of four churches who claims that he has a right to participate in any **other church** privilege, in churches of which he is **not** a member, save this? He, as their official servant, administers their baptisms, but does he claim the right to vote on the reception of candidates for baptism? He, as **pastor,** is the moderator of their business meetings, and can preside and put motions, but can he vacate his chair and vote with these churches, or as moderator, in case of a tie? Certainly he can not. He **knows,** if he knows enough to be a pastor, that he can not enjoy church rights and privileges save in the church of which he is a member, and no church has the authority to give him the right to do it.

3. Another objection—and I expect lies at the bottom of all the objections and opposition to **church** communion—

"**It is a new thing, and contrary to our denominational usage.**"

This is singular language in the lips of Baptists who oppose infant baptism and affusion! Tens of thousands of Pedobaptists would renounce affusion and infant baptism to-day were it not for the argument from "usage of the church." The teachers who mislead and cause them to err, reason thus with them: "Can you believe that infant baptism is unscriptural and injurious, when the church (this means Catholic as well as Protestant), for so many ages has practiced it, and so many thousands of their most learned and pious ministers have taught and administered it? Will you say that the church has, all these ages, been in deadly hostility to God's word, and these, the most learned ministers of earth, all ignorant of God's word, and the few illiterate Baptists alone right?" It is a powerful argument with the multitude. And then their ministers, in renouncing either error, would have to humiliate themselves before the people and confess that, for years, they had taught and practiced contrary to the teachings of God's word. The cross is fearful. Yet there are Baptist ministers who are using this self-same argument (?) with their own brethren to prejudice them against **examining the scriptures** to see if these things are so!

But I have shown that church communion is not a **new,** but an **old,** practice, from which our churches have been turned aside in these latter days.

No true man can feel that it is a shame to him to confess and turn from an error, when he is satisfied it is an error, though he may have advocated it for years, but it is the mark of a conscientious, Christian man, who loves the truth.

The objection implies that our churches have been and are **infallible,** which is not the exact truth. Paul was compelled to correct the erroneous faith and practices of the churches in his day. John, in addressing all the churches in Asia, found something to correct in the practice of the very best of them, and of these were symbols of the churches of Christ in seven different ages of this dispensation. Then it is unscriptural to believe that the churches of Christ have ever been infallible. But it is well known that within this century our fathers were wont to close their District Associations with the observance of the Lord's Supper; the Association appointing the ministers and deacons to administer it. Nor was this practice discontinued without sharp discussion and powerful opposition. The present practice of **denominational** communion retained by some associations and conventions is a relic of **associational** communion. Convinced that it is a church ordinance, it is virtually contravened by indirection. The church appoints a communion to be observed at the close of the session, and then invites all the members of the Association or Convention, with all the visiting Baptists present, to commune with her! The West Tennessee Convention, a quarter of a century ago, consented to this, and the Alabama State Convention still is wont to observe such communions, or was until recently, and how many Associations we know not. There are several other unscriptural practices that our churches were **generally** guilty of thirty years ago, as sending their licentiates to the Association to be ordained by a council appointed by the Association, or a standing presbytery, on the reception of alien immersions as valid baptism, and several other quite as unscriptural, and evil practices. We have lived to see many of these abandoned, and many who read this book years hence will wonder what could have influenced our churches to practice Intercommunion.

I conclude my defense with the latest expression received from Dr. Gardner on this subject:

"RUSSELLVILLE, KY., Feb. 18, 1881.
"REV. J. R. GRAVES, LL. D.,

"*My Dear Brother:*—In compliance with your request, I would state that I have long regarded **Intercommunion** among Baptists at the Lord's Table as **unscriptural, and of evil tendency.** It does no good, but **much harm,** and ought to be abandoned in all our churches. There is neither precept nor example for it in the New Testament; it is a modified form of **loose** Communion wholly **at war** with church discipline. The **limits** of church discipline are the scriptural **limits** of Communion at the Lord's Table.

"I take this ground in my Book on **'Church Communion,'** and in the **new and revised edition** it will be more clearly and fully presented.

"Yours, fraternally,
"W. W. GARDNER."

A late editorial expression of the "*Central Baptist,*" St. Louis, Mo., gives me additional encouragement to expect that the force of habit and prejudice touching this question will, ere long, give way. The editor, Dr. Ferguson, says:

> "A local, ceremonial institution must of necessity be in the hands of a definite class. Jesus committed the Supper either to local churches or to the ministry. If to the latter, the priest is right in carrying the bread and wine from house to house, and in giving to, or witholding from, whom he pleases. If to the former, then Communion is **by the nature of the law restricted to the local church, and can not be carried beyond unless there is positive warrant.** If any kind of Communion is to have a title to denote that it is exceptional or peculiar, that kind is 'loose' Communion. **Church** Communion, we repeat, is the indisputable law of the New Testament on the subject. Any invitation must be upon the wholly **gratuitous supposition of an implied, not expressed, liberty; and it does not then follow that the minister has any more right to invite than the humblest member.**"

CLOSING WORDS TO MY BRETHREN.

Some of you have, and ere long many will cordially embrace the views herein set forth before possibly your pastor, or a majority of the church of which you are members; and, in your zeal, you may be tempted to **force** your church to change its long standing practice. I wish to caution you against rashness, and to advise patience and forbearance. All permanent reformations move **slowly** but **surely.** If you **faithfully,** but **kindly,** bear your testimony against Intercommunion at home and abroad as a good witness for Christ, you will not be partakers of her fault. Do you not commune with your church, although she retains in her fellowship, contrary to the explicit teachings of God's word, the hard drinker and the drunkard, the covetous and the dancer, with whom Paul commands it "not to eat?" (1 Cor. v). Labor, my brethren, in all kindness to convert your brethren, by presenting the truth to their understanding, and praying for them. In this way you will soon see, and rejoice in its triumph over deep-rooted habit and prejudice. It was in this way you secured the abandonment of pulpit affiliations and "union meetings," and the rejection of "alien immersions," without the division of one church. Remain with your church, and thus labor and pray for another triumph. Very soon your brethren of sister churches will become so well informed that they will not offend you by accepting the invitation of your church, should it have so little regard for **your** feelings as to continue to invite them.

To the pastors and **deacons** of our churches who generally control these invitations without consulting the church, as such, let me in all kindness say: Granting that you believe it is **not wrong** to give Intercommunion invitations; if intelligent in our church polity, you know that you withhold no **right** from brethren of other churches by declining to invite them to the Supper of your church; because the Scriptures give them no right, and you also know it is wrong and sinful for you to **knowingly** do any thing that you may omit without blame, that will offend the least one of your brethren for whom Christ died. To do this because you have the power to do it, and when you know it will offend, you should remember Christ's words. Dear brethren, be considerate and kindly affectioned towards your brethren, and decide if you should not have more regard for the rights and the feelings of the brethren and sisters, and the peace and fellowship of your own church, than even for the feelings and questionable rights of strangers or members of other churches? Ought not brotherly kindness and respect for the rights and feelings of our brethren to begin at home? It certainly is not the spirit of the meek and loving Christ; because you can influence a majority in the church to sustain you to be willing to trample upon and wound the feelings of a minority of your brethren, and destroy their peace of mind and enjoyment of this sacred feast, by doing what you can leave undone without the least blame or sin.

May the all-loving Jesus, to whom the least of his flock is more precious than his own blood, influence us all to do those things most pleasing in his sight, and thus to dwell and to work together in unity

"TILL HE COMES."

APPENDIX A.

PULPIT RECOGNITION.

Dr. John A. Broadus, Professor of Theology in the Southern Baptist Theological Seminary, Louisville, Ky., delivered the following statements to his class, upon pulpit affiliation, which have been kindly furnished us by Elder S. M. Province, of Brownsville, Tenn., an old student:

"Illustrating the adherence to principle which the apostle Paul showed in refusing to circumcise Titus, while in the case of Timothy, where no principle was involved, he allowed the rite to be performed, Dr. Broadus said: 'A Baptist preacher may invite a Pedobaptist to preach for him, so long as **it is understood** that he does not thereby indorse the latter's ordination—*i. e.*, when no principle is involved.' I quote from my notes. In reply to the question of a student, the professor said subsanttially: 'If I were to invite a Pedobaptist to preach in **my** pulpit, and should afterward learn that he construed the invitation into a recognition of his claim to be a properly ordained minister of a New Testament church, I should not only not repeat the invitation, but I would take pains to tell him **why** I did not.' I quote from memory, but this is what he said in substance."

It must be presumed that the answers of Dr.

Stuart Robinson (O. S. P.) Louisville, Ky., and Dr. Charles Hodge, Princeton, N. J., forever determine this matter. Says Dr. Robinson:

"The idea of inviting one to preach in the character of a **layman seems to me a paradox.**"

Dr. Hodge says:

"When one minister asks another to exchange pulpits with him, **such invitation is, in fact, and is universally regarded, as an acknowledgment of the scriptural ordination of the man receiving the invitation.** . . .

"No man, who believes himself to be a minister, can rightfully, expressly, or by implication, deny the validity of his ordination; and, therefore, if invited to lecture or speak in the character of a layman, he must decline."

The *Texas Christian Advocate*, on being specially asked, answers thus:

"When one gentleman invites another to his house, receives him into his parlor, and seats him at his table, **he** recognizes him on terms of perfect **social equality.** So, when one Christian minister invites another to occupy his pulpit, **all who witness the courtesy thus extended regard it as a proclamation of perfect ministerial equality.** Only Christian ministers are invited to the pulpit. If, however, the one who gives the invitation is a Jesuit, and a hypocrite, who wishes to make a show of liberality he does not feel, and believe the brother he thus **pretends** to honor as a minister is only 'an unbaptized religious teacher, without church membership or ecclesiastical authority of any sort,' he should be treated as all hypocrites and pretenders deserve to be treated."

The *Texas Presbyterian* indorses the same.

Rev. A. M. Poindexter, D. D., the most intellectual and logical man old Virginia ever produced, wrote this:

"Now, if the bodies, to which reference has been made, are not scriptural churches, their ministers can not be scripturally ordained ministers. The ordination can have no force or validity beyond that which is imparted by the body whose act it is; and, if that body is not a scriptural church, of course its ordination can not confer scriptural authority.

"In view of these considerations, it follows that scriptural churches should not recognize, in any way, these unscriptural organizations as scriptural—either by word or action, as to the bodies themselves, or their officers. The churches of Christ are to oppose all departures from the faith as delivered in the New Testament. They may not fraternize with, or connive at heresy. And the obligation thus resting on scriptural churches bears also upon every member and every officer of those churches. The whole body, and each individual, are called upon, by fidelity to Christ and the truth, to make a solemn, consistent and unceasing protest against fundamental error, whether relating to doctrine or to practice; and, in the case reviewed, both doctrine and practice are involved. No Baptist can, rightly or consistently, recognize a Pedobaptist church as a scriptural church, or a Pedobaptist minister as a scriptural minister."

APPENDIX B.

NO CHURCH AT TROAS IN THE FIRST CENTURY.

"There is no evidence that he [Paul], or any other apostle, ever gathered a church there. On the contrary, there is **ample testimony** that, during the first century, no church is recognized as existing in this emporium, the seat of the ancient and classical Troy. The references in the New Testament to the labors of Paul evidently intimate that, when at Troas, he was only as at a point of transit, or brief sojourn for occasional preaching, while on his way to places where he had a destined mission. Thus, for example, in 2 Cor. ii: 12, Paul says: 'When I came to Troas to preach Christ's gospel, and a door was opened unto me of the Lord, I had no rest in my spirit, because I found not Titus my brother; but taking my leave of them, I went from thence to Macedonia.' [The reader can see why he did not preach at Troas, and how a door was opened unto him into Macedonia, by reading Acts xvi, and Conybeare and Howson, vol. 2, chap. xvi.] However inviting this field of labor may have been, Paul had a definite purpose in going onward to another place.

No proof exists that a church was formed at Troas during any part of the Apostolic Period, or during the first century. All the churches in that part of Asia Minor, then called Asia, are expressly named in the earlier church writers, or in the New Testament; and the seven churches to which the seven epistles in the Apocalypse were addressed, were all, we have reason to believe, which existed in that province when the Apocalypse was written (A. D. 68 or 96)." * * *

"We have here also the explanation why John was divinely directed to address his epistles only to those seven churches named in the Apocalypse, and to none besides; and it is from the simple fact, that no other churches were then existing in the province known as 'Asia.' The other five churches elsewhere mentioned in the Scriptures, or in ancient history, existed in this same province, but not at the time of the writing of the Apocalypse, when there were only 'the seven churches in Asia.' But Troas, which was the most northern bulwark or out post of this Asia, had no church, either before or after the date of John's epistle."—*From the Christian Review*, vol. 18, 1853.

An able advocate of a church at Troas urges the fact that it is known that there were other churches in Asia, though not mentioned by John, as the church at Colosse, Hierapolis, Miletus, Magnesia, and Tralles. The writer in the *Review* quotes Strobo and Eusebius in proof that during the reign of Nero, and before the visit of Paul, fourteen cities in proconsular Asia were destroyed by earthquakes in as many years, and that Colosse, Hierapolis, and Laodicea were among them, but Laodicea alone was rebuilt before John wrote the apocalypse; and that, according to Ignatius, there were no churches organized at Tralles, Magnesia, and Miletus till a few years after. The evidence that there were seven, and only seven, churches existing in Asia when John wrote, is abridged and critically stated by Dr. Cummings, of London, in the lectures on the Seven Churches in Asia. This writer concludes:

"But even allowing the later period [96–100] for the date of John's recognition of the Asiatic churches, it will be perceived that all the essentially important facts go to show, that both at the date of John's epistles, as well as in the preceding and following parts of the first century, **there were no other churches in Asia but the seven which are addressed in John's epistle**, and the other five authentically mentioned in sacred and contemporaneous history. We could carry this detail of specific evidence into many additional particulars, showing that there could have been no organized and existing church at Troas during the period of the apostolic labors, when we have such conclusive evidence of what churches did exist, or did not exist, in that circle of Asiatic cities, of which Troas was the northern key and outpost.

"The extent to which we have carried this investigation as to 'the churches in Asia,' is justified, not only by the intrinsic interest of the inquiry, but especially as furnishing decisive proof that there never was any regularly formed church in Troas; and, of course, the gathering of brethren there * * was only occasioned by the presence of Paul, while tarrying to meet the disciples, who then came together from many contiguous quarters."

APPENDIX C.

THE BEAUTIES OF OPEN COMMUNION.

In all those communities and sections of the South, where Baptists are in a helpless and unaggressive state, Presbyterians and Methodists are generally engaged in the most deadly hostilities, and there is no open communion among them, and can but indicate the character of the warfare that has been waged in East and West Tennessee in my day.

Dr. Ross, formerly of Knoxville, Tennessee (now of Huntsville, Alabama), who has for forty years been regarded as the brightest star in the intellectual firmament of Presbyterianism in Tennessee, and whom his people **love,** and whose views touching Methodism they fully indorse, in the second volume of the "Calvinistic Magazine," which he edited before the war, and wrote a series of articles against the unscripturalness of Methodist doctrine and its dangers as a system and church to true religion and to the state! From No. 8 I give this sample extract:

"**Methodism in this aspect (its worldly policy) as well as others, is a dangerous power to the piety and peace of the community.**

"The facts we have exhibited are startling. Methodism is a huge trading company. Its preachers have immense capital usurped from their people. They can constrain the people to submission by title deeds they hold for all the church real estate, and they may bind them by terrors of salvation, to buy and sell at their bidding. Thus they have the machinery, temporal and spiritual, to enlarge to overshadowing power, held by men, numbers and wealth. Is not this money power, held by men, utterly irresponsible, dangerous to piety? Once more: Methodism cultivates the fanaticism of human nature, and the money-seeking and power-loving energies of fallen man, exactly as Rome has ever done. Is not this church, then, dangerous to the peace of the community? Who says this? Answer, All Christian denominations in the United States say this. Methodist writers themselves have said this. They themselves have written it, that the itinerancy is rapidly tending to monarchy and Romanism in our country! Shall we fear Rome, and shall we not watch Methodism? Look! Roman Catholicism may be compared to some huge boa-constrictor serpent which, terribly scorched by the flames of a burning forest, has dragged its bloated mass into our green fields. We gaze and assail, in alarm, the dying folds of the monster. But shall we cherish the young Anaconda which has crawled from the same den? Shall we destroy Rome and cherish Methodism?

"We solemnly call upon the thinking men of our land to understand this power, and speak out against it. We call to the pulpit, the bench, the bar. We call to the people. Look! You have been told that Romanism is like that wave rolling back to the ocean. Look! It is coming again from the abyss. Methodism is heaving up another wave of death. You see it in the distance—swelling and glittering in light. Wake up, and all is well."

Now let the reader imagine that he is attending a communion Sabbath's service of Dr. Ross, and after exposing the unscriptural and **soul-destroying** doctrines of the Methodists, as he was wont to do, with a power and force that few men could command, he closes his sermon with the above periods. Coming down from the pulpit, and wiping the perspiration that stands in large hot drops from his brow, he benignly glances over his congregation, and lo, he sees the young anaconda, in tremulous coils, in the remote part of his congregation, and he commences, in dulcet tones, to woo it gently as a parent bird, and it a sucking dove, and charms it with the spell of a charmer, until it draws near to his communion table, and there he lovingly caresses and embraces it, in token of Christian and church fellowship,—calls it his own dear **brother, and feeds its snaky mouth with the bread and blood of the Lord's Supper!!** He calls upon the Baptists present to come and embrace and cherish it; and when they decline he glares at them over his glasses, and pronounces their conduct as inconsistent, illiberal, and unchristian, for all should commune together!

The sabbath ended, Dr. Ross sits down, in the calm of his office, dips his pen, and writes:

"We feel it our Christian and patriotic duty to warn the people against Methodism. It is destructive of the Christian religion in its doctrine, and as a religious system a dangerous power to the piety and peace of the community. We solemnly call upon the thinking men of our land to understand this power and speak out against it. We call to the pulpit, the bench, the bar. We call to the people. Look! You have been told that Romanism is like that wave rolling back to the ocean. Look! It is coming again from the abyss. Methodism is heaving up another wave of death. You see it in the distance, swelling and glittering in light. Wake up, and all is well."

So we see this anaconda serpent of Methodism is nowhere safe from the deadly weapons of Dr. Ross, except under shelter of his communion table. There he loves, there he cherishes it, as a part of the very body of Christ. There he embraces it with tears of affection, inhales its snaky breath, and feeds it with the body and blood of Christ! We turn away from the scene with disgust and horror!

Now look at a companion scene. The next sabbath is quarterly meeting, and is held in that same "Union House," and the presiding elder is solemn and terrible. He has heard of Dr. Ross's sermon, and by way of "tat," he selects Wesley's sermon on "Free Grace," which Wesley aimed and delivered with terrible effect against predestination, as held and taught by Presbyterians. I copy a few sentences:

"This doctrine not only tends to **destroy** Christian holiness, happiness, and good works, but hath also a direct and manifest tendency to **overthrow** the whole Christian revelation. * * It represents our blessed Lord * * as a **hypocrite**, a deceiver of the people, a man void of common sincerity."

He says the Presbyterians, by their doctrine and teaching, not only destroy Jesus Christ and the whole Christian system, but God himself!

"It destroys all his attributes at once; it overturns both his justice, mercy, and truth; yea, it represents the most holy God as worse than the devil, as more false, more cruel, and more unjust. * * This is the blasphemy for which I abhor the doctrine of predestination."

And he closes by indorsing, with great emphasis, the sentiment attributed to Dr. H. Bledsoe: "I would prefer to worship a huge gorilla than the Presbyterian's God."

Before he leaves the pulpit, he announces the communion to be observed, and most affectionately invites Dr. Ross and his people, as well as the Baptists present, to gather around the "sacramental board," and thus show to an unbelieving world that we are all one—all hold and preach the same essential doctrines—fighting against the same enemy, and on "our pleasing march" to the same heaven.

Now if it is asked, why we present this language and these scenes, that resemble blasphemy and sacrilege more than any thing else, we answer, to prove to all men that Baptists are at least consistent in the terms of their church communion, and that open communion among churches of opposing creeds is **contradictious** and **absurd** ; and, if we may be allowed to use one scriptural word, though a hard one—hypocritical. There seems to be to us a tremendous discrepancy between the **preaching** and **writing** of open communionists, and their **addresses** at the communion table. When does Dr. Ross and all others tell the truth—when they write and preach against each other, or when they deliver their loving addresses at their communion tables?

If these facts are not sufficient to put a full end to open communion, then truth and reason and common sense are powerless to do it.

INDEX OF AUTHORS.

Adkins, Prof., 111, 131, 290.
"Advocate, Texas Christian," Appendix A.
Alford, D.D., Dean, 20, 123, 154.
Alzog, 200.
Anthon, D.D., C., 194.
Arnold, D.D., 36, 289.
Augusti, 200.
Bannermann, D.D., 47.
Barnes, A., 242, 266.
Basnage, J., 202.
Beecher, D.D., E., 192.
Bellermine, Cardinal, 102.
Bingham, 200.
Blackstone, 117.
Bloomfield, 242.
Boardman, G. D., D.D., 100.
Broadus, Dr. Jno. A., Appendix A.
Breaker, D.D., J. M. C., 110.
Bretschneider, 242.
Buck, D.D., W. C., 269.
Calvin, J., 62.
Campbell, Alexander, 337.
Campbell, D.D., Geo., 196.
Canisius, 102.
Coleman, 200.
Clark, Adam, 132, 266, 337.
Colby, D.D., H., 38, 39, 79.
Conant, D.D., T. J., 193.
"Congregational Review," 282.
Cremer, D.D., 195.
Crosby, 107.
Cummings, D.D., Appendix B.
Curtis, Prof., 32, 33, 35, 41, 47, 80, 109, 148, 175, 177, 178, 181, 266, 267, 272, 278, 290, 292.
Dagg, D.D., 108, 146.
Dayton, D.D., A. C., 112.
Doggett, Bishop, 21, 288.
Donegan, 120.

Dudley, D.D., R. M., 81, 82.
Dwight, Dr., 61.
Dyck, D.D., A. Van, 278.
Ernesti, 117.
Everts, D.D., Wm., 110.
Fish, D.D., E. J., 100, 113, 148, 160.
Floyer, 204.
Fuller, D.D., R., 224, 268.
Gardner, D.D., W. W., 44, 77, 78, 79, 84, 131, 142, 160, 290, 298, 352.
Gavazzi, 280.
Gieseler, 168, 200.
Grimm and Wilkes, 195.
Grotius, 242.
Harvey, D.D., H., 138, 158, 160, 243, 268, 290, 297.
Hase, 200.
Hedding, Bishop, 335.
Heinricks, 346.
Henry, Matthew, 60.
"Herald, Religious," 185.
Hibbard, D.D., 78.
Hodge, Dr., 62.
Hodge, Dr. C., 52, Appendix A.
Hovey, D.D., 36, 80, 290.
Howell, D.D., R. B. C., 31, 59, 76, 312, 313, 330.
"Independent, The," N. Y., 82.
Jeter, Dr., 312.
Jones, D.D., T. G., 79, 223.
Kendrick Bishop, 204.
Knapp, D.D., 265.
Leigh, 197.
Liddell & Scott, 120, 194.
Macknight, 265.
Melville, 70.
Methodist Conference, 73.
Methodist Discipline, 293.
Millman, 200.

(367)

INDEX.

Milner, D.D., 203, 227.
Monfort, D.D., 331, 332.
Morris, Bishop, 67.
Morus, 118.
Mosheim, 169, 200.
Neander, 200.
Nevin, Dr., 62.
Norton, Wm., Eng., 60.
"Observer," N. Y., 95.
Olshausen, 265.
Osgood, D.D. H., 38, 48, 51, 52, 63.
Owen, D.D., 169.
Paine, D.D., L. L., 199.
Paxton, 290.
Pendleton, D.D., J. M., 109, 290.
Poindexter, D.D., A. M., 91, 92 Appendix A.
Pothier, 191.
Presbyterian Confession, 46.
"Presbyterian, Texas," Appendix A.
Presbyterian General Assembly, 328.
"Prot. and Herald," 332.
Pusey, Dr., 62.
"Review, Christian," Appendix B.
Rice, D.D., 237.
Robinson, D.D., E., 198, 202, 206.

Robinson, Stuart, D.D. 196, 200, 357.
Rosenmuller, 242, 346.
Ross, D.D., Appendix C.
Savage, D.D., G. M., 297.
Samson, D.D., 37.
Schleusner, 197.
Schaff, D.D., 200, 201.
Smith, D.D., Bible Dictionary, 200, 281.
Smith's Law of Contracts, 191.
Sophocles, Prof., 198.
Spencer, D.D., D., 181.
Stanley, D.D., 205.
Stokius, 198.
Suwanee Baptist Association, 292.
Synodical Enactments, 330, 331.
Taylor, D.D., G. F., 16, 88, 147, 160.
Trench, Dean, 120.
Tucker, D.D., H. H., 190.
Wahl, 198.
Wall, D.D., 204, 238.
Wayland F., D.D., 109.
Wesley, 46, 66, 67, 112, 336.
Williams, D.D., A. P., 141, 142, 150, 160, 183, 268, 289, 334.
Willmarth, Rev. J. W., 278.
Whitney, 90.

SECOND EDITION.

Mercer, Jesse, Rev., ... 266, 267, 273

A Biographical Sketch of James Robinson Graves (1820-1893)

By

John Franklin Jones

A Biographical Sketch of James Robinson Graves (1820-1893)

James Robinson Graves was born in Chester, Vermont April 10, 1820. Left fatherless at two weeks, his widowed mother defrauded of her husband's estate by the husband's business partner, the young Graves moved with his mother and sister to northern Ohio at nineteen. Of Congregation heritage, he had joined a Baptist church at age fifteen *(ESB)*.

He became principal of a school, despite his being without significant schooling himself. Graves learned the night before the subject matter he taught each day. He took charge of the school at Nicholasville, Kentucky in 1841. He taught himself a language each of the next four years and completed a college-degree equivalent. He studied the Bible in detail and joined Mount Freedom Baptist Church. That church licensed him to preach and ordained him in 1844 *(ESB)*.

John moved to Nashville, Tennessee in July 1845 to teach, and he joined the First Baptist Church of that city. He became the pastor of Second Baptist (later, Central) and served that church for approximately one year *(ESB)*.

Graves became assistant editor of *The Baptist* upon its being given to the Baptist General Association of Tennessee and North Alabama in 1846 by Robet Boyté Crawford Howell. Along with A. B. Shankland, he was made publisher and depository agent for the paper and established a bookstore *(ESB)*.

John Franklin Jones

Graves succeeded Howell as editor in June 1848 and edited the paper through its tenure as *The Baptist* and the *Tennessee Baptist* until August, 1889, when it became the *Baptist and Reflector*. For a number of years after 1869, it was the official paper for the Baptists of Arkansas, Louisiana, Mississippi, and Tennessee *(ESB)*.

Graves led the Landmark movement from its beginning in 1853, working fervently to make it the dominant perspective among Southern Baptists. He led a pointed, but unsuccessful, effort to remove from the Foreign Mission Board the power "to examine, choose, support, and direct missionaries." He was convinced that those actions belonged exclusively to churches, associations, or groups of churches. Though they debated Graves' proposal for several hours at Richmond, Virginia, in May 1859, the messengers of the Convention voted to continue the its current practice related to missionaries *(ESB)*.

Strongly committed to the importance of Sunday schools and Sunday school libraries, Graves became "a severe and sustained critic" of the "theological deviations" and insensitivity to existing needs by the SBC's publishing arm, the Southern Baptist Publication Society, Charleston, South Carolina. He led the effort to establish a thoroughly Landmark competitor in the Southern Baptist Sunday School Union (1857) and two associated publishing houses. One effort collapsed in 1871 and the other in 1877 *(ESB)*.

He organized three tract societies (1847, 1869, 1883) and the Nashville Indian and Missionary Association (1846), enabling him to maintain his continuing interest in the Indians. He was one of several leaders who started Mary Sharpe College for women at Winchester, Tennessee (1850) and raised funds to endow a theology chair at Union University. He also founded, edited, and published (for six years) the quarterly, *The Christian Review* (1855-60) *(ESB)*.

A Biographical Sketch of James Robinson Graves

Graves authored *The Desire of All Nations, The Watchman's Reply, The Trilemma, The First Baptist Church in America, The Great Iron Wheel, The Little Iron Wheel, The Bible Doctrine of the Middle Life, Expositions of Modern Spiritism, The Little Seraph, Old Landmarkism, What Is It?,* and *The Work of Christ in Seven Dispensations*. With James Madison Pendleton, he published *The Southern Psalmist* (1858) and compiled/published *The New Baptist Psalmist for Churches and Sunday Schools* (1873) (*ESB*).

J. R. Graves "influenced Southern Baptist life of the 19th century in more ways, and probably to a greater degree, than any other person." An agitator and a controversialist, he kept Southern Baptists in "almost continual and often bitter controversy for about 30 years." He frequently and prolongedly debated persons of other denominations. Though magnetic and dynamic, he was "acrimonious in his disputations and attacks." He often held large crowds raptly attentive for hours during his lengthy orations (*ESB*).

Graves suffered a paralyzing stroke August 17, 1884 while preaching at First Baptist Church, Memphis. He experienced a side-crushing fall in his yard in early 1889, which fall left him confined to a wheelchair for the remainder of his life. Though he continued to publish *The Baptist*, he gave less attention to controversial matters. He died June 26, 1893 in Memphis, Tennessee (*ESB*).

BIBLIOGRAPHY

Cathcart, William, ed. *The Baptist Encyclopaedia: A Dictionary of the Doctrines, Ordinances, Usages, Confessions of Faith, Sufferings, Labors, and Successes, and of the General History of the Baptist Denomination in All Lands, with Numerous Biographical Sketches of Distinguished American and Foreign Baptist, and a Supplement.* Philadelphia, Louis H. Everts, 1881; reprint, Paris, AR: Baptist Standard Bearer, 1988. S.v. "Graves, J. R., LL.D."

JOHN FRANKLIN JONES

Encyclopedia of Southern Baptists,. S.v. "Graves, James Robinson," by Homer L. Grice.

BY JOHN FRANKLIN JONES
CORDOVA, TENNESSEE
JUNE 2006

THE BAPTIST STANDARD BEARER, INC.

a non-profit, tax-exempt corporation
committed to the Publication & Preservation
of the Baptist Heritage.

CURRENT TITLES AVAILABLE IN
THE BAPTIST *DISTINCTIVES* SERIES

KIFFIN, WILLIAM   A Sober Discourse of Right to Church-Communion. Wherein is proved by Scripture, the Example of the Primitive Times, and the Practice of All that have Professed the Christian Religion: That no Unbaptized person may be Regularly admitted to the Lord's Supper. (London: George Larkin, 1681).

KINGHORN, JOSEPH   Baptism, A Term of Communion. (Norwich: Bacon, Kinnebrook, and Co., 1816)

KINGHORN, JOSEPH   A Defense of "Baptism, A Term of Communion". In Answer To Robert Hall's Reply. (Norwich: Wilkin and Youngman, 1820).

GILL, JOHN   Gospel Baptism. A Collection of Sermons, Tracts, etc., on Scriptural Authority, the Nature of the New Testament Church and the Ordinance of Baptism by John Gill. (Paris, AR: The Baptist Standard Bearer, Inc., 2006).

CARSON, ALEXANDER	Ecclesiastical Polity of the New Testament. (Dublin: William Carson, 1856).
BOOTH, ABRAHAM	A Defense of the Baptists. A Declaration and Vindication of Three Historically Distinctive Baptist Principles. Compiled and Set Forth in the Republication of Three Books. Revised edition. (Paris, AR: The Baptist Standard Bearer, Inc., 2006).
BOOTH, ABRAHAM	Paedobaptism Examined on the Principles, Concessions, and Reasonings of the Most Learned Paedobaptists. With Replies to the Arguments and Objections of Dr. Williams and Mr. Peter Edwards. 3 volumes. (London: Ebenezer Palmer, 1829).
CARROLL, B. H.	*Ecclesia* - The Church. With an Appendix. (Louisville: Baptist Book Concern, 1903).
CHRISTIAN, JOHN T.	Immersion, The Act of Christian Baptism. (Louisville: Baptist Book Concern, 1891).
FROST, J. M.	Pedobaptism: Is It From Heaven Or Of Men? (Philadelphia: American Baptist Publication Society, 1875).
FULLER, RICHARD	Baptism, and the Terms of Communion; An Argument. (Charleston, SC: Southern Baptist Publication Society, 1854).
GRAVES, J. R.	Tri-Lemma: or, Death By Three Horns. The Presbyterian General Assembly Not Able To Decide This Question: "Is Baptism In The Romish Church Valid?" 1st Edition.

	(Nashville: Southwestern Publishing House, 1861).
MELL, P.H.	Baptism In Its Mode and Subjects. (Charleston, SC: Southern Baptist Publications Society, 1853).
JETER, JEREMIAH B.	Baptist Principles Reset. Consisting of Articles on Distinctive Baptist Principles by Various Authors. With an Appendix. (Richmond: The Religious Herald Co., 1902).
PENDLETON, J.M.	Distinctive Principles of Baptists. (Philadelphia: American Baptist Publication Society, 1882).
THOMAS, JESSE B.	The Church and the Kingdom. A New Testament Study. (Louisville: Baptist Book Concern, 1914).
WALLER, JOHN L.	Open Communion Shown to be Unscriptural & Deleterious. With an introductory essay by Dr. D. R. Campbell and an Appendix. (Louisville: Baptist Book Concern, 1859).

For a complete list of current authors/titles, visit our internet site at:
www.standardbearer.org
or write us at:

he Baptist Standard Bearer, Inc.

NUMBER ONE IRON OAKS DRIVE • PARIS, ARKANSAS 72855

TEL # 479-963-3831   FAX # 479-963-8083

EMAIL: Baptist@centurytel.net   http://www.standardbearer.org

Thou hast given a standard to them that fear thee; that it may be displayed because of the truth. — Psalm 60:4

www.ingramcontent.com/pod-product-compliance
Lightning Source LLC
Chambersburg PA
CBHW031703230426
43668CB00006B/89